Music in Eighteenth-Century England

Essays in memory of Charles Cudworth

A Concert in Cambridge: etching by Sir Abraham Hume
after Thomas Orde (*see the note on pp. xv–xviii*)

Music in Eighteenth-Century England

Essays in memory of
Charles Cudworth

Edited by

Christopher Hogwood
and
Richard Luckett

Cambridge University Press

Cambridge

London   New York   New Rochelle

Melbourne   Sydney

Published by the Press Syndicate of the University of Cambridge
The Pitt Building, Trumpington Street, Cambridge CB2 1RP
32 East 57th Street, New York, NY 10022, USA
296 Beaconsfield Parade, Middle Park, Melbourne 3206, Australia

First published in 1983

Printed in Great Britain at the University Press, Cambridge

Library of Congress catalogue card number: 81–21612

British Library Cataloguing in Publication Data
Music in eighteenth-century England: essays
  in memory of Charles Cudworth.
  1. Cudworth, Charles   2. Music, English
  – Addresses, essays, lectures
  I. Hogwood, Christopher   II. Luckett,
  Richard   III. Cudworth, Charles
  781.742   ML286
ISBN 0 521 23525 1

Contents

Illustrations

Foreword

Charles Cudworth, to whose memory the essays in the present volume are dedicated, was a force in music studies in Cambridge and in a wider world over three decades. His background was unconventional. Charles (his full true name was Cyril Leonard Elwell Cudworth) was born near Cambridge on 30 October 1908, the son of a policeman. At the time when he might have opened up educational opportunities for himself by winning a scholarship to a secondary school, he was unable to do so as he had been ill and confined to bed for the preceding year. His eagerly inquiring mind and his intellectual interests led him to obtain jobs in bookshops; he later embarked on a novel (though he never finished it) calling, amusingly and observantly, on his experiences of those days. Working in a shop gave him a free afternoon each week, and he used those afternoons to copy into keyboard scores music of the kind that attracted him – at first in those Cambridge libraries to which he had access, later by taking a half-day return train ticket to London and working in the British Museum Reading Room. This way he built up a large collection of rough scores of eighteenth-century symphonies and concertos, and laid the foundation of his encyclopedic command of this repertoire. He was particularly encouraged by E. J. Dent. Later he took posts in university departments, and in 1943 became assistant in the music section of the University Library; three years later, with the option of a superior post there or the librarianship of the Pendlebury, the Music Faculty library, he chose the latter – because, he later said, he liked to be in daily contact with young people. In 1957 he was appointed Curator.

Since he possessed no degree or other formal qualification, Charles's situation was in a sense anomalous. As librarian of the University Music School, he was constantly in demand for help at every level, and he gave such help unstintingly: to lecturers, to research students, to undergraduates, to performers of every sort, to numerous amateurs of music who needed guidance and knew where it could readily be found – for example, in looking out repertoire suited to the improbable combinations of instruments and voices liable to crop up at college concerts. Circumstances, abetted by his own generosity and enthusiasms, were such that he was called upon too often to lend himself for these lesser chores; his kindliness, his friendliness and his unpretentiousness invited people to take advantage of him. He did no formal teaching until 1953 (when the present writer became the first research student to be supervised by him). In 1957 his scholarly distinction was belatedly recognized by the university and he was awarded the honorary MA degree.

The list of Charles Cudworth's publications (pp. 245–58) demonstrates his range, as man and scholar. This range was wide, in several directions. He could write plays, novels and verse on the one hand; on the other, he could amass accurate and painstaking bibliographical lists. He could investigate and illuminate remote corners of music, and he could throw light on familiar masterpieces. His interests began in the early seventeenth century, grew in intensity for the period between Purcell and Mozart, and continued through the Romantics to the English song writers of the early twentieth century. He could equally write a serious scholarly paper or a chatty magazine article.

One thing that ran through all his works, and permeated his teaching too, was a deep feeling for the quality of written English. His literary inclination shows in the fascination that connections between writers (Shakespeare, Gray, Dickens and Housman, for example) and music held for him. There was no self-conscious elegance about his own prose, but a constant concern for simplicity and directness and for saying precisely what he meant. He wrote much as he spoke. And that meant that his eagerness for what he had to say always came through. Only fairly late in his life was his talent as a broadcaster fully exploited; there his enthusiasm, along with his direct, kindly manner, and the hint of East Anglian in his voice, made him an ideal communicator because so natural a one. He often broadcast on non-musical topics, especially to do with his beloved East Anglia, its traditions and its architecture.

Among his favourite anecdotes was one about a meeting between Arne and Boyce: while Dr Arne pointed out the errors in a score, Dr Boyce was content to note its merits. Charles Cudworth belonged to the Boyce party. This possibly made him less than ideal as a critic, for he erred on the side of lenience or generosity. He hated to be unkind, and sought good even when it was hard to discover. Writing about performance in any case interested him much less than writing about music itself.

It is sad that Charles Cudworth never produced a substantial book. Much of his wisdom on the subject of eighteenth-century English music – always at the centre of his interests and affections – died with him, on Boxing Day 1977. But there are several important studies, including much pioneering work, remaining. Some of his energies were devoted to questions of authenticity, notably the Pergolesi articles, the Trumpet Voluntary ones, and above all the famous *Notes* article 'Ye Olde Spuriosity Shoppe; or, Put it in the Anhang' (1954–5), whose title not only typifies his wit but has added a new word to musical discourse. His concern with terminological precision is demonstrated in his brief but pointed *Monthly Musical Record* article of 1953, 'Baroque, Rococo, Galant, Classic', which played a crucial role in establishing regularity and propriety in the use of those words. His most important original research is to be found in the articles on the English symphony and keyboard concerto in the eighteenth century, in the *Proceedings of the Royal Musical Association* (1951–2) and *Score* (1953) respectively; some of this work has of course been superseded, and indeed some of it is supplemented in this very volume, but its importance in opening up new fields cannot be overstated. He wrote countless dictionary articles, in different editions of *Grove*, in *Die Musik in Geschichte und Gegenwart*, in the Belgian *Algemene Muziekencyclopedie*, in the *Encyclopedia Britannica* and elsewhere, many of them embodying new research of his own, and all of them showing his characteristic concern not only with accurate fact but also with historical and stylistic placing – for Charles, values were central, and good writing about music necessarily contained an evaluative element. Possibly the most important of all his dictionary contributions, and certainly the one he himself reckoned the most widely used and appreciated, was the 'Libraries' entry in the fifth (1954) edition of *Grove*; it involved massive international correspondence with librarians at a time when the libraries and the scholarly world were still in a state of disarray after World War II, and it helped Charles build up friendships in many countries especially in the community of music librarians, where he was always an outstandingly popular figure.

The present tributes to Charles Cudworth come partly from his friends and pupils, partly from his colleagues and acquaintances, partly from those who have pursued lines of research that interested him. It is characteristic of the direction in which musical scholarship has moved since the middle of this century that several of them deal with detailed questions surrounding texts and editions, especially those contributed by the younger generation of Handel scholars. Handel's relations with English music were a topic that fascinated him; that he felt Handel to be more affected by his English surroundings than vice versa was typical of his readiness to challenge idly and uncritically received opinion, and of his feeling for the integrity of English traditions, before, during and after Handel's time. These lines of thought are in different ways picked up in several essays offered here, covering Purcell, Tudway and John Christopher Smith (an Englishman in musical regards even if German-born), and of course the next English generation, the early symphonists on whom he himself did the pioneer work. His literary side too is reflected in the studies of the relation of music to text and context; so is his enthusiasm for local history and social history as manifested in provincial concert life. Charles's interests ranged later, too – to the *galant* era, John Christian Bach especially, to his English contemporaries and successors (men like Stephen Storace, Samuel Arnold and in particular John Marsh, whose manuscript memoirs he helped bring to light and took delight in), and of course on to Mozart. This side is less fully pursued in the present volume, though here too Charles's enthusiasm and example have awakened scholarly activity. Charles Cudworth's interests and influence are aptly commemorated here; but they were also more widely spread, and will continue, through his numerous and affectionate friends, pupils, and intellectual and musical debtors, to irrigate British musical scholarship and musical life for many years.

Stanley Sadie

Editorial Note

Charles Cudworth made a unique contribution to the study of music in eighteenth-century England, through his writings (both scholarly and popular), through his teaching, and through the enthusiasm that he inspired in others (particularly by his broadcasts). Indeed it can be said that to a large extent he created a new field for serious musicological study, and created a public to profit by such study. The object of this collection is to commemorate his work by extending it, and to provide a *point d'appui*, a volume that can be used both as a work of reference and as a stimulant for further enquiries.

Our procedure, therefore, has not been to assemble at random a distinguished group of Cudworth's friends and pupils, but to approach some of those scholars whose work we felt to be most likely to be substantial, even though they may have had no personal connection with Cudworth. The essays concern themselves with what seem at present the principal areas of both academic and practical interest: the Purcellian inheritance; Handel and the Handelian legacy; J. C. Bach and the English symphonists; Haydn in his English aspect. In each of these areas Cudworth had done pioneer work, whether through his infectious delight in the music in performance, or through his scrupulous scholarship – though the two things, in Cudworth's case, were scarcely separable.

This collection, then, is neither a Festschrift nor a commemorative tribute in the conventional sense: rather, it attempts a laying of bearings, or perhaps a highlighting of problems, at a moment when the study of eighteenth-century English music, largely as a result of the work of the man to whose memory it is dedicated, is unprecedentedly vigorous.

C.J.H.
R.L.

A note on the frontispiece:
A Concert in Cambridge

Christopher Hogwood

The well-known caricature *A Concert* has been variously described as showing 'an amateur concert party', 'Gentleman players' and 'a University recital', and as featuring 'an unknown form of dulcimer' played by 'an English performer'. Since three and possibly four of the players were foreign, all were professionals, and the curious instrument has been proposed not only as the immediate predecessor of the piano[1] but also as 'the largest stringed instrument ever made',[2] a summary of the documentary evidence identifying the scene, the players and the instrument might not be out of place.

Two concerts were advertised in *The Cambridge Chronicle and Journal* during the summer of 1767 featuring Mr Noel, 'the celebrated Performer of the Panthaleon'. The first, to be given on 28 May in 'Trinity College-Hall', was announced on the 23rd, but without details of programme. For the second appearance, on 8 June, the paper was more specific:

> For Mr. NOEL / At CHRIST College-Hall, on Monday / next the 8th of this Instant June, will be per / formed, a CONCERT of / Vocal and Instrument MUSIC. / ACT I / Overture Samson. / Song composed by Mr. Jackson. / Concerto Panthaleone. / Solo Violino by Mr. Hellendaal. / Fourth Overture by Mr. Abel, Op. 1. / ACT II. / Overture Bach, Manuscript. / Solo Panthaleone. / Second Concerto Geminiani, Op. 2. / Cantata accompanied by the Panthaleone Obligato. / Overture Mr. Noel. / Tickets to be had at Mr. Wynn's Music Shop, at / the Union, Dorkell's, and the Rose Coffee-Houses, / and of Mr. Noel at Mr. Mackenzie's, at 2s 6d. each. / To begin precisely at Eight o'clock.

Mr Noel, or Nowell as some sources had him, was actually Georg Noëlli, a Portuguese Jew who had studied the pantaleon with its inventor, Pantaleon Hebenstreit. (Louis XIV, hearing this elaborate version of the dulcimer in Paris in

---

1. Christoph Gottlieb Schröter in *Neu-eröffnete Musikalische Bibliothek* (Leipzig 1736–54), vol. 3, pp. 474–6; and *Marpurg's Kritische Briefe* (Berlin 1764), vol. 3, p. 85.
2. *Guinness Book of Musical Facts and Figures* (London 1976), p. 47.

1705, had displayed his approval by decreeing that it take the Christian name of its inventor.) After studying with Geminiani, Padre Martini and Hasse, Noëlli began to tour as a virtuoso player and improviser: his contemporaries considered him the equal of W. F. Bach, and he was associated with Telemann, Handel and C. P. E. Bach. In 1752 and again in 1757 a 'Mr Noel' appears as composer and performer on the 'cymbalo' in London (New Haymarket Theatre); he may even have been heard earlier in Birmingham, where 'several pieces of musick on the Cymbal by Israel Nowell' were advertised in a concert on 16 July 1747.[3] In Norwich in 1753 we hear of 'several grand Concerto's on a foreign Instrument, call'd Cymballo, by Mr. Noel: Which Instrument has given general Satisfaction . . . in London, and . . . Cambridge: Also some favourite Airs on the said Instrument, with Mr. Noel's own Variations' (*Norwich Mercury*, 7 July 1753), from which we deduce that the 1767 concerts did not mark Mr Noel's Cambridge début.[4] Despite these appearances, the instrument could still be described in Worcester in 1767 as 'newly invented' when Noëlli played 'several Grand Overtures' there. Many contradictory descriptions of the pantaleon can be found;[5] the same Worcester paper claimed that 'The instrument is eleven feet in length and has 276 strings of different magnitudes', but Burney was able to report on the original instrument which he found in a ruinous state when he visited Dresden in 1772:

> it is more than nine feet long, and had, when in order, 186 strings of catgut. The tone was produced by two *baguettes*, or sticks, like the dulcimer; it must have been extremely difficult to the performer, but seems capable of great effects. The strings were now almost all broken, the present Elector will not be at the charge of furnishing new ones, though it had ever been thought a court instrument in former reigns, and was kept in order at the expence of the prince.[6]

Kuhnau, who owned a 'Pantaleonisches Cimbel', praised it for its powers of *forte* and *piano*, but admitted that the effort of striking the strings with small hammers was 'herculean' (in Mattheson, *Critica Musica*, 8 December 1717); in the same year Christoph Gottlieb Schröter, by mechanizing its hammer action, claimed to have invented the fortepiano.

Sadly, no description of the English performance has yet come to light, but a long and ecstatic account of the instrument's powers can be found in a letter of Diderot to Sophie Volland (17 November 1765) reporting on a recital in Paris:

> Imaginez un instrument immense pour la variété des tons, qui a toutes sortes de caractères, des petits sons faibles et fugitifs comme le luth lorsqu'il est pincé avec la dernière délicatesse; des basses les plus fortes et les plus harmonieuses, et une tête de musicien meublée de chants propres à toutes sortes d'affections d'âme; tantôt grand, noble et majestueux, un moment après doux, pathétique et tendre, faisant succéder avec un art incompréhensible la délicatesse à la force, la gaieté à la

3. See J. Sutcliffe Smith, *The Story of Music in Birmingham* (Birmingham 1945), p. 15.
4. See Trevor Fawcett, *Music in Eighteenth-Century Norwich and Norfolk* (Norwich 1979), p. 44.
5. For a summary, see Sibyl Marcuse, *A Survey of Musical Instruments* (Newton Abbot 1975), pp. 225–7.
6. Charles Burney, *The Present State of Music in Germany, The Netherlands, and United Provinces*, 2nd edn (London 1775), vol. 2, p. 57.

mélancholie, le sauvage, l'extraordinaire à la simplicité, à la finesse, à la grâce, et tous ces caractères rendus aussi piquants qu'ils peuvent l'être par leur contraste subit. Je ne scais comment cet homme réussissoit à lier tant d'idées disparates; mais il est certain qu'elles étoient liées, et que vingt fois, en l'écoutant, cette histoire ou ce conte du musicien de l'antiquité qui faisoit passer à discrétion ses auditeurs de la fureur à la joye, et de la joye à la fureur, me revint à l'esprit et me parut croyable. Je vous jure, mon amie, que je n'exagère point quand je vous dis que je me suis senti frémir et changer de visage; que j'ai vu les visages des autres changer comme le mien, et que je n'aurois pas douté qu'ils n'eussent éprouvé le même frémissement quand ils ne l'auroient pas avoué. Ajoutez à cela la main la plus légère, l'exécution la plus brillante et la plus précise, l'harmonie la plus pure et la plus sévère, et de la part de cet Osbruck une âme douce et sensible, une tête chaude, enthousiaste, qui s'allume, et qui se perd, et qui s'oublie si parfaitement qu'à la fin d'un morceau il a l'aire effaré d'un homme qui revient d'un rêve.

The etching of the Cambridge concert, presumably made *c.* 1767, is attributed to Sir Abraham Hume, based on a drawing by the young Thomas Orde, later Lord Bolton, who was an undergraduate at King's College.[7] Two states of the print are known, several of them carrying later inscriptions added in pencil or ink; in examples of the first impression in the British Museum and the Fitzwilliam Museum, Cambridge, the inscription is completed in pencil to read 'A Concert at Cambridge'. 'Publish'd According to Act of Parliament' is added bottom left, and the presumed engraver 'Bretherton' bottom right (spelt 'Bretherston' on the Fitzwilliam copy).[8] The second impression (British Museum and Rowe Library, Cambridge) has the Parliamentary privilege engraved, with a pencilled 'Bretherton' on the Rowe copy.

Also inscribed on both impressions are identifications of the musicians; in the spelling of the Fitzwilliam copy, these are, from left to right:

HELLENDALE / NEWELL SEN[R] / RENNISH / WEST / WYNNE / NEWELL JUN[R] / WOOD

The Dutch violinist and composer Pieter Hellendaal, after succeeding Charles Burney as organist at St Margaret's Church, King's Lynn, lived in Cambridge from 1762 until his death in 1799, and was responsible for the promotion of many of the professional concerts in East Anglia.

John Frederick Ranish (originally Wranisch?) had been flautist with the Covent Garden orchestra, but was much associated with East Anglia. He can be seen in the painting by Heins of the 1734 concert party at Melton Constable,[9] and on his death in 1777 the *Cambridge Chronicle* described him as 'an eminent teacher and performer on the German flute in this town. He always supported the character of a gentleman . . .'. This etching shows that he, like many eighteenth-century wind-players, doubled on oboe and flute.

John Wynne, playing the double-bass, was a music publisher and kept his

7. F. G. Stephens and E. Hawkins, *Catalogue of Prints and Drawings in the British Museum. Division I. Political and Personal Satires*, vol. 4 (London 1883), p. 698, no. 4479.
8. See *Gainsborough, English Music and the Fitzwilliam* (Cambridge 1977), pp. 26–7.
9. See Fawcett, *op. cit.*, p. 43, and Prince F. Duleep Singh, *Portraits in Norfolk Houses*, ed. E. Farrer (Norwich n.d.), vol. 2, p. 20.

'Music Shop, at the sign of the Harp and Hautboy [also the device of John Walsh], near the Senate House' (advertisement in the *Cambridge Chronicle*, 7 April 1764).

Both 'West' and 'Newell Sen''', present difficulties; no mention of a West is to be found in Cambridge documentation, and no report suggests that Noëlli travelled with his father. (We know that family groups, such as the clarinettist 'Mr. Charles' and his wife and son, received good publicity.) Alternative identifications of these players, however, have recently come to light inked in the margin of a newly discovered copy of the second impression of the etching (reproduced as the frontispiece of this volume), where the second violinist is 'Keymur' and the bespectacled cellist 'Alexis'.

John Keymer (also spelt Kymer and Keymour) was a chorister at Norwich Cathedral, and for many years a Lay Clerk at King's College. According to his obituary (*Norwich Mercury*, 8 September 1770) he also sang in the choirs of St John's and Trinity Colleges.[10]

'Mr. Alexis' appears regularly in the Cambridge concert scene of 1767, but without surname; a benefit on 21 February 'For Mr. Alexis', a concert with 'violoncello Mr. Alexis' on 28 March and, more conclusively, a benefit concert in Trinity on 6 July involving 'Messrs. Hellendaal, Alexis, and Ranish' (*Cambridge Chronicle*, 27 June). An undated publication from about this period solves the mystery: 'Six Sonate for the Violoncello e Basso, composed by Alexis Magito, Opera Prima' issued by 'John Wynne, for the Author: Cambridge' (copies in the Rowe Library and the British Library).[11] It seems likely from the limited number of appearances in Cambridge and the hybrid Italian–English of his title that Magito was a visiting Italian, probably invited by Hellendaal for the 1767 season.

10. More biographical details are to be found in A. H. Mann's MS Notebooks in the Rowe Library, King's College, Vol. I.
11. See Charles Humphries and William C. Smith, *Music Publishing in the British Isles*, 2nd edn (Oxford 1970), p. 344.

The beginnings of provincial concert life in England

Michael Tilmouth

Much has been written of the early development of the public concert in London, from the modest endeavours of John Banister at Whitefriars, after Charles II's return to the throne, to the positive ferment of activity which made Handel's London and the city Haydn came to know one of the most musically alive centres in Europe. But what of the provinces? A start has been made on documenting the great festivals which were held in places like Salisbury, Winchester, Oxford, Cambridge, Liverpool, Manchester, Birmingham, Derby, Newcastle and York in the post-Handelian era,[1] and Stanley Sadie has discussed the activities of the music clubs and societies which were mainly responsible for promoting concerts in the second half of the eighteenth century over the length and breadth of England, sometimes in quite surprisingly small village communities.[2] Information about these concerts comes mainly from the newspapers of the period, but since few provincial papers were established before the 1720s the first two or three decades of the eighteenth century are poorly documented; for our knowledge of them we have to rely mainly on a few notices that happened to reach the London press, odd references in letters or account books, or the chance presence of a diarist among the enthusiasts who promoted or attended musical events at the time.

Undoubtedly the Restoration, following the resumption of court activities in London, had seen a centralization in the capital of affairs musical and otherwise, a centralization at first perilously like that in Paris and perhaps all the more welcome to Charles II on that account. A rapidly expanding commerce, a growing population, the reaction against the restrictions of the Puritan regime of the Commonwealth, an increasing throng of supplicants for some kind of court

1. See various articles by Douglas J. Reid and Brian Pritchard in *Royal Musical Association Research Chronicle* Nos. 5, 6, 7 and 8 (1965–70).
2. 'Concert Life in Eighteenth-Century England', *Proceedings of the Royal Musical Association* LXXXV (1958–9), pp. 17–30.

preferment – all these created in London a relish for entertainment of every kind and in particular the circumstances which ensured the success of the new public concerts. The emphasis in music-making shifted too, with the modest attainments and self-enjoyment of the amateur all too often discounted in comparison with the more brilliant and extrovert achievements of the professional virtuoso. In the concert rooms music was to be bought and sold like any other commodity, and its wares and practitioners tended towards the fashionably foreign, whether real or feigned.

There were some who regretted the change. Roger North pointed out that

> when music was kept in an easy, temperate air, practicable to moderate and imperfect hands, who for the most part are more earnest upon it than the most adept, it might be retained in the country. But since it has arrived at such a pitch of perfection, that even masters, unless of the prime, cannot entertain us, the plain way becomes contemptible and ridiculous, and therefore must needs be laid aside. By this you may judge what profit the public hath from the improvement of music.[3]

As English Restoration drama shows, the tides of fashion swept more slowly through the country than through the capital itself, and this was as true in the changing taste for music as for clothes or furniture. In a play of Thomas Baker's, Woodcock, a yeoman of Kent, remarks:

> And pray, what are your Town Diversions? To hear a parcel of Italian Eunuchs, like so many Cats squawll out somewhat you don't understand – The Song of my Lady's Birth-Day, by an honest Farmer, and a merry Jig by a Country-Wench that has Humour in her Buttocks, is worth Forty on't.[4]

But resistance was vain. In its seasonal peregrinations London society took its pleasures with it, and the new-fangled concerts soon became as much a reason for going to Tunbridge or Bath, and perhaps as mildly curative in their way, as the waters ever had been before. Inevitably, too, the new provincial concerts began by following the pattern set by those in London. There may have been more amateurs among the performers, but the leading professionals were there too. A generation earlier European musicians had begun to discover the financial rewards which awaited them in London. Now we find players like Geminiani and Dubourg enjoying the delights of a more varied itinerary and reaping the rewards to be gained in cities like Bath, Wells and Salisbury.

Before the end of the seventeenth century the London 'season' had settled down into a routine that has scarcely changed since. Concerts were given there from October to May, but during the rest of the year, with concert rooms and theatres for the most part closed, many musicians had to seek employment elsewhere. At the very lowest level there was of course the music at the annual fairs in London itself. It formed a prominent part of the entertainment at May Fair; at Bartholomew Fair music for the masses was purveyed from Heatly's Booth,

3. *Autobiography*, ed. A. Jessop (London 1887), p. 70.
4. *Tunbridge Walks* (London 1703), p. 4.

Crawley's Booth, and the Gun Musick Booth, eliciting some vastly amusing if not altogether printable comments from Ned Ward and Tom Brown.[5]

Further afield, circling London in a green belt much of whose rural charm has long since disappeared, were the wells and spas at Islington, Epsom, Lambeth, Richmond and Hampstead. Sadler had rediscovered the medicinal wells at Islington in 1683. He laid out pleasure gardens there and built a music house. He was later succeeded by the musician Francis Forcer, who from 1699 was joint proprietor with James Miles – hence the occasional references at the time to 'Miles's Musick House'.[6] The wells were open each summer and free treatment was provided for the poor.[7] Perhaps for this reason Sadler's Wells was never a fashionable resort (some say it never has been). In 1697 Misson wrote with the detached eye of a foreigner that 'Les Gens de qualité ne vont guères là.'[8] It is not surprising to find that early gutter pressman Ned Ward there two years later purporting to give an account of the scene in the music house when 'Lady Squab', a singer, has just resumed her place by the side of the organ – yes, the organ, not the harpsichord:

> With hands on her Belly, she open'd her Throat,
> And silenc'd the Noise, with her Musical Note:
> The Guests were all Hush, and Attention was given,
> The Listening Mob thought themselves in a Heaven;
> If the Ravishing Song which she Sung, you wou'd know,
> It was 'Rub, rub, rub; rub, rub, rub; in and out ho'.[9]
> As soon as her sweet, modest, Ditty was done,
> She withdrew from her Wicker, as Chaste as a Nun.
> The Butchers so pleas'd with her warbling strains,
> Both Knock'd her, and Clap'd her all round for her Pains.
>   Then up starts a Fiddler in Scarlet, so fierce,
> So unlike an Orpheus, he look'd like a Mars.
> He runs up in Alt, with a Hey-Diddle-diddle,
> To shew what a Fool he could make of a Fiddle,
> And has such an excellent hand at a Pinch,
> He hit's Half a Note, to a Quarter of an Inch.[10]

Music of a sort was not the sole entertainment provided at Sadler's Wells: there was also a sword-swallowing girl, and in 1699 – the principal attraction that year – an 'ingurgitating monster', a gentleman who, for five guineas, undertook to swallow a live cock, feathers, spurs and all. The first regular concerts there, as distinct from the provision of music for dancing, started in 1697, when every Monday morning a performance of vocal and instrumental music was given,

5. E. Ward, *The London Spy 1698–99*, ed. R. Strauss (London 1924), p. 258; 'Monsieur Voiture', *Familiar and Courtly Letters*, trans. Dryden, Dennis *et al.* (including letters by T. Brown) (London 1700), pp. 184, 194.
6. *The Post Boy*, 21 March 1702.
7. *The London Gazette*, 11 May 1693.
8. Henri Misson, *Mémoires et Observations faîtes par un Voyageur en Angleterre* (The Hague 1698).
9. The refrain of a most indecent song, 'A lusty young Smith', by Richard Leveridge (D. Wright, London 1705).
10. E. Ward, *A Walk to Islington with a Description of New Tunbridge Wells and Sadler's Musick House* (London 1699), p. 13.

'dubbling the usual number of performers'.[11] The price for admission was sixpence only. The following year the concerts were held twice a week, and the
instrumental forces included violins, flutes (recorders), hautboys, trumpets and
kettle-drums.[12] After 1700, with increasing competition from the other wells, the
importance of Sadler's Wells declined, though it is clear that music of a sort was
still being given, as many sheet-song publications describe the contents as having
been sung there.

Epsom Wells falls into the same category as Sadler's. It became popular from
about 1705 and was open each year from Easter Monday until Michaelmas. A
consort of music played there every day during the season, of which the proprietor seems to have been rather proud: it consisted of 'Eight MUSITIANS and a
TRUMPET, (the like Number is not at any other Place in Epsom, nor at any other
publick Wells in England)'.[13] Occasionally concerts of a more ambitious sort were
announced. In 1708 a performance in the Great Room by the bowling green
included

> a Sonata on the Flute Almain, by Mr Lature [La Tour], several Songs, sung by Mr
> Wheley, being the First time of his Performance in Publick. A Solo on the Flute,
> Compos'd by Mr Pepusch, Perform'd by Mr Massey, being the Second Time of his
> Performance in Publick, since his Arrival in England. A Sonata for 3 Flutes,
> entirely new. A Sonata for a Haut-boy, and Flute. Some select Songs out of the late
> Opera's with their Symphonies. A Double Solo of Corelly's, by Mr Beeston.[14]

Lambeth Wells were opened in 1696. 'The Place is extremely pleasant, and
fitted for the Entertainment of Persons of all Qualities', or so the proprietor
pretentiously claimed. 'On Tuesdays, Wednesdays and Fridays the Musick will
be continued till 4 after Noon, and the other 3 days till 7.'[15] These wells, like those
at Epsom, were open from Easter Monday until Michaelmas, and in 1697 a series
of weekly concerts was given in the great room there, 'consisting of about Thirty
Instruments and Voices, after the method of the Musick meeting in York Buildings. The price only excepted, each person being to pay for coming in but one
Shilling.'[16] Two of the entertainments that year consisted of 'Warlike Musick, with
Trumpets, Kettle Drums, and other Instruments'.[17] Such concerts seem to have
had a considerable attraction to a nation whose norm of existence was a state of
hostilities with at least one of its neighbours. No one was admitted in a mask,
which indicates that the proprietor wished to raise the tone of the proceedings.
These weekly concerts were given again in 1698 but after that seem to have been
abandoned. As a fashionable resort Lambeth soon lost ground although it continued to be patronized by the less well-to-do.

Musical performances at Richmond seem to have begun in 1696 when 'the Ode

11. *The Post Man*, 24 July 1697.   12. *The Post Man*, 21 May 1698.
13. *The Daily Courant*, 27 July 1710. Epsom Wells had, of course, been a seat of pleasure long
    before there was much musical activity there – see, for example, Thomas Shadwell's comedy
    Epsom Wells (1672).
14. *The Daily Courant*, 26 July 1708.   15. *The London Gazette*, 30 April 1696.
16. *The Post Boy*, 11 May 1697.   17. *The Post Man*, 20 July 1697.

made on Mr H. Purcel, the Words by Mr Dryden, and set to Musick by Dr Blow, in 30 Pages' was given 'in all its Parts'.[18] These wells (there were two, described as the 'Old Wells' and the 'New Wells' respectively) generally opened each year on Whit Monday, and attempts were made to attract well-to-do people to stay there over the summer as they did at Bath or Tunbridge, for there were 'very Large Lodgings well furnished, fit for Persons of Honour, &c'.[19] Concerts were given spasmodically up to about 1705. In 1697 two performances of Purcell's 'Ode for the Duke of Gloucester's Birthday' were given at the New Wells in which the celebrated trumpeter John Shore took part.[20]

The only performance at Richmond which seems to have been advertised between 1705 and 1720 was a benefit concert for the singer Tenoe given in the Great Room in 1711,[21] but this does not mean that no others took place. Lady Hervey wrote from Richmond to her husband in July 1719 commenting on the fine music she had heard there. But she, though a celebrated beauty, was a domestic creature at heart and 'would willingly have exchanged it all to have heard [him] pipeing in the Summer-house' at home.[22] These concerts were given by visiting musicians and not by those employed to provide the regular music for dancing. The usual price of tickets was one shilling, but when Abell performed there in 1701[23] and when Elford, Weldon, Dieupart and 'Gasperini' (Gasparo Visconti) were there in 1703[24] this sum was advanced to five shillings. The latter concert was 'to be perform'd but once, because of the Queen's going to the Bath'. The movement of the court to one of the spas was a signal for a general exodus of society in the same direction, and naturally the best musicians, as experienced as any of the camp-followers of society, went too.

Richmond did not depend entirely on resident guests: it was within easy reach of London, and there was a daily influx of visitors from the city by water, for 'the Tide served at 11 a clock in the Morning and Light Night' at certain times during the year. There is no reason to suppose that concerts such as those given by Abell at Richmond were of a less high standard than those given in the London concert rooms, but some of the other music, if we may believe Thomas Brown (admittedly making the most of it) writing to Moult in 1699, was of a very poor quality:

> as for the Musick, it was so abominable, that half a dozen Welsh-harpers met upon St David's Day, to make merry over a Mess of Leek-porridge, could not have tormented the Ears of a Purcel with more discording Thrumthrum. I dare almost ingage, had the same Fellows play'd upon the same Instruments before the Town of Jerico, the Walls would have paid the same Compliment to their Harmony, as they did to that of the Levites, for nothing could have patience to stand still and listen to their Performances.[25]

18. *The Post Boy*, 25 July 1696. (The ode is the one beginning 'Mark how the lark and linnet sing'.)
19. *The Post Boy*, 20 May 1697.   20. *The Post Man*, 18 and 25 September 1697.
21. *The Spectator*, 19 July 1711.
22. *The Diary of John Hervey, 1st Earl of Bristol*, ed. S.H.A.H. (Wells 1894).
23. *The English Post*, 8 September 1701.   24. *The Daily Courant*, 7 August 1703.
25. 'Monsieur Voiture', *op. cit.*, letter of 25 July 1699, p. 171.

Hampstead Wells were opened in 1701 and, as at Richmond, there was 'all manner of accommodation for Gentlemen and Ladies that intend to drink [the] Waters, and very good Musick for their entertainment'.[26] Concerts were given there in the Great Room at any rate until 1713, and were a weekly event in 1701 and 1702. The artists named included the ubiquitous Mr Abell, Jemmy Bowen, Dean the violinist, and John Eccles. They were widely advertised: 'Great Bills' were certainly employed to give details of the programmes,[27] and some concerts were advertised in as many as five different newspapers.

Some of these entertainments continued to be of a very mixed nature. For example, in 1706 a benefit for Mr Robinson included, apart from the music, an exhibition of tumbling, and Mr Robinson's 'Ladder Dance' – the latest success from the dancing rooms.[28] But this was an age when proper pastimes for gentlemen included cock-fighting and goose-riding, when nauseating exhibitions such as the consumption of a live cock, 'wonders' like the threading of a needle with his feet by an armless dwarf,[29] or gaping at the unfortunate inmates of Bedlam were thought quite proper pursuits for all classes. Considered against such a background, the average concert programme of the time, interlarded as it might sometimes be with quaint spectacles, seems on the whole a model of good taste. But the refined works of art and craft which characterize the Augustan Age – the furniture of Chippendale, Wedgwood china, a portrait by Reynolds, the music of Purcell and Handel – were made for a community which paradoxically, as J. H. Plumb has pointed out,[30] in other respects could manifest a boorishness which has rarely been paralleled in English history. If not exactly the rule, Squire Blifil in Fielding's *Tom Jones* was certainly not the exception.

The ruderies of the fairs provided summer entertainment for the poor, and the wells at Islington, Epsom, Hampstead and Richmond progressively more acceptable pleasures for the better-off; the real quality began to create the custom they have followed ever since of removing themselves as far as possible from the normal scene of their activities:

> . . . the Quality from Court,
> To Tunbridge, or the Bath resort,
> And all Mankind that are at leisure,
> Pursue some distant Rural pleasure . . .
> And to those Pleasures you may join,
> Good Musick, Dancing, and good Wine;
> Fine Beauties to delight your Eyes,
> Some vertuous, and some otherwise.[31]

26. *The Post Man*, 5 June 1701.
27. *The Daily Courant*, 5 August 1705. No examples seem to have survived.
28. *The Daily Courant*, 16 August 1706.
29. This unfortunate individual was an object of curiosity all over Europe: see H. Acton, *The Last Medici* (London 1958), p. 200.
30. *The First Four Georges* (London 1956), pp. 13–22.
31. Anon., *A Rod for Tunbridge Beaus, Bundl'd up at the Request of the Tunbridge Ladies* (London 1701), pp. 1–3.

Tunbridge and Bath in other words can be seen simply as an extension of the London pleasure haunts, providing musical and other entertainments for that element of fashionable London society which, every summer, transplanted itself to them with almost clockwork regularity.

Tunbridge had long been fashionable as a resort – ever since Charles II, in fact, had developed the habit of putting his queen out to grass there. No doubt the queen took her own private musicians with her, but there would be some public music too, though since there was no Tunbridge newspaper until much later, very little is known about it. In 1690 a 'Mr Rose over-against the Musick on Tunbridge Walks' is mentioned.[32] In 1696 the music seems to have been very poor, for in order to reassure intending guests for the next season, the following notice appeared in June 1697:

> The Musick that were at Tunbridge Wells last Year having given a Dissatisfaction to most of the Nobility, &tc. that were then present, there is now a new Consort goes down this Year, which have been approved of by several Noblemen and Gentlemen, and by License of the Lord of the Manner [sic]: And all Noblemen, Ladies and Gentlemen are desired that they will be pleased not to take notice of any other Musick, but such as shall play at the Walks, who are Deputed so to do by the Lord of the Manner abovesaid: They intend to begin to play on the 24 June next in the Musick Room upon the Walks, as usual.[33]

Celia Fiennes[34] noted that music was maintained by the company 'to play in the morning so long while they drink the waters, and in the afternoon for dancing', and it is doubtless this sort of entertainment to which the above notice refers. But formal concerts given each week had started by 1703, as the following puff indicates:

> They write from Tunbridge Wells, That there is arrived there that famous Italian Lady Signiora Francisca Margaretta de l'Epine, that gives every week Entertainments of Musick, all Compos'd by that great Master Signior Jacomo Greber, perform'd to the content and great satisfaction of all the Nobility and Gentry, which are in such great numbers there, as has not been seen these many years; the said Music is perform'd at New-Bounds, at Southborough, near the said Wells.[35]

Again, in the case of Bath, the absence of local papers makes information about music there rather sketchy. But there must have been many concerts in the season, especially when the queen and her court came to take the waters in 1703. As early as 1668 Pepys, after sweating for an hour after his first bath, tells us that 'by and by, comes musick to play to me, extraordinary good as ever I heard at London almost, or anywhere: 5s.',[36] and Defoe too describes how 'the Musick plays you into the Bath'. According to Ned Ward, behaviour here was not altogether above reproach, for the Cross Bath, to which most of the quality resorted, was 'more fam'd for *Pleasures* than *Cures*'. Here were 'Languishing eyes, Darting Killing Glances, Tempting Amorous Postures, attended by soft Musick,

32. *The London Gazette*, 28 July 1690.   33. *The Post Boy*, 15 June 1697.
34. Celia Fiennes, *The Journeys of Celia Fiennes*, ed. C. Morris (London 1949).
35. *The Post Man*, 12 August 1703.   36. *Diary*, 13 June 1668.

enough to provoke a *Vestal* to forbidden Pleasure, Captivate a Saint, and charm a *Jove*'.[37] Clearly the rule of a Beau Brummel was needed before, a century later, Jane Austen's Catherine Morland could be so well polished by the proprieties of Bath as to make her a fitting mistress for the parsonage of Woodston. But to be fair to Ward, he also mentions the 'Consort of Delicate Musick, Vocal and Instrumental, perform'd by good Masters' which was generally played at the balls given by members of the nobility. Many people came simply to enjoy such pleasures as the balls and the company afforded, and ignored the presence of the baths and waters altogether.

Lady Cave, writing to her father in September 1709, helps to complete the picture:

> This town is extream full of company, and highly entertained with Singing and Musick, by the famous Nicoleno & Valentinio, besides plays, baths, puppet-shows, ladder-Dancing, &c.[38]

As we shall see later, in 1712 Claver Morris, the musical doctor from Wells, met Corbett the violinist in Bath[39] and subsequently heard Matthew Dubourg there and Geminiani – the latter 'the best Player on the Violin in Europe', or so he maintained.[40]

Although Bath and Tunbridge were certainly the most fashionable resorts of their kind outside London, another spa was discovered at Astrop, near King's Sutton in Northamptonshire, in 1664; by 1697 it had 'grown as Famous (almost) to emulate Tunbridge its self'.[41] Celia Fiennes described it as 'Much frequented by the Gentry . . . there is a fine Gravell Walke that is between 2 high Cutt hedges where is a Roome for the Musick, and a Roome for the Company besides the Private Walkes'.[42] In fact, there was a rapid increase in the number of wells and spas becoming known and frequented all over England at this time,[43] and music was one of the entertainments which all of them provided, though only at the greater spas was one likely to hear lavish concerts performed by the 'best masters' such as might have been heard in London.

Clearly, the presence of visitors, many of them from London itself, was responsible for the promotion of a good deal of concert activity in the provinces in the summer months. But some of the larger and more prosperous towns had musical societies which promoted concerts for local residents during the winter months too, though the performers often included a high proportion of amateurs. The choirs in the cathedral towns provided a basis which could be built upon, and there were several provincial 'Societies of Gentlemen, Lovers of Musick' mod-

37. E. Ward [attrib.], *A Step to the Bath, with a Character of the Place* (London 1700).
38. *Verney Letters of the Eighteenth Century*, ed. Margaret Maria Lady Verney, 2 vols. (London 1930), I, p. 187.
39. 'The Account Books of Claver Morris', *Notes and Queries for Somerset and Dorset*, vols. 14, 22 and 23 (1914–15, 1936–8 and 1939–42): entry for 12 September 1712.
40. [Dr Claver Morris], *The Diary of a West Country Physician*, ed. E. Hobhouse (London 1934): entries for 26 September 1718, 6–7 October 1721.
41. R. Peirce, *Bath Memoirs* (London 1697).   42. Celia Fiennes, *op. cit.*
43. See *Englishmen at Rest and Play*, ed. R. Lennard (Oxford 1931), especially Appendix I.

elled upon that in London, which promoted quite respectable vocal and in-
strumental concerts with a particular effort being made when it came to
22 November, the festival of St Cecilia. Husk has given details of some of the St
Cecilia's Day concerts at Oxford, Salisbury and Winchester.[44] These perfor-
mances, however, may often have received additional polish from the presence of
London musicians. For St Cecilia's Day 1704 the organist of Winchester, Vaughan
Richardson, composed music, but for the performance at Winchester 'Mr John
Shore, the Famous Trumpeter, and Mr Elford, were sent for down by the Gentle-
men of the County'. The expense was apparently worthwhile, for 'the whole
Performance was very satisfactory, and received with the general Applause of the
Audience'.[45]

National rejoicings too were often celebrated musically up and down the
country:

> They write from Oxford, that they have made extraordinary rejoycings there
> upon account of the Glorious success of her Majesties Arms, and especially for the
> late Action at *Vigo*, in which his Grace the Duke of *Ormond*, Chancellor of the
> University, gained so much Honour. Those rejoycings have lasted a whole week,
> and were concluded on Saturday night by a magnificent Consort of Vocal and
> Instrumental Musick performed by Mr Abel.[46]

Mr Abell seems always to have contrived to be in the right place at the right time to
demonstrate his abilities to the full, and no journey daunted him: he even
planned a concert in Aberdeen where he proposed to be, 'with the Help of GOD',
on 3 November 1705.[47]

Royalist Oxford had welcomed the king's return in 1660 with a concert in the
Music School which, under the enthusiastic guidance of Edward Lowe, became
the focus of much fruitful musical activity. But the Sheldonian Theatre, after
Smith's organ was set up there in 1671, increasingly became the scene for the
larger public concerts, and from 1679 the Music Acts took place there too. Wood
describes such an event in 1680: 'Here were 2000 people at least; all well done and
gave good content.'[48] The two odes of William Croft's *Musicus Apparatus Academi-
cus* performed at Oxford on 13 July 1713 show the ambitious scale of the Music
Acts by that date.

But yet again, Oxford and Cambridge musical events often seem to have relied
rather heavily on London musicians. The Oxford St Cecilia's Day celebration of
1696 was probably simply a transplant from London.[49] And when William Turner
went to Cambridge in the same year to present his public exercise for his Doctor's

44. W. H. Husk, *An Account of the Musical Celebrations on St Cecilia's Day in the 16th, 17th and 18th
    Centuries* (London 1857).
45. *The Diverting Post*, 25 November 1704.   46. *The Post Man*, 12 November 1702.
47. *The Edinburgh Courant*, 26 October 1705.
48. E. F. A. Williams, *A Short Historical Account of the Degrees in Music at Oxford and Cambridge*
    (London 1893), pp. 28–9.
49. See M. Tilmouth, 'Nicola Matteis', *Musical Quarterly* XLVI (1960), pp. 30–1. The music of
    Matteis's ode, 'Assist, assist! You mighty Sons of Art', hitherto believed to be lost, has been
    identified by Alan Browning in the Bodleian Library, Oxford, MS Mus.c.16, fols. 3ff.

degree it was clearly just as much an outing for the royal musicians, for he was assisted 'by Dr Blow, the Gentlemen of the Chappel Royal, and the chief Musicians about Town'.[50]

Races and assizes, in towns where these were held, provided the kind of gathering of society that made concert promotion worthwhile:

> York, August the 8th. During the Sizes will be perform'd a Consort of Musick, by Mr Holcomb, Mr Corbet, &c. Who will perform the same in Nottingham August the 16th, 17th, 18th, and 19th, after the Races are over, viz. All the choicest Songs out of all the new Operas, in Italian and English, with their proper Sinfoney's as they are play'd in the Queen's Theatre.[51]

At Nottingham, music during August race week may have been a regular thing. In 1707 the musicians Hughes, Corbett and Babell visited the town.[52] That they placed notices in the London press shows that it was the patronage of visitors to Nottingham as much as that of the local populace that was being sought. On another occasion Colonel Molesworth's regiment was quartered near the town:

> On Friday the Sixth Day of January next. At Mr Porter's Dancing School in the High-Pavement, Nottingham, (for the Benefit of his Majesty King George's Hautboys, belonging to the Honourable Colonel Molesworth), Will be perform'd, A very good Consort of, Instrumental, Musick: With several of Corelli's, Vivaldi's, and Albinoni's Concerto's: And one of Corelli's Solo's by an extraordinary Hand. And a Gentleman of the Town to play the Harpsicord. NB. After the Consort is over, to oblige the Quality, there will be Country Dances. Tickets 2s 6d to be delivered at the Door.
> Beginning at Five a Clock.   Vivat Rex.[53]

This mixture of amateurs and professionals in a concert-cum-dance was to become typical of eighteenth-century provincial music-making.

In East Anglia, then the centre of a vastly profitable wool trade, concerts and even operas were promoted in the larger towns from an early date. One Norwich performance in 1700 was duly noted in the London press:

> On the 17th of January the Opera Dioclesian, was acted at Norwich, by Mr Dogget's Company, the Duke of Norfolk's Servants, with great Applause, being the first that ever was attempted out of London.[54]

Whether much of Purcell's elaborate score was played seems doubtful, but ten years later Leveridge's *Macbeth* was given at the Queen's Arms with, it is claimed, 'all the Witches, Songs and Dances, as they were originally performed at the Theatre Royal in London';[55] and *Abra-Mule* in the following year incorporated 'that Excellent Song set by Mr Henry Purcel, "From Rosie Bowers"'.[56]

50. *The Flying Post*, 2 July 1696.   51. *The Daily Courant*, 1 August 1709.
52. *The Daily Courant*, 23 July 1707; see also *The Nottingham Weekly Courant*, 26 June 1718.
53. *The Nottingham Weekly Courant*, 22 December 1715.
54. *The Flying Post*, 23 January 1700.
55. *The Norwich Gazette*, 16 December 1710. (This and other East Anglian references are drawn from A. H. Mann, 'MS Notes on East Anglian Musicians and Musical Events', Norwich Public Library, 22 vols.)
56. *The Norwich Gazette*, 13 January 1711.

Taverns were often the scene of the early provincial concert promotions just as they had been in Banister's days in London, and no doubt the locals lent a similar informality to the proceedings:

> At the Greyhound, in St Stephens [parish, Norwich], is a curious new Organ set up, there is also the Hautboy, Violin, and Harpsicord, and the Harp played on to great perfection by Charles the Harper's own Son; where all Gentlemen and others may be entertained with a Lesson of Musick at their Pleasure, and find kind an[d] Civil usage.[57]

Clearly at the Greyhound you could ask for a hornpipe or a jig with your pint of ale much as we would ask for a packet of crisps or (sad comment on our times) press a coin into the inevitable jukebox.

The City Waits seem to have persisted as an active body rather longer in Norwich than in many other towns. In 1714 they gave monthly concerts, charging a shilling for admission, the proceeds from which helped to pay for the St Cecilia's Day feast. In 1717 there were two concerts given 'for Mr Dahwson's [Dahuron's?] benefit' at Mr Boseley's Rooms in Norwich.[58] The harpist Morphew also played several times at the King's Arms there in 1718, and Thornowitz followed him in 1724. By this time sufficient interest seems to have been aroused to warrant weekly music meetings similar to those which had taken place at York Buildings in London some twenty years before, even if the scale was more modest, the musicians generally less eminent, and the audience less sophisticated.[59]

In 1721 there was a proposal to start regular concerts at Bury St Edmunds, to include 'the newest Solos, Sonatos, Concertos and Extravaganzas extant'. They were to be weekly or monthly, as the subscribers thought fit, and the promoter hoped that 'by the encouragement of this intended subscription, the best and newest Music that can be got, will be procured and performed to satisfaction'.[60] A little later, works by Corelli, Vivaldi and Alberti were given by 'the best masters from Norwich' in the Great Hall at Yarmouth.[61] As London had been to Norwich so Norwich became to the smaller towns in its vicinity.

Clearly East Anglia was developing musical activities quite rapidly and, as we know from the programmes, musical taste was not conspicuously lagging behind that of London. This is emphasized by the activities of local booksellers as well as other general shopkeepers who, from the close of the seventeenth century, added a selection of music books to their stocks. George Barton, for example, had shops in Huntingdon, Peterborough and St Ives and had a stall at St Neots on market days; apart from selling musical instruments he announced that he would send to London 'for Music-Books of all sorts'.[62] Such examples could be multiplied. By 1723 Crossgrave of Norwich, the printer of the local *Gazette*, found it worthwhile to insert a list in his paper of the music he could supply. As well as items predictably catering for amateur diversion such as 'Lessons for the German Flute' or Keller's indispensable 'Compleat Method . . . for Thorough Bass', this in-

57. *The Norwich Gazette*, 25 August 1711.   58. *The Norwich Gazette*, 29 December 1706.
59. *The Norwich Gazette*, 31 October 1724.   60. *The Suffolk Mercury*, 13 November 1721.
61. *The Norwich Gazette*, 9 November 1728.   62. *The St Ives Post Boy*, 27 October 1718.

cluded Corelli's Opp. I–V, some of the trio sonatas arranged for flutes and bass, Thornowitz's 'Solos', Handel's *Radamisto* (presumably the songs in the opera), and other current favourites.[63]

Sometimes concerts in the provinces, as in London, were frankly promotional. When the London instrument-maker Ralph Agutter returned to his native parts in 1712 he advertised his wares in no fewer than thirty-one issues of the *Newcastle Courant*[64] and was almost certainly responsible for the meetings at Mr Harris's Dancing School in Westgate, Newcastle, when there was performed 'a CON-SORT of Instrumental Musick; As Opera-Tunes, Italian-Solio's, Sonata's, Over-tures &c upon the following Instruments, viz. Spinett, Trumpet, Hautboy, Violins, Bass-Viols, Bassoon, &c'.[65]

One of the chief differences between the London concert scene and that in the provinces was in the extent of amateur participation both in promotion and in actual performance. True, the 'Society of Gentlemen Lovers of Musick' which organized the St Cecilia's Day celebrations in the capital was compounded of amateurs and professionals, and if we may believe accounts of the celebrated meetings at the house of Thomas Britton, musicians from the meanest to the mightiest rubbed shoulders there with a society of amateurs at least as diverse in social standing. But many London concerts were purely commercial ventures undertaken by musicians themselves primarily for financial benefit. The same may have been true of such concerts as some of those run by the Norwich City Waits, but by and large provincial concerts depended much more upon the existence of a flourishing music club or society, and as the fortunes of such clubs waxed and waned with the arrival or disappearance of a notable enthusiast so did the tide of their musical activity ebb and flow.

Surprisingly little attention has been paid to the papers of the Wells physician Dr Claver Morris,[66] though they provide us with a vivid picture of his own musical activities as well as those of the Wells music club of which he was clearly the leading spirit. Before coming to Wells in 1686 Morris lived in Salisbury and in his later years returned there several times on the occasions of the Salisbury St Cecilia's Day celebrations, the influence of which perhaps helped to shape the pattern of activities in the Wells music club. Morris had studied medicine at Oxford, but music was clearly his first love: he sang, played the harpsichord and organ, and seems to have had some capacity on the violin, bassoon, oboe and flute. The music club met every Tuesday night in the Vicars' Hall at Wells – the Close Hall – though it moved to the Deanery for a time in 1704. The early diary of 1709–10 records details of Morris's own private music-making as well as meetings of the club the climax of whose activities was on 22 November 1709 when 'Purcel's Cecilia Song and much other musick' was performed. Somewhat obscurely he writes that 'We had of Half-Crown Men 62. The Women faild to pay by

63. *The Norwich Gazette*, 1 June 1723.   64. From 30 April 1712 to 30 July 1712.
65. *The Newcastle Courant*, 21 May 1712.
66. The ensuing quotations and allusions are from the two sources named in notes 39 and 40 above.

getting some of them into the place; so that there were of them when fairly in, but 33.'

The later diary, covering the years from 1718 to 1726, is of the greatest interest. In 1718 Morris visited Bath and made music with Dubourg and heard Walter and Besiwillibald play Schenk's sonatas for two bass viols. Back in Wells the St Cecilia's Day music was improved by the presence of 'Mr Duglass the Black-moor Trumpeter', whom Morris thought the best trumpeter in England; he played two trumpet sonatas for them as well. The following year Dahuron joined them in 'Dr Croft's Song for his Degree, and a great Deal of other Musick. We advanced the Tickets to 2s, and had as much Company as the last year.'

Morris had a mechanical turn of mind: he experimented with a sprung brass tangent (perhaps inspired by clavichord mechanism) to replace the normal harp-sichord quill, he devised 'a stand to set a Bass-viol on to make it sound louder in playing on it', and he saw to the repair of a mechanical time-beater for use in the church in 1720. He was intrigued too by 'an Upright Harpsichord mix'd with an Organ' (apparently a claviorganum) built by Schwarbrook in 1725 when he was in Wells working on the cathedral organ. Morris was a devotee of modern music, much of which he had brought by carrier from London. His account books enable us to form a very exact idea of his library, which included the operas *Thomyris*, *Almahide*, *Telemachus* and *Rinaldo*, motets by d'Eve, Fiocco, Mont de Caix and Cherici, sonatas by Tibaldi, Bassani (some copied for him 'with his Graces express'd'), Valentine, Reali, Corbett, Sherard and Schickhardt, and solos by Corelli, Valentini and Mascitti. We can also identify much of the music which he and his friends played with such pleasure privately or at the music club, works like Vivaldi's 'Cuckoo' Concerto, or concertos by Valentini, Albinoni and Alberti. Some of their meetings must have been veritable marathons. Once nine of Valentini's concertos were played at a sitting, and on another occasion 'we play'd the 6th Opera of Bomporti all over, Finger's two Sonatas which I would should be play'd at my Funeral, & two of Bassani's Sonatas'.

Morris himself tried never to miss an opportunity of hearing leading perfor-mers when they were in the neighbourhood. He met Corbett in Bath in 1712, though in 1723 he just missed the chance of hearing Cuzzoni sing there. In 1724 Francischello and Fiocco came to Wells, and the club rose to the occasion by performing the latter's 'Serenade, & some other of his Compositions'.

A great occasion was in October 1721 when Morris went to Bath to hear Geminiani. He was privately introduced to the violinist who, he writes, 'enter-tain'd us with the utmost Civility as well as his wonderful Hand on the Violin'. The Wells music club seems to have been a friendly affair, always ready to welcome guests whether as performers or listeners. In 1723 'General Evans's Hoboys were there & enter'd Clubbers': one wonders what stirring sounds filled the air that night.

In 1725 the death of Morris's wife interrupted the meetings of the club for ten weeks, an indication perhaps of how dependent it had become on his energy and drive in the management of its affairs. The meetings were eventually resumed, but in the next year there seems to have been some difference of opinion with the vicars and the club moved to the Mitre nearby. Perhaps Morris's own private concerts became his chief solace – and not a purely musical one either, to judge by the truly Pepysian repast he served up on 11 July 1726:

> I had a Consort of Musick at my House; & I invited Mr Taylor, Mr Prickman, Mr Nikells, Mr Boulting, Mr Tutton, Mr Broadway, Mr Slade, Captain Penny, Mr Lucas, Mr Burland, & Mr Comes junr, who all came: I gave them for Supper a Cold Shoulder of Mutton, a Cold Breast of Veal, a Sallet, a Couple of Neat's Tongues; & I had for them a Bowl of Punch, a Bottle of Claret, Many Bottles of October-Beer, & Ale. We play'd all Tibaldi's Sonates. And the Company, many of them stay'd till past 1 a clock.

Morris's account books, apart from listing his purchases of music, are a mine of information about the prices he paid for instruments or for modifications to them and accessories for them. He died in March 1727; but if the last request in his will was observed, even his death did not quite end his activities as concert-promoter:

> My desire is that there might be no Appearance of Concernment or Grief amongst even my nearest Relations or Friends But if it might be possible, there might be a Concort of Musick of three Sonatas at least in the Room where my Body is placed before it be carryed out of my House to be Interred.

Morris's papers give a vivid picture of the activities of the Wells Music Club and once again show that, provincials though they might be, the members were not noticeably behind a London audience in their musical tastes. Were such clubs common at this time? Certainly at Worcester by 1720 there was an active musical society and enough local interest to encourage Claudius Phillips to give a benefit concert in the Great Room in the Tower.[67] At Shrewsbury too there was a musical society which met to give performances of vocal and instrumental music in Shrewsbury and Hereford.[68] No doubt a thorough search in local archives would produce evidence from diaries and letters that the picture painted of Wells by Claver Morris was by no means unique in the early years of the eighteenth century.

Another factor which inevitably influenced provincial concert life was the growing fashion for patronage of musicians by the nobility who, in travelling to their country seats or to the fashionable resorts, might include them in their retinues of servants. In *The Maid's Last Prayer, or Any, Rather than Fail* (1693) Thomas Southerne satirizes the domestic concerts of 'gentleman performers', the tone of which in this instance had perhaps not been raised by the addition of professionals to the little band. Act IV scene 3 represents a musical party at Sir Symphony's ('A *fanatico per la musica*'). Sir Symphony plays the violin – 'a Cremona, and cost me fifty pounds' – and the bass viol. He has difficulty in getting any sound out of the viol since one of the 'bullies' in the overcrowded room has inconsiderately drawn the bow through candle-wax, but eventually they start:

SIR SYMPHONY: Come, pray, let's begin. (*All the while the symphony plays, he beats*

67. *The Worcester Post Man*, 26 August 1720.   68. *The Worcester Post Man*, 1 April 1720.

time and speaks in admiration of it.) O Gad: there's a flat note! there's art! how surprisingly the key changes! O law! there's a double relish! I swear, Sir, you have the sweetest little finger in England! ha! that stroke's new; I tremble every inch of me; now ladies, look to your hearts – softly, gentlemen – remember the echo – captain, you play the wrong tune – O law! my teeth! my teeth! for God's sake, captain, mind your cittern – Now the fuga, bases! again! Lord! Mr Humdrum, you come in three bars too soon. Come, now the song.[69]

Sir Symphony's antics, if not very typical, are at any rate amusing. Moreover, if domestic music of this sort had not been a fairly common form of entertainment this passage, and others like it in other Restoration plays, would never have been written.

Turning to real life, the addition of a few professionals could of course improve the result greatly, and, as James Brydges found, retaining only the most capable sort of fiddling valet could result in a very impressive concert for him and his privileged guests at his semi-rural retreat at Cannons.[70] Others might be more modest. The domestic music of John Hervey, 1st Earl of Bristol, must have been in marked contrast with its setting at stately Ickworth in West Suffolk. Hervey played the recorder and the violin; he bought a harpsichord by Player for his wife and between 1702 and 1735 paid Ralph Courtivill, Francis Dieupart and Joseph Kelway considerable sums for teaching his daughters to sing and play. In London he employed Schudi to tune the harpsichords, subscribed to the building of Vanbrugh's Haymarket Theatre and even had Bononcini's *Crispo* performed at his house by Senesino and Mrs Robinson accompanied by the Castruccis. But his music-making in the country seems to have been altogether less flamboyant, his own participation making it a matter for the personal pleasure of his friends and himself alone.[71]

Very much the same could be said of Sir Harbottle Grimston of Gorhambury near St Albans somewhat earlier, during the 1680s, when his employment of Diessener as harpsichord teacher to his daughter and other small expenditures seem to recognize in music a matter for private relaxation rather than public show.[72] This sort of attitude was shared later by Sir Dudley Ryder,[73] whose contact with two professional musicians, Demoivre and Cynelum, gave him a tolerable skill on the flute and the bass viol without hindering his legal studies so much as to prevent him reaching the top of his profession as Chief Justice in 1754.

Yet others were more influenced by what they had observed on the Grand Tour. If Cardinal Ottoboni could keep Corelli in his service as a showpiece for his guests, then an English duke might do likewise. In 1700 Wriothesley Russell returned from Rome to inherit the Dukedom of Bedford. Two years later he attached to his household two Italian musicians and composers – Nicola Cosimi

69. The song is Purcell's 'Tho' you make no return to my passion', z601/1.
70. See C. H. C. Baker and M. I. Baker, *James Brydges, First Duke of Chandos* (Oxford 1949).
71. See note 22 above.
72. Account books of Sir Harbottle Grimston in *Historical Manuscripts Commission*, Manuscripts of the Earl of Verulam, p. 209 *et seq.*
73. See *The Diary of Dudley Ryder 1715–16*, ed. W. Matthews (London 1939).

the violinist, and Nicola Francesco Haym the cellist, who later collaborated with Handel – as one of his librettists; Haym received £100 per annum as 'Master of the Chamber Musick' at Southampton House. Just as earlier when the Duke of Buckingham had gone racing at Newmarket he had been accompanied by his own band of fiddlers,[74] so Cosimi and Haym formed part of Bedford's retinue on his journeys about England. The 'Eytalians' were not popular with the rest of the duke's household. Both spoke English badly, Haym was apparently over-weeningly arrogant (especially for a mere musician, as no doubt most of the English servants thought of him), and everything had to be done for them when they accompanied the duke to Bath or to visit the Duke of Beaufort at Badminton.[75] But the presence of such excellent musicians as Cosimi and Haym in Bath must undoubtedly have helped to raise the level of public and private musical entertainments there, or indeed wherever they went in the provinces, and added another factor in the furtherance of the Italian orientation of English musical taste at this time.

The growth of provincial musical activities in the early part of the century no doubt also fostered the development of native talents that might otherwise have lain dormant. Inevitably, and sometimes inadvisedly, some were drawn to seek their fortune in London, still the nation's musical capital, as an anecdote from Dudley Ryder's later, unpublished journal suggests:

> A young singer in the choir of Worcester came to London with [a] recommendation to Mr Handel as [a] great genius. Handel asked him to sing; he did so. Handel said: 'This is the way you praise God at Worcester?' 'Yes', he answered. 'God is very good' [replied Handel], 'and will no doubt hear your praises at Worcester, but no man will hear them at London.'[76]

Handel's somewhat enigmatic advice might not have held good for very long, for the cut-throat competition of the London scene was already beginning to spread further afield. In the 1740s and '50s Sir Dudley Ryder was able to hear singers like Senesino and Galli and the oboist Martini at York and Lincoln when he was on circuit in the North.[77] Senesino had attended Lord Burlington to York but initially greatly offended the company by arrogantly refusing to sing even though (or perhaps because) the Duke of Rutland had offered to accompany him on the violin: four nights later he unbent and sang at the assembly room. Ryder states that he had never heard him to so great advantage: 'It was surprising how his voice filled that vast room, though itself full of company.' Even if it never came to dominate the provincial scene, the professional concert, often with a foreign

---

74. J. A. Westrup, 'Domestic Music under the Stuarts', *Proceedings of the Musical Association* LXVIII (1941–2).

75. See G. S. Thomson, *Life in a Noble Household, 1641–1771* (London 1937), and *The Russells in Bloomsbury, 1669–1771* (London 1940).

76. Undated anecdote in the Ryder Papers (shorthand journal). I am indebted to Mr K. L. Perrin for the transcript of this passage and to the Earl of Harrowby and the Harrowby MSS Trust for permission to reproduce it.

77. Ryder Papers (see note 76). Martini and Senesino performed in York on 18 August and 19 August (year unspecified) respectively; Galli sang in Lincoln on 4 September 1747.

virtuoso heading the bill, was gaining ground in the provinces just as it had done earlier in London.

The middle years of the century, however, remain largely unexplored. A thorough examination of the files of local newspapers which proliferated from the 1730s onwards and of the letters and private papers held in public and private archives should add enormously to what is known of the lives and activities of musicians and the quality and extent of musical culture in what is still sometimes so oddly and undeservedly described as the 'land without music'.

Thomas Tudway's History of Music

Christopher Hogwood

'In matters of Antiquity there are two extreams, 1. a totall neglect, and 2. perpetuall guessing; between which proper evidences are the temper; that is, if there be any, to make the best of them; if none, to desist.' Roger North's blunt opening to his 'Memoires of Musick' (in the final 1728 version) hardly conceals the exasperation of a sceptical professional lawyer with the speculations of the musical antiquarians; 'another', he declares, 'may squeese out some further misty conjectures, and so with labour in vain, tire upon the subject till doomsday'.[1] Within fifty years of his remarks the English public was to be presented with not one but two complete histories founded on the 'proper evidences' that North prescribed. While Sir John Hawkins was certainly more sympathetic to the qualities of earlier music than Charles Burney, both men took the approach (then relatively novel with reference to music) of generalizing on collected evidence; both employed the comparative method, with musical examples to support their arguments (though not in both cases with the intention of proving 'progress' in the arts);[2] both histories accepted that the 'ancient' in music could not reasonably be equated with the ancient in literature or architecture. But this change of attitude was no sudden reform of the 1770s. Both Burney and Hawkins built on earlier efforts to systematize with 'proper evidences' the old Quarrel of Ancients and Moderns.

A polarization of views had been apparent since the beginning of the century. On the one hand there was the view held by Dr Pepusch, possibly the best-informed and certainly the most influential of the musical antiquarians:

> He asserted, that art of music is lost: that the ancients only understood it in its perfection; that it was revived a little in the reign of King Henry VIII, by Tallys and

1. *Roger North on Music*, ed. John Wilson (London 1959), pp. 317, 325.
2. Prior to 1770 it was rare for historical argument to resort to musical examples. The title-page of Peter Prelleur's *Brief History of Musick* (1738) 'collected from Aristoxenus, Plutarch, Boetius, Bontempi, Zarlino, Tho: Salmon and many others' speaks for itself. See also Warren Dwight Allen, *Philosophies of Music History* (New York 1962), pp. 245ff.

his contemporaries; as also in the reign of Queen Elizabeth, who was a judge and patroness of it: that, after her reign, it sunk for sixty or seventy years, till Purcell made some attempts to restore it; but that ever since the true, ancient art, depending on nature and mathematical principles, had gained no ground, the present masters having no fixed principles at all.[3]

On the other hand, in practical circles, both professional and amateur, there is ample evidence of disillusionment with the transmitted views of the ancients on musical theory. Pages of leaden prose on the system of modes, scales, tetrachords and the gamut had already driven Pepys to think of devising a more intelligible 'Scheme and Theory of Music', complaining that 'though it be a ridiculous and troublesome way . . . [yet] like the old Hypotheses in philosophy [i.e. natural science] , it must be learned, though a man knows a better' (8 April 1668). By 1719, Handel could firmly maintain the irrelevance of the Greek modes and solmization: 'as we have [now] been liberated from the narrow limits of ancient music, I cannot see what use the Greek modes can be to modern music' (letter in French to Johann Mattheson, 24 February 1719).[4]

The gulf between these two schools was a major obstacle to the practical historian of music in the early years of the eighteenth century. Roger North was certainly unusual in asking that for historical inquiry 'gentlemen must put off their *anno domini* . . . and put on the time and garb of the age they are to deal in', and as an intelligent performer and connoisseur of all arts he found the Quarrel exaggerated and futile, since 'in matters of taste, there is no criterium of better and worse'.[5] But he also noted one of the main dangers in perpetuating the controversy: that the same enthusiasm for the modern and practical that was disposing of the inconvenience of the modes was also removing the very evidence needed for a scientific appraisal of musical composition.

> This so generall abrenonnciation of all elder, tho' lately by-gone musick, is the cause that almost all the ancient copys, tho' very finely wrote, are lost and gone; and that litle which is left, by pastry and waste paper uses, is wearing out, and in a short time none at all will be left. The musick in Henry 8th's time hath bin mentioned as in some degree valuable, but where shall wee find it?[6]

He would in fact have found it (and much more) not so many miles from his house at Rougham, in the Earl of Oxford's library at Wimpole Hall, a short distance beyond Cambridge.

North in fact was not 'the first to recognize the merits of old English musicians whose works had been neglected'.[7] Primacy in this, and in the association of a history of music with musical examples, belongs to Thomas Tudway, trained as a chorister of the Chapel Royal, and appointed to the honorary position of 'Musick-

---

3. Reported by John Wesley, *Journal*, 13 June 1748. Writers such as Vossius (*De Poematum*, 1673), Sir William Temple (*Essay on Ancient and Modern Learning*, 1690) and Arthur Bedford (*The Great Abuse of Musick*, 1711) were even more dogmatically devoted to the 'degeneracy' theory.
4. Quoted in O. E. Deutsch, *Handel: A Documentary Biography* (London 1955), pp. 86–8.
5. *Roger North on Music*, pp. 284, 317.
6. *Ibid.*, p. 284.   7. Allen, *op. cit.*, p. 71n.

Professor to the University of Cambridge' in 1705. Between 1715 and 1720 he assembled a manuscript collection of services and anthems, both ancient and modern, for the Harleian library, and in the (unpublished) prefaces to these volumes he set out his views on the history of music from earliest times to the present day. It is an idiosyncratic viewpoint, and one that can be seen to change as the collection progressed. Tudway's vision was limited, and his standpoint, at least at first, reactionary. But his reference to 'proper evidences', his adoption of chronological limits to 'ancient music' which held good for the remainder of the century, and the gradual change of position that enables us to measure the gap that separated Handel from Pepusch make his idiosyncrasies and inaccuracies doubly useful. The modern historian could well consider how Tudway arrived at his view of history, and also what pressures – musical, antiquarian and aristocratic – influenced the compilation of this first English history of music in the eighteenth century.

The Harleys had, from Stuart times, been a family of bibliomanes, and well documented though the growth of the library is (through the diaries of the librarian, Humfrey Wanley, in particular),[8] throughout the time of Tudway's association with the family it is never clear to whom the library actually belonged – to Robert Harley, Lord Treasurer until his impeachment in 1714, and virtual ruler of England, or to his son Edward, who became 2nd Earl of Oxford on his father's death in 1724.[9] Although Tudway wrote to Wanley congratulating Robert Harley for going 'vigorously on . . . In furnishing his Library with ev'rything that is curious' despite the events of 1714 (Tudway to Wanley, 10 September 1714: British Library, Harl. MS 3782, fol. 29), Robert Harley's imprisonment in the Tower the following year must have put an end to his direct supervision of the library. Edward Harley, a devoted antiquarian and unenthusiastic politician, and the scholarly and loyal Wanley appear to have controlled the policy of the collection, and it was through Wanley that Tudway began his connection with the Earl of Oxford.

At first he was employed as a negotiator in the difficult dealings between Harley and John Covel, Master of Christ's College, Cambridge, over the sale of the latter's Greek manuscripts. Covel, who had travelled widely in the East (spending some six years as chaplain in Constantinople), knew the niceties of haggling and prolonged the negotiations with 'Whofflings and Shifts', as Tudway put it.

These delays, however, gave Tudway the opportunity to develop with Wanley a scheme for a collection of 'Ancient compositions of Church Musick' that would be 'worthy of so renowned a Library as my Ld's is'. The assembling of this material, Tudway's growing enthusiasm for ancient manuscripts and the widening of his circle of sources as the collection grew can be traced through his correspondence with Wanley. The (sometimes strained) relationship between the

8. *The Diary of Humfrey Wanley 1715–1726*, ed. C. E. Wright and R. C. Wright (London 1966).
9. On Edward Harley and his circle, see James Lees-Milne, *Earls of Creation* (London 1962), pp. 173–218.

protagonists is summarized by Edward Turnbull in 'Thomas Tudway and the Harleian Collection',[10] but it is clear from the Epistle Dedicatory to Volume I that Tudway acknowledged Wanley, rather than the Earl or himself, as 'the first proposer of this work'.

Wanley was a noted antiquarian (he was co-founder, with John Talman, of the Society of Antiquaries of London), an expert palaeographer and an authority on Anglo-Saxon. As a cataloguer he was unrivalled, and as a librarian immensely well read, but his interest in music seems to have been slight.[11] Nevertheless, as we shall see later, his musical taste was to exert a direct effect on Tudway's project.

Wanley had first worked in the Bodleian Library, Oxford (1695–1700), where he met Henry Aldrich, Dean of Christ Church from 1689 to 1710, and one of the first connoisseurs of early vocal music. His collection of transcriptions from sixteenth-century partbooks (Palestrina, Marenzio, Victoria and Gesualdo, for instance), which he left to Christ Church Library, contained (in the words of his will) 'things of value in themselves and to be found in very few libraries'.[12] The 'Papers prepared for a treatise on music' listed under his name in the library catalogue (Ch.Ch. 1187) and summarized in Burney[13] are largely in the hand of James Talbot, but they nevertheless provide evidence of the spirit of inquiry flowing from the Christ Church circle via Wanley and Harley himself to encourage Tudway's scheme. Certainly Aldrich's collection supplied the measure against which Wanley was later to note the lacunae in the Harleian collection, and therefore the catalyst for his proposal to Tudway.

Against this background of antiquarian inquiry into the actual nature of 'ancient' music, but still hampered by a natural conservatism and the historio-graphical uncertainties of the 'ancient versus modern' conflict, Tudway takes the expected reactionary stand in his dedicatory preface to 'A Collection of the most celebrated services and anthems used in the Church of England from the Re-formation to the Restoration of K. Charles II' (B.L. Harl. 7337, fols. 3–4).[14]

[f3]   To The Right Hon[ble] Edward Lord Harley
         My Hon[or]d very Good Lord

10. *Journal of the American Musicological Society* VIII (1955), pp. 203–7.
11. In a short essay on the problems of 'judging the Age of MSS, the Style of Learned Authors, Painters, Musicians &c. by Mr. Humfrey Wanley' (written in 1701 and published in *Philosophical Transactions* XXIV (1706)), directed to Narcissus Marsh, Archbishop of Dublin, he took palaeography rather than musicology as his theme.
12. See W. G. Hiscock, *Henry Aldrich of Christ Church, 1648–1710* (Oxford 1960), and Percy Lovell, '"Ancient" Music in Eighteenth-Century England', *Music & Letters* LX/4 (October 1979), p. 408. For a suggestion that Aldrich's taste and collection derived from music imported by Robert Martin in the mid seventeenth century, see D. W. Krummel, 'Venetian Baroque Music in a London Bookshop: The Robert Martin Catalogues, 1633–50' in *Music and Bibliography. Essays in Honour of Alec Hyatt King*, ed. Oliver Neighbour (London 1980), pp. 5–7.
13. Charles Burney, *A General History of Music from the Earliest Ages to the Present Period (1789)*, ed. Frank Mercer, 2 vols. (New York 1935, repr. New York 1957), vol. 2, p. 480n.
14. I am grateful to Tim Crawford and Nicholas Clapton for help in transcribing the Tudway extracts and the Tudway–Wanley correspondence.

I shall think my self much Hon[or]^d & very happy, if any endeavours of mine, in Obeying your Lordships commands, may contribute anything to your Pious designe, of rescuing from ye dust, & Oblivion, our Ancient compositions of Church Musick; at this time, so much mistaken, & dispis'd.

The Pious Reformers of our Church, from ye Errors of Popery, haveing settl'd ye Doctrines thereof, thought it very necessary, & advisable allso, to appoint a standard of Church musick wch might adorn ye dayly service of God, by such a solemn performance, as might best stir up devotion, & kindle in mens hearts, a warmth for devine worship.

I dare affirm my Lord, that there cou'd never have been any thing better devis'd, than what was compos'd first of that kind, by Mr Tallis, & Mr Bird. They were both Servants, & Organists, to her Majesty Queen Elizabeth, & employ'd by her in composing for ye service of her Chappell Royall; & though both of them Papists, have sett an inimitable Pattern of solemn Church musick, wch no one since, has been able to come up to, & remains to this day, a demonstration of their exalted Genius; of wch two excellent persons, give me leave to give your Lordship some further

[f3v] Account. Mr Tallis was ye senior, & began to appear eminent, in Harry ye 8th, & Edward ye 6^{ths} time; But ye greatest part of his compositions, were made in Queen Elizabeths time, & for ye use of her Chappell, as I have allready mention'd.

Mr Bird was his schollar, & allso a Contemporary wth him; He imitated so well ye copys his master set him, that tis a hard matter to know wch exceeded; I think Mr Bird outliv'd his master, & was Servant & Organist to King James ye 1st.

Your Lordship will find in this Collection, the works of all that liv'd at ye same time, wth these Excellent men; such were cheifly, Dr Tye, Dr Bull, Dr Giles, Mr Barcroft, Mr Stonard, Mr Morley, wth severall others; These, no more than those who succeeded them, cou'd ever make appear so exalted a faculty in compositions of Church Musick; I must here however, except, that most Excellent Artist, Mr Orlando Gibbons, Organist & Servant to King Charles ye 1st, whose whole Service, of *Venite Exultemus, Te Deum, Benedictus,*[15] *Kyrie Eleyson, Credo, Magnificat, Nunc Dimittis,* wth severall Anthems &c, are ye most perfect peices of Church Compositions, wch have appear'd, since ye time of Mr Tallis, & Mr Bird; The Air so solemn, the fugues, & other embellishments so Just, & Naturally taken, as must warm ye Heart of any one, who is endu'd wth a Soul, fitted for devine raptures.

I must allso further acquaint your Lordship, that this standard of Church musick, was not left at random, to ye fancy & invention of ye Composers of those times; But was circumscrib'd, among other Ecclesiastical matters, by Authority; As your Lordship will find, by a Book entitl'd

---

15. Tudway selected only the Benedictus for inclusion in his collection.

Reformatio Legum Ecclesiasticarum; wch has been publish'd three sever-all times; first in ye reign of Queen Elizabeth, And twice by King Charles ye 1st; the Original Mss. of w^{ch}, is in ye Harlyan Library, as I'm inform'd, by the most Ingenious and Learned, Mr Humfrey Wanley, your Lordships Librarian, the first proposer of this work.[16]

The Governours of our Church in those dayes, wisely forsaw, that any deviation in matters of Church Musick, woud soon destroy, the cheif designe, & use therof; And therfore, guarded against all innovations, & [f4] encroachments, of ye Composers of Musick; They prohibited all vibra-tive, & operose musick; things perfectly secular; And ty'd 'em down, as near as possible, to ye Planus Cantus; that those who sung, as well as such as hear'd, might have ye Benefitt of ye result, in their Pious Exercises, & stir'd up to a devout sence, & frame for religious worship.

They knew well, that operose, or Artificiall musick, woud have no effect, to inspire true devotion, but wou'd rather excite delight, and Pleasure; And therfore not fitt, or proper to be admitted, wthin the doors of ye Church; They kept closs [sic] therfore, ev'n to ye Character, or Notes, long before us'd in Church Musick; viz: Breif, semebreif, minum &c, & forbid ye makeing use of Notae deminutionis, that they might not in any wise, mix devine musick, wth secular.

Your Lordship will find therfore, through this whole Collection, the same Style, & Character, as at first appointed to be us'd, & wch lasted wthout deviation, for above a 100 years; How we are come to a kind of Theatrical, & Secular way, in our Modern Compositions of Church Musick, I shall presume to acquaint your Lordship, in my Collection, of ye next volume, wch I intend to present to y^r Lordship; beginning at ye Restauration of King Charles ye 2^d.

Apart from Tudway's over-enthusiastic punctuation, the only surprise in the dedication would seem to have been the promise of another volume. 'When the Doctor undertook to make the Collection of services, &c The Principal Pieces only were to be transcribed, & the whole to be contained in one volume', Wanley complained to Harley, when the project had, as he saw it, got out of hand.[17] The extension of the scheme to include music since the time of Charles II was an embarrassment to Tudway as well: having condemned the degeneracy that had overtaken church music in his time, he now had to excuse the repertoire on which he had been brought up as a child of the Chapel Royal and as a colleague of Blow, Turner, Wise, Purcell, and Child. He was, moreover, now in a position to include his own compositions in the collection, which feature the very 'symphonys wth

16. First published in 1571, with later editions of 1640 and 1641. The manuscript of the text (prepared for the use of Archbishop Cranmer) is now B.L. Harl. MS 426. For the full text and a commentary on the manuscript, see E. Cardwell, *The Reformation of the Ecclesiastical Laws* (Oxford 1850).

17. B.L. Harl. 3782, fol. 89v.

instruments', 'light solos' and 'Retornellos' that he professed to deplore. The King's taste is adduced as prime excuse, and royal ceremonial music is excepted; lesser establishments without sufficient resources should stick to their own 'heavy, & indeed shocking way, of Psalm Singing' (could this be directed at Thomas Mace?). What was right for Whitehall was improper elsewhere. His first escape from the dilemma is, therefore, to create a separate and special category of ceremonial music, for use in the king's presence (preface to B.L. Harl. 7338).

[f2]   King Charles ye 2^d being restor'd to his Just Rights, & wth him ye Church of England to its Ancient use, & dissipline; The 1st thing thought of, was to settle ye divine service, & worship, in his Majestys Chappell Royall, after such a Modell, as ye Cathedralls in England, and Ireland, were to Establish theirs by.

The Horrible devastations, ye sons of violence had committed, on all
[f2v] things sacred, in ye time of ye Usurpation, had disfurnish'd all ye Cathedralls throughout both Nations of their Organs &c, so necessary for ye solemnization of divine service, in singing of Hymns, & Psalms. 'Twas in those dark & Gloomy days, The Church of England was sad, & disconsolate, & Robb'd of all its melody; Twas then ye Church of England, was in ye same afflicted State, as ye Jews were in ye Babilonish Captivity, when they Hung their Harps upon ye trees, & coud not sing ye songs of Sion in a strange land; But as soon as ye King was restor'd, the Church reviv'd, And Cathedral worship, was again Establish'd.

In ye beginning of ye year 1662, ye first Organ was Erected in his Majestys Chappell in White Hall; The King took great delight in ye Service of his Chappell, & was very intent upon Establishing his Choir, and had ye goodness to make such an addition, as allmost to double ye number of Gentlemen, & Children of ye Chappell wch it consisted of before ye Rebellion, to make room for those, who had bin sufferrers, & had surviv'd ye wars, & allso for ye best voices that were then to be found.

The Standard of Church Music, begun by Mr Tallis & Mr Bird, &c. was continued for some years, after ye Restauration, & all Composers conform'd themselves, to ye Pattern wch was set by them;

His Majesty who was a brisk, & Airy Prince, comeing to ye Crown in ye Flow'r, & vigour of his Age, was soon, if I may so say, tyr'd wth ye Grave & Solemn way, And Order'd ye Composers of his Chappell, to add Symphonys &c wth Instruments to their Anthems; and therupon Establis'd [sic] a select number of his private music, to play ye Symphonys, & Retornellos, wch he had appointed.

The King did not intend by this innovation, to alter any thing of the Establish'd way; He only appointed this to be done, when he came himself to ye Chappell, wch was only upon Sundays in ye morning, on ye great festivals, & days of Offerings; The Old Masters of Music viz: Dr Child, Dr Gibbons, Mr Law, &c Organists to his Majesty, hardly knew how, to comport themselves, wth these new fangl'd ways, but proceeded in their Compositions, according to ye old Style, & therfore, there are only some services, & full Anthems of theirs to be found.

[f3]   In about 4 or 5 years time, some of ye forwardest, & brightest Children of ye Chappell, as Mr Humfreys, Mr Blow, &c, began to be Masters of a faculty in Composing; This, his Majesty greatly encourag'd, by indulging their youthfull fancys, so that evr'y Month at least, & afterwards oft'ner, they produc'd something New, of this Kind; In a few years more, severall others, Educated in ye Chappell, produc'd their Compositions in this Style, for otherwise, it was in vain to hope to please his Majesty.

Thus this Secular way was first introduc'd, into ye Service of ye Chappell, And has been too much imitated ever since, by our Modern Composers; After ye death of King Charles, symphonys, indeed, wth Instruments in ye Chappell, were laid aside; But they continu'd to make their Anthems wth all ye Flourish, of interludes, & Retornellos, wch are now perform'd, by ye Organ.

This However, did not Oblige ye Cathedrals throughout England, to follow such an Example; for indeed such an Example was very improper for their imitation; because they had none of ye fine voices, wch his Majesty had in his Chappell, to perform light solos, & other slight Compositions, And therfore it had been much better for them, to have kept closs to ye old, Grave, & Solemn way; w^{ch}, such voices as they had, were more capable of p[er]forming; But ye Composers of those, and later times, being Charm'd, wth what they heard at White Hall, never consider'd how improper such Theatricall p[er]formances are, in religious Worship; How such performances, work more upon ye fancy, than ye passions, and serve rather to create delight, than to Augment, & actuate devotion; And indeed all such light, & Airy Compositions, do in their own Nature, draw off our minds, from what we ought to be most intent on, & make us wholy attend, to ye pleasing, & Agreeable variety of ye sounds, and from hence sprang all that contempt, wch Cathedral Service is fall'n into; The fanaticks, & other enemies of our constitution, seeing ye bungling work, that many, if not most of our Cathedrals made of the Service, by following a Style, wch was neither suitable to devotion, nor capable of being perform'd by Ordinary voices, have had ye confidence, to preferr their own

[f3v]   heavy, & indeed shocking way, of Psalm Singing, to ye best of our performances; Wheras, such Compositions as are Grave, solemn, & fitted to devotion, have allways been valu'd, & esteem'd, ev'n by our enemies, for that they naturally have a mighty force, & Energy to excite, & heighten all our passions, wch are devotionall; The Notes seeming so Adapted to ye words, that they do in some measure, express ye seriousnes of ye matter, wch goeth along wth y^m, wch make strange impressions upon a mind religiously affected, & make it more in Love, wth those things, about wch it is conversant.

This is that Harmony, that doth not only strike, & please ye Ear, but is from thence carried to our spirituall facultys, & is wonderfully efficacious, to move all our affections, & oftimes, ev'n to draw forth tears of devotions. This is y^t Harmony, wch as a Divine of our Church expresses it, warms ye best blood we have w^thin us, & is fitt for a Martyr to sing, & an Angel to hear.

The musical contents of Volume II of Tudway's collection ('A Collection of the most celebrated services', B.L. Harl. 7338) are broader than his title would suggest, since he includes sixteen anthems 'by Carissimi, Palestrina, Stradella &c' (nos. 23–38), taken from Dean Aldrich's collection, with English words substituted for the original Latin. These clearly define the 'Grave, solemn' style that he recommends, although he makes no mention of the clear differences between, say, the four extracts from Carissimi's *Jephte* (nos. 35–8) and the Palestrina motets which open the volume.[18]

Dean Aldrich is joined with exalted company in the preface to the succeeding volume (which, Tudway assures Wanley, is to be the 'third and last') in a brief account of those 'Emperou[r]s, Kings, Popes, and great D^rs of ye Church' who have not thought it beneath them to compose church music. Harley, a graduate of Christ Church, had obviously asked for the inclusion of Aldrich's own compositions, and the opportunity to applaud aristocratic involvement was important to Tudway, who was anxious to secure Harley's approval for an expansion to six volumes, despite his assurance to Wanley. Harley himself now began taking an active interest in the content of the collection. This increased Tudway's circle of sources, since the Earl could intercede on his behalf with owners of manuscripts: 'Some very fair scores of Dr. Creighton's' were obtained in this way from Wells (Tudway to Wanley, 24 May 1716). Tudway could now afford to devote himself to the more difficult task of prizing compositions out of living composers in London. This required his personal attendance in the capital, and a letter of 17 February 1717/18 explains his strategy:

> I have happily fix'd my Lords busines since I came to Town at St Pauls, Westminster Abby, & ye Royall Chappell, & have got Catalogues of ye peices [that] Will be sent after me, to Cambridg, by wch I'm enabl'd to proceed, w^thout delay; I have not been wanting in spending of money in treating these Masters, of wch Dr Croft's is cheif, & I have now a faithfull promise from his own Mouth, to send me his Thanksgiving Te Deum & Jubilate, whenever I give him notice that I'm ready for it; A Glass of Wine &c, has brought all these Masters together to drink my Lords health, & has kept 'em in humour, & open hearted; . . . [P.S.] But for this Journy, & Method I've taken wth these Gentlemen, I shoud never have been able to have got anything certain of them, wch woud have confounded ye Method, I'm in, of makeing a Catalogue before I set about a volume, that I may see what Materialls are ready, to fill it w^th; And moreover, I shoud in vain, have troubl'd my friends to solicit for me, w^thout any effect . . . [B.L. Harl. 3782, fol. 89]

18. The contents of Tudway's collection are listed in full under 'Tudway' in *Grove's Dictionary*, 4th edn (London 1940).

Wanley notes rather sourly (for Harley's benefit) on the reverse of this letter the original arrangement, which consisted of a single volume, collected by Tudway himself, and hints that the monies given him for expenses have been used for other purposes. Two days later, however, Tudway reports that all is well and presumes that Wanley has 'done the friendly office, wch I desir'd of you'. Wanley himself is drawn into the operation, and Tudway writes to him in London, asking whether he will 'drink a Token of half a guinea, wth Dr Crofts, Mr Church, & one or two more' at a tavern in Charing Cross, which 'I will repay you at y^r first appearance here [Cambridge] or at Wimple' (17 March 1717/18: *ibid.*, fol. 92). From what we are told elsewhere of Wanley's drinking habits, we can be sure that he obliged. With this and other assistance, Tudway was deluged with manuscripts: 'I shall desire my Corespondents to stopp their hands, who are pouring in peices upon me, from all parts, if my Ld shou'd not be pleas'd to enlarge my Comm^{ssion} . . .' (Tudway to Wanley, 5 March 1716/17: *ibid.*, fol. 71v).

Volume IV (B.L. Harl. 7340) was announced as finishing Tudway's search after 'Ancient Compositions of Church-Music, In wch I think I may boast, in ye success I've had, that there is scarse a Cathedrall in England, from wch I have not drawn some Copys or Mss or hardly an Author, or Composer of Church Music, from ye Reformation to ye Restauration of King Charles ye 2^d Of whose works, I have not in these volumes, recorded, more or less of their Compositions' (fol. 2). His bib-liophile's urge for completeness forces Tudway once more to shift his ground. He first explains to Harley 'how much better it had been, for ye promotion of Divine Worship as well as Hon[or] to ye Authors of such Compositions, as were made for ye service of ye Church; If all ye Composers, since ye Restauration, had thus distinguish'd their works, from ye Secular, by keeping up to the standard of Mr Tallis, Mr Bird, & Mr Gibbons &c;' (fol. 2v).

From this he moves on to elucidate counterpoint (from four to twelve parts) together with the allocation of voices, and maintains that this is what disting-uishes sacred music from secular.

[f3]   The bus'nes of secular composers, was only, to furnish out Tunes, for Masks, & dances, for interludes, & ye like; Their skill usually reach'd no further, than makeing different sorts of Tunes, fitted, for such & such purposes of danceing &c; They woud have been too much fetter'd, and Hamper'd, wth many parts, wth Canons &c; Their bus'nes of Tunes, & Madrigals, or Songs, was to be free in their inventions, & flights, and not ty'd down to intricate rules of Composition &c; In a word my Lord, tis not above a Century since, there was Nothing compos'd of music, in parts, But what was made for divine Uses;

In order to defend this statement, Tudway concludes his dedication, and the volume (fol. 264v), with the example of Purcell's setting of 'Thou knowest, Lord, the secrets of our hearts', 'accompanied wth flat Mournfull Trumpets', an anthem composed

[f3] after ye old way; & sung at ye interrment of Queen Mary in Westminster
Abby; A Great Queen, & extreamly Lamented, being there to be interr'd,
ev'ry body p[re]sent, was dispos'd, & serious, at so solemn a service, as
indeed, they ought to be, at all parts of divine Worship; I appeal to all y^t
were p[re]sent, as well such as understood Music, as those y^t did not,
whither, they ever heard any thing, so rapturously fine, & solemn, & so
Heavenly, in ye Operation, wch drew tears from all; & yet a plain, Naturall
Composition; wch shews ye pow'r of Music, when tis rightly fitted, &
Adapted to devotional purposes; I think I need say no more but this, to
evince, what I have been endeavouring to prove, that woud men come to
Church, so prepar'd, wth a pious, & devout disposition, The old compositions, of Tallis, Bird, Gibbons, wth such as have imitated them, woud have
ye same Effect, as this of Mr Purcells, I've just now given an instance in.

Tudway has now reached a curious dilemma: instead of recommending the
'ancient' style, and by extension those contemporary works which imitate it, he
has now to approve a modern colleague (who, as he well knew, produced only
occasional pieces in the 'antick' manner) and via his success advocate a return to
Tallis, Byrd, *et al.* After eschewing 'any deviation in matters of Church Musick' in
Volume I, and disapproving of 'all vibrative and operose musick', Tudway had
first to relent in Volume II in the case of court compositions in deference to
Charles's taste for interludes and 'Retornellos'; next, to admit to Volume III the
music of his contemporaries and himself which, to a greater or lesser degree,
subscribed to the secular idiom; and by Volume IV to so modify his stance that it
amounts merely to a dislike of too overtly theatrical a manner in church. While
there is little logic in his arguments, the cause of the dichotomy in his position is
quite apparent: having been drawn to the old manner (one might say the *prima
prattica*) by taste, academic surroundings and upbringing, Tudway is deflected
not only by the demands and tastes of a 'modern' aristocrat, with lively contacts in
the contemporary arts, but also by the renewed contacts he has had to make with
the London scene and 'living Authors'.

How much Tudway's partial 'conversion' was due to his own discoveries and
how much it arose from pressure from Harley is difficult to establish. Although
Tudway claimed that the choice of music for inclusion in the volumes was entirely
his own, we know that Harley, for instance, asked for Aldrich's compositions and
adaptations to be featured, and from the correspondence of December 1717 we
discover that Wanley took it upon himself to persuade Tudway to include
Roseingrave's 'Arise, shine'. Tudway, although resigned to accepting it, cannot
resist a last-ditch protest:

> I thank you very kindly for Mr Rosengraves peice, wch my L^d deliver'd to me; The
> Artfull part is very fine, & he has show'd himself, a great Master, but for want
> I beleive, of being us'd to set Church Music, He keeps too theatrical a style, And
> introduces, in most places, his words, wth very great Levetees [sic]; I shall better
> explain my self, when I have ye happines of an hours conversation; this is also M^r
> Hendals fault, if I may be permitted to call it so; Mr Purcell I think keeps a Nobler,

& more Elevated style, quite through his Te Deum, & Jubilate, & has not so much of ye flutter &c. [16 December 1717: B.L. Harl. 3782, fol. 86]

By 1717 Tudway had persuaded Harley to extend his commission to six volumes in all, and the fifth of these, finished in 1718, consisted of music 'Compos'd for the most part in the Reigne of . . . Queen Anne' (B.L. Harl. 7341). Understandably, Tudway offered no prefatory comment on this repertoire, but reserved his energies for the extended introduction he was planning for the final volume.

For this he worked equally on modern and ancient repertoire. He was enthusiastic to obtain a copy of 'Mr Hendal's famous Te Deum' via Dr Arbuthnot (23 February 1716/17: B.L. Harl. 3782, fol. 70), but even more delighted to run to earth Tallis's forty-part motet 'Spem in alium' which answered to all his requirements of 'artfull' music (save that, instead of the original Latin, its English text was in praise of the Princes Henry and Charles, and he thought it 'not strictly Church music').[19]

> I'm very glad that my friend Mr James Hawkins[20] has ye good fortune to get into his hands, ye original score, of Mr Tallis's 40 parts Anthem, tis a Unic made & scor'd in Queen Elizabeths time, I think it will incomparably be proper to go along wth that great body of Compositions, wch I have prepared for my Lord, & a greater rarity, there cannot be, in its kind, it haveing never been attempted by any one, & is indeed fittest to be laid up, among so many valuable manuscripts, wch you have wth so much Judgm^t, pains & Industry procur'd for my Lord; The designe of Composeing it, was not, we may be sure, to be perform'd; but to remain a Memoriall, of ye great skill and abillity of ye composer, who was able to find wayes for so many parts to move differently, in their own spheres; I had been often told of this Composition, but I coud never beleive ther was any such thing; [Tudway to Wanley, 1 May 1718: B.L. Harl. 3782, fol. 95]

Presumably because of its size, however, Tudway decided some two weeks later that 'it is utterly impracticable, to transcribe his manuscript of 40 parts, into my Lords volumes; & I Judg it rather better to be laid up in my Lords Library in ye Original Mss because of ye Antiquity of it than to have it copied'.

In any case he is now overwhelmed with contemporary contributions for the final volume: 'Copies now Crowd in so fast upon me, from liveing Authors, that I forsee, I must enlarge this last volume, wch I've just begun' (Tudway to Wanley, 27 July 1718: B.L. Harl. 3782, fol. 101).

The preface that Tudway supplied to Volume VI, by far the longest of his introductions (B.L. Harl. 7342, fols. 2–13v), consisted of a summary account of the entire history of music, from its supposed origins in the ancient world up to his own day. In scope, if not detail, it surpasses the writing of the authorities he quotes (Mersenne, Kircher, Holder and Bedford, for instance) and covers more ground than the historical section of Malcolm's *Treatise* (published in 1721) or Prelleur's account (see above, note 2).

19. See Bertram Schofield, 'The Manuscripts of Tallis's Forty-Part Motet', *Musical Quarterly* xxxvii/2 (April 1951), pp. 176–83.
20. Organist of Ely Cathedral (d. 1729).

In common with the majority of earlier writers, Tudway adopts the biblical chronology for his early sections, together with a digest of the theories of Greek musical development that had originated with Boethius and had served to perpetuate the legend of Pythagoras ever since the sixth century. But rather than postulate conditions for the invention of music (a topic that North rightly abandoned), Tudway concentrates on the 'divine use of music', and for the first time subjects the biblical accounts to commonsense scrutiny. Tudway's account of Greek musical theory, the modes and *genera*, together with the distinctions of diatonic, enharmonic and chromatic is largely derivative. His sceptical approach to the musical talents of the Greeks betrays a mind that despised 'solitary [i.e. solo] music' (to use the terminology of Holder and North) and found the limited compass of the Greek scale too restricted to allow 'music in parts'.

Tudway is consistent in his pursuit of the use rather than the invention of music through the early days of the Christian Church. The traditional historians of music, with their philosophical and biblical roots firmly in medieval sources, had always found an obstacle in justifying the existence of their music, lacking the prototype that the legend of Orpheus had provided for the world of the Greeks, and David the Psalmist for the Jews. Tudway skirts the problem in a single sentence, with the idea that 'Music in imitation of ye Church Triumphant, made a part of ye worship of ye Church Militant', and proceeds to examples of its use, and the incorporation of its greatest musical asset, the organ, in fulfilling a heavenly harmony.

Even when dealing with relatively recent events and personalities, Tudway can still display surprising ignorance of facts (over the dates of the Lawes brothers' deaths, for instance). But although it is tempting to excuse these lapses as provincial lack of information, we have no evidence to suggest that Tudway's views would have differed from those of Blow, Purcell, Croft and many other professional musicians of his generation, who from the same upbringing in the Chapel Royal had not proceeded to academic positions. His opinions provide us with a necessary measure of historical awareness at the beginning of a century that was to see the simultaneous publication of two exhaustive histories; Tudway is the necessary deterrent to the assumption that every musician was as knowledgeable as a Hawkins or a Burney, as sceptical as a North or as expertly informed as a Pepusch.

Tudway's history summarizes a view of the state of church music in England which owes more to practical experience and sentiment (both important ingredients for later investigators) than to archival research. What is original is his linking of these views with a corpus of music, in the acquisition of which he is drawn to a more tolerant and 'advanced' assessment of the virtues of the modern style. The fact that the credit for this liberalization should putatively be shared with an aristocratic patron and an antiquarian librarian merely emphasizes the unique procedures of patronage in an eighteenth-century English household.

[f2] I have, wth ye Blessing of God, brought to a conclusion, a Collection of all

ye most eminent Church Music, wch has been compos'd, for ye use of ye Church of England, as well ye Services, as Anthems, from ye Reformation, to ye end of ye reigne of our late souvereigne Lady Queen Anne; wch coud not be contain'd in less, than a thousand sheets; Your Lordships known Piety & Zeal, for ye Hon[or] of Cathedral Service, I make no question, inspir'd you wth thoughts, so peculiar to y^r Lordships religious disposition, of makeing an Everlasting Memorial of these sacred Compositions; The Glory of ye Church of Englands publick worship, particularly at this time, when Cathedral Service, lyes under so many & great discouragem^ts & disregards; Nay ev'n when, (so little is Church Music understood), it is much to be feard, ye use of it, may soon be going to be laid aside;

[f2v]   The Revd Dr Holder in his Treatise, of ye Naturall Grounds and Principles of Harmony sayes, that Music, is so Essential a part of worship, & Homage, to ye divine Majesty, y^t there was never any religion in ye World, Pagan, Jewish, Christian, or Mahometan, y^t did not mix some kinds of Music, wth their devotional Hymns, of Praise & Thanksgiving;[21]

The first divine use of Music, wch we read of among ye Jews, was for that wonderfull deliverance, wch God wrought for Israell, when he overthrew Pharaoh & ye Egyptians, in ye red sea; This song of Praise & Thanksgiving, was w^thout doubt, penn'd by Moses, who was learned, in all ye wisdom of ye Egyptians; This was sung, wth great Exultation, by all ye Host of Israell, & answer'd by Miriam, ye sister of Aaron, who took a Timbrell in her hand; & all the women came out, & follow'd her, wth Timbrells, & Dances, repeating alternatly those Glorious, & Triumphal verses, viz: The Horse, & his rider, hath he thrown into ye sea, &c, The Poetical part of this song, may be accounted for, since we see, some of ye beautys therof, in our own Language, But as to ye Musical part, viz: ye Air, or tune, we must be contented to be ignorant of, since, that is long ago, vanish'd, into its Original, Air;

How therfore to account for ye Music, on this great Occasion, there lyes the difficulty; They might tis true, borrow from ye Egyptians,[22] some Kind of Air, or tune, wch they might observe, was made use of by them, on ye like occasions of victory &c, but how this was manag'd in relation to Harmonious concent can't be imagin'd; There coud be no Modulation of voices, in such a Multitude, & therfore very far, from being under any regulation; we must therfore conclude, that this exultation, as to ye musical part therof, was no other, but a vast, and Tremendous sound or Clangor, wch issued from ye mouths of so great a Multitude, & when Join'd by ye women wth their shrill voices, their Timbrells &c, it all serv'd but to increase ye Noise; so that they who think Harmony, had any part on this occasion, must be much mistaken, haveing no Notion of Harmony,

---

21. Holder (published 1694), p. 203.
22. See Bedford, *The Great Abuse of Musick*, p. 6, quoting Kircher's *Oedipus Aegypticus*.

or the Propertys therof; As a Revd Divine, who lately writ a Book, against
the abuse of Music, woud insinuate, viz: that this Triumphall Song, was
perform'd, by a Consort of vocal, & instrumental Music;[23] No, Music was
then, but in its infancy, & had no Art, or Science, to help & assist it, &
consequently, must have been, very barbarous & rude; besides, their
Timbrells & Harps, & what other instruments they had, we may much
rather suppose, were us'd wth their voices, because of their dances, w^ch
they always mixt, wth their songs of Triumph, it being a custom among y^e
Eastern Nations to express their Joy and satisfaction, by diverss postures,
& Gestures in danceing, wch was always a part in their Triumphal Exulta-
tions; As I shall have further occasion of showing, in many instances,
from severall places of Scripture;

Fols. 3–5 contain further extracts from the Old Testament. Tudway mentions
that 'The Psalms, compos'd by David, & others, were w^thout doubt, sung, or
Chanted upon divers great occasions, & events in ye Tabernacle, and I suppose
verse by verse, alternately; as are ye Psalms in Cathedralls at this day', and
concludes that the divine use of music was 'not very artfull' but rather a 'Tumul-
tuous mixture; evr'y one being left to their own humour, to express themselves
upon their severall instruments, as fancy shou'd suggest'.

On the secular use of music by the Jews, Tudway interestingly adduces
evidence from contemporary Turkish practice (acquired from the well-travelled
Dr Covel), in addition to asides on the standing of popular music in England.

[f5] The use of Music then among ye Jews, tho on a religious account, (otherwise, than that inspir'd for ye service of ye Temple) not being any way
regular, or Harmonious; it cannot be suppos'd, they were more exact, or
Artfull, in their secular uses of it; a remarkable instance wherof, I shall
give in the Babylonish Captivity.

Nebuchadnezzer setteth up, & dedicateth a Golden Image, & command-
eth all Nations & Languages, under his Government & Jurisdiction,
That at what time they hear ye sound of ye Cornet, Flute, Harp, Sackbut,
Psaltery, dulcimer, & all kinds of Music, they were commanded to fall
down, & worship the Golden Image, that Nebuchadnezzer ye King, had
set up, Dan: ye 3^d. v: ye 5th. You see here, a great assemblage of Instruments of Music, as they call'd them, But for what? not sure to make a
Consort w^th, But rather a Tintimarre, or Clangor, to be heard far & near, to
[f5v] give Notice to all, w^thin ye reach of y^t Noise, at that instant, to fall down &
worship ye golden Image, that Nebuchadnezzer ye King had set up; the
whole Copia Sonorum of Instruments of Music, were there summon'd to
make this Bruit, or Noise; for there is not only mention made, of ye Cornet,
flute, Harp, &c But all kinds of Music; that is, of ev'ry instrument then
us'd, whither of sounding Brass, or tinkling Cymbals; I suppose, all these

23. Bedford, *op. cit.*, p. 5.

Join'd, were not to make Harmony wth, but all ye Noise, & Clangor possible, wch ye Eastern Nations, & turks do still at this day; As a very learned, & great man, altogether a Judge, in these matters, has most fully informd me, viz: Dr Covel Master of X^{ts} College in Cambridg;[24] He sayes, that when ye Grand Signiors Music play to him, wch is as great a solemnity as any they have for Music, they stand in a Court of ye seraglio, & wth all ye Clangor, & din, they can possibly make, wth shawms, & loud screaming Pipes, & wth uncouth Jarring instruments, & gingling Noises, they make all ye most Horrible noise they possibly can, and this they take thô thus Barbarous rude to be ye glory of their performances; they have indeed a tune, wch goes along wth this mixture of Noises, wch is ye subject, & wch all these rude, & uncouth instruments imitate, in ye measure, or time; like those at country Wakes, here in England, where, they play upon Tongs, & other Mixture of Noises, for ye diversion of ye vulgar; such a company of Barbarous, discordant, & inharmonious sounds, clapt together, is hardly possible to be born by any Ear, that can distinguish, one sound from another, & this I'm confident, was ye way of ye Jews, & Eastern Nations, nay, ev'n of ye whole world, at y^t time, in their secular uses of Music.

From whence tis pretty plain, we must not go to those Ages, to seek for Harmony, or music in any perfection; After ye destruction of ye Temple, The Jews being carried into captivity, what remaind to y^m for their honest & civil uses, & diversions, were those instruments of Music, so often mention'd in Scripture, viz Tabrets, Timbrels, Harps, cymbals, dulcimers, these I suppose were string'd instruments; Trumpets, Cornets, Flutes, were some at least of their wind Music; upon these, or ye like instruments, they play'd their tunes, for ye leading of their dances, wch was one of their chief solaces, & delights, as it is at this day, among ye Greeks, who are in like mañer subjected to ye Turks; wth these also, they celebrated their new moons, their Sabbaths, & all their solemn feasts; These iñocent injoyments, God threatens them for their sins to take away; As in ye Prophet Isaiah, Jeremiah, Osea, Amos, ye book of ye Macchabees &c. I will cause all their mirth to cease, I will turn their feasts into

---

24. Dr John Covel, a frequent source of reference for Tudway, gives a fuller description of the Turkish music in his diaries (Hakluyt Society vol. 87, pp. 211–12):

> The G[rand] S[igno]r, Vizier, Kaimachans, etc., musick is all alike. 1st, there are trumpets, which come in onely now and then to squeel out a loud note or two, but never play a whole tune. 2d, pipers – their pipe is much the same with our trebble shaurne [shawm] or Hoóboy; these play continually without any pause. 3d, great drums, but not bract [metal-plated] as oures, nor corded at the bottom; they beat them at both ends, the top with the right hand with a great stick at every long or leading note, the bottom with a little in their left hand at every small or passing note; these have their pauses often. 4thly, little kettle or dish drums (for they have both) dissonant one to the other, for they are in paires; these rest sometime likewise. 5thly, they have 2 brasse platters about foot wide, which they hang loose in their hands, and clatter them one against the other.
> I am very inclinable to believe all this Musick old, and mention'd in Scripture.

mourning, & their songs into Lamentation; The mirth of their Tabrets ceaseth, ye Noise of them y^t rejoyce endeth; The Joy of ye Harp ceaseth &c; Now from hence tis a great peice of fondnes in any, to inferr, that ye music of those Ages, must needs be very exquisite, & melodious because, it was so delightfull, to those who heard it, & enjoy'd ye diversions of it; wheras, there is nothing more evident, ev'n at this day than, that people wthout skill, are delighted, wth what they hear of this kind, according to their apprehension, & Capacity; does a Lancashire Hornpipe, wch ten thousand people, especially of that Country, woud choose to hear, before ye most exquisite Consort, Compos'd, & perform'd, by ye best Masters, Argue, or prove that y^t therefore is ye best Music. anymore than ye three Children of ye wood, or any other Stupid Ballade, woud prove, y^t to be best Poetry, because ye vulgar, are generally most delighted wth it;?

Fols. 6–7 contain an account of the Greek scale and its development derived from standard sources. Tudway considers the legends of Timotheus and Amphion 'but flights in Poetry, & figures in Oratory'. To speculate upon Greek compositions is, he declares, 'out of ye reach of any, at least, at this time o' th' day, to discover'.

[f7v] In prosecuting this discourse, I shall rather take upon me to say, what they did not, or coud not do, than what they did; and by that time I come to give your Lordship, an account, how far practical Music has been improv'd, & carried, by ye Moderns, since a little above a Century, there will be no occasion, as I conceive, to lament ye loss, of ye knowledg of ye Greeks in ye practical part especially, of this Science;

What has been said of ye ratios of sound wthin ye compass of an Octave, relate altogether to ye Diatonic scale, wch ye Modern Musicians use, to this day; The Diatonic scale, as I've said, rises, from ye Unison, or given Note, by 4 progressive sounds, consisting, of 3 whole Notes, or Gradus's, & one Hemitone, or half Note; wch wth ye given Note, make Diapente, or a 5th; they then added, an other tetrachord, or 4 sounds; the first of w^{ch}, began upon Diapente, or ye 5th sound, & consequently, a Unison to it, therfore, ye Diatesseron, or 4th consisted, but of two whole Notes, & one half Note, or Semitone; So that Diapason, wch contains, Diapente, or a 5th & Diatessron, or a 4th is made by 5 whole tones & 2 semitones; The Moderns, who use only this scale, acknowledge, as Gradus's, only whole tones, & semitones;

The Greeks had also, two other scales, or Ascents; viz: Chromatic, and enharmonic; the Chromatick, ascended, by half notes, or semitones only, wch upon occasion, as wth us, at this day, being now & then mixt, wth ye Diatonic genus, make ye sweetest Harmony; And as ye brightest colours, when us'd wth Art, make ye most beautifull pictures, so the Chromatic genus, being now & then mixt, wth ye Diatonic, make the most charming parts, of a musical Composition;

The enharmonic scale wth them, had ascents, by less degrees, than Hemitones, viz: by Commas, & Diesis's; wch because, such degrees, are incommensurate & their ratios, hardly to be found; they are therfore in their Nature, ascent, and progressive Order, disagreeable to ye Ear, & inharmonious;

The scales then of Ascents, or Gradus's of their Sounds being found; we are still at a loss, & in ye Dark, for their time, or measure, wthout w^{ch}, sounds, are but a Jargon, & an undistinguishable mixture, wthout Method, or Order; & cannot possibly make tune, & consequently, coud not be exhibited to us, in any uniform Air, to be understood; And this makes it further impracticable, to give any certain Account of their Music; My Opinion only, in this matter, is, that ye way they had, was to measure, or set their tunes, by ye measure of their verse; so that as verses run, both in Duple, & triple measure, so their tunes, as at this day, were cheifly in those measures; And in this probably, was Poetry, & music, more nearly Allied, than any other way; for as words are made musical, by being put into verse, or numbers, so sounds are made tune, or Music, by being put into time, or measure;

[f8]   The 5 famous Moods, or kinds of Music, among ye Greeks, were wthout question, according to ye mode, or mañer of those 5 Nations & places, bordering upon them; viz: Doria, Lydia, Æolia, Phrygia, Ionia; from thence, ye Dorick, Lydian, Æolick, Phrygian, & Ionick Moodes; we may ye better understand this, by shewing ye like kind at this day, when we say, a French Courant; a German Almaign; a Spanish Sarabrand; a Scotch Jigg, &c; The French in a Galliardizing, & Courtlike Air, or Style; the Germans, in a more rough, & warlike mañer; The Spaniard, or Moris- co, in a more Stately, & lofty way of Danceing; the Scotch, after a Mimical, & Antick mañer; This is enough, as I imagin, wherby to form an Idea, of those Moodes of ye Ancients; wch is all y^t we really know of them; some, it is said, of their Ancient Musicians, made use Only of ye Dorick, & Phry- gian Moods, referring to, & concludeing ye others in them; The Dorick, for their Grave, & Secular uses, & ye Phrygian for their Martial, & warlike Occasions;

As to ye compositions of ye Greeks, & ye Harmony, & Melody, result- ing from them, there cannot be found, any tracks, or footsteps, wher- by to Judge of them; Only their scale; wch indeed we have of them. But alass, what can be gather'd from thence? The scale itself, is only an Arangement of sounds, fitted by calculations, to produce Melody, or Harmony; If I may be allow'd to give my opinion, betwixt ye Greeks, & Moderns in this particular; The Greeks, were by much, ye greatest Mas- ters in ye Mathematical part of Music; in their calculations of ye ratios, & proportions of all intervals, or Gradus's, comparing them together, & giveing ye ratios of them, in their Geometrical, & Arithmetical propor- tions; They were likewise, ye greatest Masters, in ye Philosophical part; in all maner of Harmonical Calculations; by discovering ye reasons, of Consonancy, & dissonancy, by ye frequency, & infrequency, of ye Coincidences of their vibrations, & undulations; wherby Concord, & discord are produc'd; These were undoubtedly, ye cheifest Talents of ye Greeks in Music, & in w^{ch}, no Age, or Nation, ever did, or coud pretend to equall them; By this, Music worthily acquir'd ye title, of a liberall Art, or Science;

But I must beg pardon, of ye cryers up of ye Greek performances, especially in practical Music, if, for severall reasons, I shall give in their due place, I cannot allow, that either their compositions, their instrum^{ts} for performance, Or their skill in performing, did any way equall the Moderns; First then, ye Greek Scale, w^{ch}, as I've said, extended at first, to no more than 4, & then 5 strings, & not till some time after, to above seven distinct sounds, or notes; these, coud not give compass enough, to show

[f8v]

any great skill, in composing, & makeing their tunes, wch require, a larger feild for musical disquisitions; And when Pythagoras, had added his Proslambanomenos, & conjoin'd, & found out, that ye first & last Note of an Octave, had ye nearest Harmonical relation, & therby open'd a way for further progression, by adding yet a 2^d or disdiapason, w^{ch}, as I've said, was reckon'd their Systema Maximum; I say, this compass, thô of their whole Scale, was not enough, whereby to form, any composition of Music in parts, wch Kercher indeed, & Mersennus, are possitive the Greeks knew nothing of, they useing only Solitary Music, as Dr Holder expresses it,[25] of tune or Air; wheras ye Moderns, by extending their Scale, to 4 & 5 Octaves, have scope, & room for ye Treble, or highest part to act in a sphere of its own; The Base or lowest part, in a sphere, proper to its self, and this highest, & lowest part, conjoin'd in an Harmonious relation, by a Tenor, or Middle part, wch acts likewise, in a different sphere, from ye other two; & notwthstanding all these 3 parts, are severall, in their style, & air, & differ from one another; yet are they in a wonderfull maner, combin'd in a musicall relation, as produces the greatest of all Harmony; Further, as to their instruments, on wch th[e]y play'd their tunes, &c, what were they? either for Capacity, or Nobleness of Sound, to those us'd at this day? what had they to compare wth that Wonderous Machine, an Organ? or wth our Harpsecords, Lutes, Violins, Basses of severall sorts,? likewise, wth our Wind instruments viz: Organs, Trumpets, Hautboÿs, Flutes, &c, all wch are enough to show, that ye practical music of ye Greeks, is not to be compar'd, wth that of ye Moderns at this day;

The Greeks, when they play'd severall instruments together, or Join'd voices wth them, sung, & play'd ye same part, or tune, differing only in ye Octave, as ye voice, or instruments, might be in pitch, viz: either in ye highest, or Lowest Octave, of their two diapasons; & this, as I conceive, was all they meant, by their Treble, & Base parts;

---

25. Roger North also used this terminology (see *Roger North on Music*, p. 257).

As to ye Romans, they were never famous, in any Musical performances; they had ye usuall instruments, for their Martiall occasions; & their Lyres, Tibia or Flutes, for their Odes, & ye Stage; but what kind of instruments their Lyres, & Flutes were, & how handl'd &c is too hard a task for me to determine; & wch however is as much as can be said of them, in this particular; so I leave them, as well as ye Greeks, & hasten to give your Lordship, some further Account of music, & how introduc'd into ye Christian Church, when it began to be settl'd, & at rest, from ye persecutions of Heathen Emperours;

[f9]   The X^{tian} Religion, wch after ye death of our Saviour, remain'd to be propagated, might rather be call'd ye X^{tian} faith, or X^{tian} beleif; wch ye Apostles, & others inspir'd by ye Holy Ghost, spent their whole lives in preaching up, & instilling into ye Primitive X^{tians}, the Doctrines of ye Cross, & Mysterys of ye incarnation &c. wch were so necessary to be beleiv'd, by ye followers of Jesus X^t.

This preaching of ye Gospell, remain'd some Ages after ye Apostles time, wthout any fixt, or constituted Church, or set form of worship, only beleivers, were added to ye Lord; But when Constantine ye great, & others succeeding him, became X^{tian} Emperours, then they began to build Churches, & establish rites, & Uniformity of worship, And Music, in imitation of ye Church Triumphant, made a part of ye worship of ye Church Militant;

The venerable Bede, a thousand years ago, gives this peculiar Testimony of ye use of Music in ye X^{tian} Church; Nulla Scientia, ausa est, subintrare fores Ecclesiæ, nisi ipsa tantūmodo Musica; Before ye Establishment of ye X^{tian} worship, The primitive X^{tians}, & ev'n ye Apostles, sung Psalmes, & Hymns, wch wthout doubt, were those us'd of old by ye Jews in ye Tabernacle; such were those sung by our Saviour wth his Disciples, before they went to ye mount of Olives; & such were those, wch Paul & Silas sung in Prison &c;

This kind of singing, is properly call'd Congregational, & is what ye vulgar & unskilfull, bear a part in, being wthout Art, & therfore styl'd very properly, planus Cantus; but what we call Church Music, is Artfull Music, compos'd, & perform'd wth great exactnes, to time, or measure, by a Choir of voices, fitted to their severall parts; This was found to raise devotion, by ye Harmony resulting therefrom, being in a style, or Air, proper to ye solemnity of ye service of God in his Church; This is by ye Italians therfore, call'd Stilo Ecclesiastico, by us, Church Music; I shall speak of this more fully, when I come down to ye Music us'd at this day, in ye service of ye Church of England;

The first singing then, or Chanting, us'd in ye X^{tian} Church, after ye Establishment therof, was ye Chanting of ye Nicene Creed about 300 years after X^t this was done, Acta voce, that is, the Preist, wth an Elevated voice, began the pitch, by chanting out, Credo in Unum Deum; & then ye Choir, or those who waited at ye altar, went on, in ye same tone, or pitch to y^e

[f9v] end of ye Creed; This is all that I can find introduc'd into ye X^tian Church, till severall centurys after, viz: about ye 6th century, when St Gregory ye great, compos'd, for ye makeing more regularly ye responses, what we call now, ye chanting of ye Service, in ye Church of England; as we may see it set down in Notes, in the Missals &c, that is, that all ye responses made to ye suffrages, or at ye end of ev'ry pray'r &c, shoud be in a Musical Uniformity of sound, or tone, & not at random, as those made by Congregations in Parochiall Churches, where, no Order is observ'd, of Uniformity, or Agreement of Sound, but only, a disagreeable murmuring Noise is heard, by a confus'd mixture of tones; tis true indeed, that this Art of makeing Musical, & regular responses, cannot be had, but where Choirs are establish'd, & therfore this is not said, to upbraid as indecent, Parochiall Service, but to show ye disparity of these two wayes;

The same St Gregory, finding ye whole System compriz'd in an Octave, or diapason, & that ye scale, was nothing else but ye replication of Octaves, wch might be repeated as far as sounds coud be made practicable, reduc'd all ye Characters of ye degrees of sound, under ye seven first Letters of ye Latin Alphabet; I have been ye more particular in this, in Order to introduce, ye Modern Scale, & the improvement therof, w^thout w^ch, it had been impossible to have given scope or compass, for all parts of ye Naturall voice, to act in their different & proper spheres;

About ye 10th or 11th Age, one Guido Aretinus, a Benedictine Monk, in ye dutchy of Ferrara took upon him, to reduce ye Greek scale, by Articulations, more proper, & sonorous, than those us'd by ye Greeks, viz; Ut re mi fa sol la, wch they add, came into his mind, by singing ye Hymn of St John Baptist

> Ut queant laxis,   Resonare fibris
> Mira gestorum   Famuli tuorum
> Solve polluti   Labii reatum
>   Sancte Joannes

wch a learned Italian, one Angelo Berardi, hath happily compriz'd in ye following verse

> Ut Relevet Miserum Fatum Solitosque Labores.

This Guido Aretinus, first fix'd ye Gamma, from thence call'd ye Gam-ut, as ye first, & lowest Note of ye Naturall voice, from thence, riseing by Diatonic degrees, they came to ye first Letter again upon ye Octave, or diapason, wch Octave being extended, & repeated as often as ye compass of ye composition requir'd, made this large, extended System of ye Modern Scale;

They give also ye reason, why ye Gamma, being ye 3^d Letter of ye Greek Alphabet, was set ye first in ye Modern scale, wch they say was, because

[f10]   his name began wth that Letter, & therby he meant to Eternize it, to succeeding Generations; others, that it was to acknowledge, that ye Originall scale came from Greece, that famous seat of ye Muses.

I might write a volume, in explaining, & reconcileing ye Greek, wth ye Modern Scale, but I pass by all further searches, & remarks, to give your Lordship, an Account of ye beginning, & progress of Music, in the X^{tian} Church.

The founding of Chanterys, & Choirs, in all, or most of our old Cathedrals was wthout question, to sing Dirges, & make musical responses, wth more exactnes, that what part soever ye Preist Chanted, might be suitably answerd, by ye choir; From this simple planus Cantus, they came by degrees to compose in parts; first, ye Base, against the Treble, or highest part, we may beleive, their skill did not reach further than Contrapunctum, y^t is, point against point, or Note against Note, of ye same value; Then by degrees, they put in, between ye Base, or lowest part, & ye Treble or highest, the Medius, or Tenor, combining these three altogether, in an Harmonious relation; The Harmony resulting, from ye Joining of these 3 parts, was at that time so astonishing, as soon determin'd them, to appropriate it, to divine Service in ye Church, as best fitting ye Solemnity therof;

Mr John Gregory, a learned & Judicious Author, will not allow, Organs to be introduc'd into ye Western Church, till about ye year 1200;[26] However it was, this Noble Machine, must be imagin'd, far short, of ye prodigious improvement that has been made of that instrument, in less than a Century, wherby tis confest, to be ye Noblest Instrument that is, or ever was in ye world, & therfore most worthily apply'd to ye service of ye Church; But I shall not in this place insist any further theron; As it was then, it was undoubtedly ye only Instrument, wch coud best express ye nature of Harmony, in ye consonancy of ye severall parts, and therfore ye most proper of all others, to Joine wth Choirs of voices, to make ye Harmony therof, full, & compleat; In those Ages, & infancy of this kind of Music, little, or no particulars can be met wth; I can't find, any ye Compositions of those times, express'd in Notes, or Characters, othe[r]wise, than those allready mention'd, compos'd by St Gregory, in ye Roman Missals; though, tis very plain, by ye Statutes of severall Colleges, of 3 & 400 years standing & upwards, in both ye Universitys, they had Choirs, Organs, & singing ye Service of ye Church; I must therfore skip over severall Ages, as Dark, where nothing can be discover'd of their proficiency in composeing,

[f10v]   and begin again about ye time of our Henry ye 8th who was himself a kind of proficient in this Noble Science; Henry ye 8th, haveing an Elder Bro^r who was to inherit ye Crown, He was by his father, Henry ye 7th design'd for an Ecclesiastick, & being brought up in their semenarys, became skillfull in Music; we have an Anthem at this day, said to be his, wch was

26. See his *Discours declaring what time the Nicene Creed began to bee sung in the Church* in *Gregorii Posthuma: or certain learned Tracts: written by John Gregorie* (London 1649/50).

compos'd in Latin, and wch they say, was sung in his own Chappell, when afterwards King of England;[27]

The King thus Honouring this Science, we may be sure, that others took great pains to approve themselves Artist in composing of Church Music; However, there are few, or no compositions to be met wth of that standing; what Dirges, or Te Deums, Jubilates &c there might be, was compos'd in Latin, for the service of ye Romish Church, & therfore, not wthin ye Compass of this Collection, wch begins at ye reformation of ye Church of England; I beleive ye improvement both of Church Music, as well as secular, did somewhat advance in this Princes time, He being a proficient himself in ye one, & keeping a splendid Court, wth music, danceings &c for ye encouragement of the other; Notwthstanding w^{ch}, there is nothing extant to be found before, or in his time, but what woud be dispis'd by our Artist at this day, either for skill in seting, or ye Air, or Style thereof; so that we must Date ye beginning, & improvem^t, of Church Music Especially, from ye Reign of Queen Elizabeth, to ye decease of Queen Ann, where this Collection ends;

Queen Elizabeth haveing then Establish'd ye reformation of ye Church of England and appointed ye dayly service of ye church to be said, & sung in English, it was altogether necessary, that ye Hymns of Morning, & Ev'ning service, as well as ye Anthems, shoud be all compos'd anew, in our own Language; Those, first employ'd in this work, were Mr Tallis, & Mr Bird, two of ye Queens own Servants, who, it is own'd at this day, set an incomparable Pattern of Church Music, in a style, befitting ye solemnity of ye service; Their compositions, are all in 4 parts, except, some Anthems in five; The adding of this 4th part, gave a wonderfull Harmony, to ye whole Chorus, wheras before, they never aim'd at above 3 parts, for wch there were 3 cliffs establish'd, suited to each part; But these skilfull Artists, finding, there might yet be a higher part, than a Tenor introduc'd, betwixt ye Tenor & Treble; compos'd a 4th part, calling it Contratenor; In these 4 parts, were all ye compositions for ye Church cheifly made in that time; But as men of Head, & skill in composition of this kind, came on, we have seen Hymns, & Anthems compos'd, of 4.5.6.7.8 &c parts; But these appear'd, rather as an Exercise of their Art, than use in ye Church.

These 4 parts then, viz: Base, Tenor, Contratenor, & Treble, were fix'd, as sufficient to make ye fullest & compleatest consonancy, & Harmony, their ratios, being all contain'd, as I've said in an Octave, the most compleat System;

These compositions of Mr Tallis, & Mr Birds, were us'd many years alone in ye Church, wthout admitting any others; However, in that Queens time, severall eminent men, for compositions in Church Music, rose up, viz: Mr Parsons, one of ye gentlemen of ye Queens Chappell; M^r

[f11]

27. 'O Lord, the Maker of all things', variously attributed to William Mundy and John Shepherd, which opens Tudway's third volume.

Morely, ye greatest Artist in fugues, Canons, & such like Exercises, of figurative Music, that ever was; Dr Bull Organist to her Majesty, ye most famous of his time, & Dr Tye, bo:h Batchellours, and D^{rs} of music; these have Compos'd also for ^{e} Church, but wthout any great effect, or success; I think never ye less, I ought not to omit ye mentioning, in this place, an Anthem of Dr Bulls, being ye Collect for ye Feast of ye Epiphany, commonly call'd ye Star Anthem, wch for Art, & Air, & other Excellent dispositions, hath maintain'd its ground, ev'n to this day; it being still perform'd, on that occasion, in many of our Cathedrals;

In King James ye first's time, there were severall Eminent composers of Church music, particularly, Dr Giles, Mr Bevin; famous for ye Art of Composing many parts; Mr Shepherd, Mr Lugg &c. The Elaborate works of these, & many others, are now allmost forgot, The new Style prevailing in all our Cathedrals, & places, where ye singing of Divine Service is us'd;

I shall pass on to name, some of ye most eminent in King Charles ye first's time, viz: the Tomkins's, 3 Bro^{rs}; very skillfull Organists, Mr Henry & Mr William Laws, both Bro^{rs}, all Servants to his Majesty; the 2 Laws's dy'd in ye feild, in ye service of that Prince;[28] But above all, I must never forget to mention, Mr Orlando Gibbons, first Organist to his Majestys Chappell, who, throughout all his compositions, has alone maintain'd, the Harmony, & dignity of ye Church Style, & I think I may Justly say, comes little, if at all short, of ye Pattern set, by Mr Tallis, & Mr Bird; Thus I have given your Lordship some account of ye beginning of Church Music, from ye Reformation; wth ye Characters of ye cheifest Composers, down to ye restauration of King Charles ye 2^d, when music, & ev'rything praise worthy, was again restor'd, & introduc'd into ye Service of ye Church;

I gave your Lordship in a former Epistle to one of my volumes,[29] some Account how, ye Alterations in ye Church Style began, wth ye probable reasons, wch occasion'd it; I may now wth more assurance, tell you, that, by what I have met wth, I find, there is hardly any flights in Music, ev'n of ye Stage, that some Composer or other, has not introduc'd into ye Church; I have seen ye most extravagant repetitions imaginable, ev'n upon a single word, repeated, eleven times, wch coud never be tollerable, but on ye account of some fantastical humour, or other, wch I'm sure, was never consistant, wth divine Service; The words, *all, now, ever, Never,* &c have had their share likewise, in these musical tautalogies; I forbear mentioning Authors; But above all; to ye corruption of that solemn, & grave style, wch was Establis'd as only proper to be us'd in divine service, there are composers, wth in ye compass of this Age, that I defye ye stage, to outdo, in Levity, & wantonnes of style; The reason of this must needs be, the little care that is taken, to inspect Compositions, before they are addmitted

[f11v]

---

28. William Lawes was killed by a stray shot at the siege of Chester; Henry Lawes died 21 October 1662.
29. Volume II.

into ye Church Service; The compositions of Mr Tallis, & Mr Bird, were so, & approv'd of, by Authority, before they were admitted, wthin ye doors of ye Church; but now, ev'ry one is become a Composer of Church Music, and I verily beleive, since ye Restauration; there are no fewer, than 500 Anthems compos'd, & have been perform'd in divine service, besides ye Hymns, of Morning, & Ev'ning pray'r, in abundance; wheras, from ye Reformation, to ye Restauration, in 1660, there is hardly forty Anthems to be found, & perhapps not half of them ever sung in ye Church; such sorry, & injudicious compositions, as before mention'd, instead of assisting, & improveing, ye performance of the Service, as is pretended, by a greater variety, do but bring a disreputation, & contempt upon it, & is ye occasion of that irreligious behaviour, wch most people make appear at Cathedral Service, where they come, rather to be entertain'd, & diverted, than wth a sence of Religion, or devotion; for finding such turns, & strains of Music, As they have been accustom'd to hear at ye play House, think it but reasonable, to make ye same use of it in ye Church; And this I conceive to be ye very reason, why Church Music, has lost, so much of its former respect, & reputation, as well as ye Composers therof, viz: by departing from that peculiar gravity of style Appropriated to it; If this had been strictly adher'd to, people had not come to Church, for diversion, but to say their pray'rs, wch Cathedral Music, was design'd, to assist them in;[30]

However, there are other reasons of ye decay of this institution, for in all Cathedralls where Choirs were first founded, I dare say, then, their stipends were a maintenance; But Deans, & Chapters, since ye Reformation, tyeing their Clerks down to ye same allowance, now, when money is not a 5th part in value, to what it was then, have brought a generall neglect of ye service, & a very mean, & lame way of performing it, for want of encouragement; I can't forbear to say, it was an oversight at ye Reformation, to constitute a dayly service, for Chanting, & Singing of Hymns, &c, & not provide a sufficient maintenance, for those, upon whom ye performance of that duty lay; wheras, before ye Reformation, their Clerks were provided for, in their way, in ye Colleges, & Cloysters, &c in wch they were Establish'd, & had their meat, drink, lodgings, &c provided; they were by y^t means at leisure to practice & prepare, what was necessary for divine Service in Publick, & were not encumber'd wth familys to provide for; This insufficient provision, I take to be, the sourse of ye decay of Cathedrall Service wth us; and what makes this, yet more evident, is, that where there is encouragement, or a maintenance, as at the Royall Chappell, St Pauls, Westminster Abby &c, they abound in

---

30. As an indicator of changing eighteenth-century taste, compare Burney's comments in his 'Extracts' taken from Tudway's volumes (B.L. Add. MSS 11587 and 11589); the jaunty obbligato marked 'Org. part. Trumpet stop' in 'Sing O heav'ns' is censured not for frivolity but for 'unnaturalness': 'The D^r forgot that the trumpet has no such notes as these in its scale.'

good voices, and the service is perform'd, wth such decency & solemnity, that God is truely worship'd, as of old, in ye beauty of Holines;[31]

[f12]   My Lord.

The Service of ye Church of England, thus suitably Compos'd, & decently perform'd, is that sort of music, wch your Lordship hath vouchsaf'd to become ye Patron of, in these Collections; and wch may truely be esteem'd, such a peculiar rarity, & curiosity, as no one, but your Lordship, in any Age, hath pitch'd upon, to make a Memoriall of; And I hope therfore will not be reckon'd ye meanest, among ye Harleyan Manuscripts.

How it comes to pass, that Church music only shoud be so little regarded, in an Age, when Music in generall, is come to such a heighth of improvement as, I appeal to all ye musical world, is incomparably beyond what ever was before, must proceed, from much ye same reason, as that of religion, viz: that in this Age also, when there was never so learned a Clergy, nor learning at so great a heighth, Religion itself shoud be so boldly attack'd, & Orthodoxy in beleif, & worship, so impudently oppugn'd; As to Church-music, I'm afraid, some have mixt, too much of ye Theatrical way, thinking therby to make it more Elegant & takeing; But by this means, the peculiarity, & gravity of style is lost, wherby it was always, worthily distinguish'd, from ye secular; The truth of all this is; the skill of Composeing is much more generall, & greatly improv'd, And ye composers of Secular Music, are become much greater Masters, than ever was known before; The Art of composeing Operas for ye stage, is a very great & masterlike performance, wch they may have had in Italy, threescore, or fourscore years, thô scarse in such perfection as at this day; I must, thô I shoud offend some of my Country men, needs say; to Compose an Opera, is a very great & masterlike work, & ye greatest of all secular performances in Music; wch few genius's ev'n among ye Italians, can reach; But I don't in ye least question, by that time these musical representations, have been a few years longer in England, & ye present encouragement continues, by ye Countenance of so great a Number of our Nobillity, & Gentry, it will appear, we have Genius's in England strong enough for y^t work; However, this can't be done, by despising of 'em, as many of our Masters do, who obstinatly deprive y^mselves of ye means of obtaining to ye perfection of them;

Our Country man, Mr Henry Purcell, who was confessedly the greatest Genius we ever had, dy'd before these musical representations, came upon ye the stage in England; He would have been so far from despiseing them, that he woud never have ceas'd, till he had equall'd, if not outdone

---

31. See Peter le Huray, *Music and the Reformation in England 1549–1660* (London 1967, repr. Cambridge 1978), pp. 36–7, for a similar complaint voiced by the anonymous author of B.L. Royal MS 18.B.XIX (an early-Jacobean treatise on cathedral music).

them; And did by ye pow'r of his own Genius, contrive very many, &
excellent compositions of divers kinds for ye stage;

[f12v]   But that wch set Mr Purcell eminently above any of his contemporarys,
was, y^t Noble Composition, ye first of its kind in England, of Te Deum, &
Jubilate, accompanied wth instrumentall music; wch he compos'd principally against ye Opening of St Pauls, but did not live till that time;[32]
However, it was sung there, severall times since, before her Majesty
Queen Anne, upon ye great Events of her Reigne; I needed not perhapps
to have mention'd this, since 'tis inserted in these Collections, but to
observe to your Lordship, that there is in this Te Deum, such a glorious
representation, of ye Heavenly Choirs, of Cherubins, & Seraphins, falling
down before ye Throne & singing Holy, Holy, Holy &c As hath not been
Equall'd, by any Foreigner, or Other; He makes ye representation thus;
He brings in ye treble voices, or Choristers, singing, To thee Cherubins, &
Seraphins, continually do cry; and then ye Great Organ, Trumpets, the
Choirs, & at least thirty or forty instruments besides, all Joine, in most
excellent Harmony, & Accord; The Choirs singing only, ye word Holy;
Then all Pause, and ye Choristers repeat again, continually do cry; Then,
ye whole Copia Sonorum, of voices, & instruments, Joine again, & sing
Holy; this is done 3 times upon ye word Holy only, changeing ev'ry time
ye Key, & accords; then they proceed altogether in Chorus, w^th, Heav'n,
& Earth are full of ye Majesty of thy glory; This most beautifull, & sublime
representation, I dare challenge, all ye Orators, Poets, Painters &c of any
Age whatsoever, to form so lively an Idea, of Choirs of Angels singing, &
paying their Adorations;[33]

Dr Crofts, and Mr Hendale, both by ye Queens Order, have likewise w^th
great Art And good success, compos'd ye like peices, of Te Deum, &
Jubilate, wch were perform'd before her Majesty, on Publick Occasions,
wth great Applause; These 3 compositions, are all of this kind at p[re]sent
were ever made in England;

Your Lordship, will distinguish, that such like peices as these, are only
proper in ye Church, for great Occasions of Publick Thankesgiveings; &c,
These Compositions therfore, are not stricktly call'd Church Music,
although, they are upon ye same divine subject; I have been ye more
particular upon them, because, they are ye production of this Age only, at
least in England; There remains for me to add, some Account of that

32. The Te Deum and Jubilate were indeed published in 1697, the year of the opening of the
    choir of St Paul's (the first portion to be completed), but Purcell's widow states that the work
    was 'Made for St. Cecilia's day, 1694'.
33. Sir John Hawkins (*A General History of the Science and Practice of Music*, 2 vols. (repr. New York
    1963), vol. 2, p. 795) quotes another comparison of Purcell's sacred and secular styles said to
    be taken from a letter written by Tudway for the information of his son. Burney (*History*, vol.
    2, pp. 344–5) quotes from the same source apropos the battle of the Temple organ, and his
    account is repeated (and corrected) by E. J. Hopkins and E. F. Rimbault (*The Organ, Its
    History and Construction* (London 1855), p. 77n); the location of the original letter remains
    unknown.

most Noble instrument, an Organ, whose Artificiall breath, will nere expire, whilst ye vital breath of singing in Choirs, remains; they seem to be made, for each other, & will hardly subsist asunder; And as Organs have been infinitly improv'd, since 50 or 60 years, by additional stops, wch imitate almost ev'ry instrument of pipe, or string; so are they become, in less than an Age allso, a very Ornamental, and ye most beautifull structure, that ever was Erected in ye Church;

[f13]   The word Organum, is of so extensive a signification, that tis almost imposible to guess what maner of instrument, a Musical Organ, so often mention'd in scripture, was; it is certain, that Organs, whatever they were, have not been us'd in ye Western X^tian Church, above 4 or 500 years, & tis as certain, that ye inventors therof, made but a small progress, in comeing to any perfection;

A Church Organ consisted then, but of 5 or 6 stops, wch might perhapps take up, 200, or 250 pipes of wood; wheras, tis nothing now, to have Organs, of 15, or 20 stopps, all, or most of Metal, consisting of 1200, or 1500 pipes; Besides those stops, properly call'd Organical, our Modern Artists, have invented stops, wch imitate ye Cornet, Trumpet, flute, Vox humane, Ecchos, Bassones, violins &c wth severall others, less frequent;[34] To dissect this Noble Machine, woud require a volume, rather than ye compass of a Dedication; but by what I have been able to say of it, Your Lordship may perceive, how much an Organ exceeds, all other instruments, And cannot be deny'd, ev'n by ye profest enemys of that, & Church Music, to be ye greatest, & most Noble instrument of Music that was ever in ye the world, & ye most worthy of all others, to accompany the service of God in his Church;

Thus, my Lord, I have endeav[or]^d to ye best of my pow'r to give your Lordship, what may be gather'd from Scripture, of ye divine use of Music, among ye Hebrews; and I think, I have not mistaken them, in representing them as knowing Nothing of Harmony, or ye propertys therof; sounding Brass, & tinckling Cymbals, is a Character, wch St Pauls [sic] gives of those instruments, & I beleive will serve, for most of their Musical instruments; However, the Harp, & Tabret are indeed mention'd in Scripture, wth Epithets of Melody, & pleasantnes of sound, wch need not be deny'd; But for any skill, or science, in ye use of Music, I must insist upon it, they were altogether Ignorant; yet, might delight y^mselves wth it, as knowing no better; Science in Music, came in afterward, by ye Greek Philosophers, and theirs, seems more a Mathematical, & Philosophical knowledge, than any exquisitenes in performance; If they knew nothing, as before hath been observ'd, of ye Harmony of parts, as many Authors confess they did not, their solitary music, of tune alone, can never come

34. Tudway's account of the Temple organ (see Hawkins, *History*, vol. 2, p. 691) mentions 'the Vox-humane, the Cremona or Violin stop, the double Courtel or bass Flute . . . These stops, as being newly invented, gave great delight and satisfaction.'

into competition, wth ye Harmony that results from a Composition in parts; Tune alone, may indeed be call'd Melody, but can't, wth any Propriety, be styl'd Harmony; wch I presume is made, from ye Agreement, & adjustment, of ye severall parts, of a Composition;

[f13v]   I have likewise brought Music, down, to ye use of it, in the X^tian Church, but wth little more knowledg for severall Ages, than a Bare Chanting or Elevation of Voice; I'm sure, they have left us no tracts, or footsteps wherby to Judg of them; But, as I've said, about Harry ye 8^ths time, Church Music, began to make some figure, He being himself a Composer of Church Music in parts; But that wch brought on ye search after knowledg, & skill in that way was, The thorough Reformation of ye Church, under Queen Elizabeth, when, as I've said, the Hymns, & Anthems, were all to be compos'd anew, in our own Language, and degrees in music, began then, again to be more frequently taken in both Universitys as an encouragement & recompence, for Composing ye Hymns of ye Church; what progress, & improvement, hath been made, down to this time, I leave to Ages to come, to make a Judgment of, from ye severall Compositions, both Ancient, & Modern, Collected in these volumes; After this breif recapitulation, there remains only, for me to add, wth great truth,

My Ever Hon[or]^d and very good Lord.

The Hon[or] your Lordship hath done Church Music, & ye Composers therof, by this Memoriall of it, I dare not take upon me, to draw a discription of; This I dare say, wth great assurance, that all true Lovers of ye good old constitution, of singing ye service of God, in ye Church, will bless your name, & memory for it; The Professors of this faculty, are infinitly Hon[or]^d by your Lordships Patronage; And as to ye unworthy Collector of these volumes, he hath no greater Ambition, than your Lordships favourable acceptance, & approbation of them; Haveing great assurance in your Lordships goodnes, I beg leave to subscribe as in duty bound;

My Ever Hon[or]^d & very good Lord
   Your Lordships most faithfull and most
      Obedient Servant.
      Thomas Tudway

Purcellian passages in the compositions of G. F. Handel

Franklin B. Zimmerman

Handel's musical borrowings, however simple or complex, usually are interesting and thought-provoking, especially when the passage in question is affective, dramatic, illustrative or scenic in expression. Whether characterized by deft retouching or by total reworking of their material, these borrowed passages usually show great improvement under Handel's care. This fact no doubt explains the perennial popularity of this borrowing question among Handel scholars, and the extensive body of literature it has accumulated over many years.

Most of Handel's massive borrowings, as in *Israel in Egypt*, or in the *Occasional Oratorio*, seem to have been urged upon him by pressure of time, with performance dates too near to allow him to compose entirely original material for a given event. However, in other instances, as in *Xerxes*[1] or in the overture to *Susannah*,[2] it may be seen clearly that Handel undertook to rework movements or other large portions of other men's compositions as if to show how these might be improved. In turning to Purcell's music, however, Handel seems to have been both more respectful and more circumspect. There are no wholesale borrowings and very few unequivocally demonstrable indebtednesses of any other sort. But there are a number of arresting similarities in the works of these two English masters, as we shall see. Often the similarities are so subtle as to be traceable only to the general effect. But the similarities are nevertheless there, as it will be the purpose of this paper to demonstrate.

In his interesting essay 'Englische Einflüsse bei Händel', Edward J. Dent suggested (p. 2) that Handel was too remote from the spirit of the Purcellian age to

1. See Harold Powers, 'Il Serse trasformato', *Musical Quarterly* xlvii/4 (October 1961) and xlviii/1 (January 1962), for a thorough examination of Handel's elaborate study and revision of Bononcini's *Serse* for his own *Xerxes*. Since Bononcini had been active in London's musical life up to the time of his departure in 1731, one may surmise that Handel felt constrained to camouflage any ideas or musical phrases he may have borrowed. One can only wish that the music examples illustrating Powers's study had been more plentiful and more persuasive.
2. See F. B. Zimmerman, 'Händels Parodie-Ouvertüre zu Susanna: Eine neue Ansicht über die Entlehnungsfrage', *Händel-Jahrbuch* No. 24 (1978), pp. 19–30.

be susceptible to its influence.[3] Whatever the merit of Dent's explanation of the apparent lack of any real Purcell influence on Handel's music, it is appropriate to add that Handel also was too much in the public eye in England, his adopted country, to risk offering such appropriations as those he had taken so little pains to disguise in *Israel in Egypt*, or in the *Occasional Oratorio*, where passages from the music of Stradella, Erba and Urio shone forth in virtually their original shape.

Dent's shrewd appraisal of Handel's position *vis-à-vis* contemporary English composers seems apt; but when one looks beyond mere melodic content in some of the works he wrote after settling in England, several interesting facts come to light.

During his first decade in London, Handel poured the bulk of his energies into the creation of Italian operas which by their very nature were not susceptible to English musical influences. However, in compositions belonging to the English ambience, such as the 'Ode for the Birthday of Queen Anne' (1713), the Utrecht Te Deum (1713), the early *Water Music* Suites (1715-17), and some of the Chandos Anthems (1714-19), it is clear that Handel deferred to Purcell's muse time after time. Then in *Esther* (1720) and *Acis and Galatea* (1718), and in the long series of English oratorios which these introduced, English influence became more and more important, and the Purcellian presence even more noticeable.

Even so, overt borrowings from English composers were rare. In fact, only the aforementioned annexation of the overture to Blow's *Begin the Song*, which Handel reworked so masterfully (as the overture to *Susannah*), can now be advanced as a parallel to large-scale appropriation of passages from German and Italian composers. To assist in gaining a true perspective on Purcellian passages in Handel's oratorios, it will be useful at this point to summarize the various kinds of Handelian borrowing that have been recognized by several authorities on the subject.

The largest and most striking class consists of those overt plagiarisms from the works of Cesti, Clari, Erba, K. H. Graun, Habermann, Keiser, Lotti, Georg Muffat, Stradella, Telemann, Urio, and others which have so exercised and incensed several generations of Handel scholars.

Next are the relatively few instances in which Handel borrowed some component of a work other than the melody – say, a bass, a cantus firmus, or an accompaniment,[4] as in the case of his borrowings from Muffat in *Alexander's Feast*, or from Reinhard Keiser in *Agrippina*. A third class comprises Handel's parodies, in which he has taken over an entire passage without any real disguise but reworked it, or added elements of his own invention which invest the borrowing with his own style and air without altering its outer attributes, as is the case with many of the larger borrowings in *Israel in Egypt*, or in his complete reworking of the Blow overture mentioned earlier.

Handel's Purcellian borrowings, however, belong to a new class, in which the

3. E. J. Dent, 'Englische Einflüsse bei Händel', *Händel-Jahrbuch* No. 2 (1929), pp. 1–12.
4. See Zimmerman, *op. cit.*, p. 30 for an interesting instance in which Handel borrowed an accompaniment only from Reinhard Keiser's *Octavia*.

original shape of the borrowed material is no longer so obvious, or even apparent, except, perhaps, to the most attentive and well-grounded listener. For want of better terminology, these might be called borrowings of scene, mood, atmosphere or affect. They represent a curious reversal of Handel's customary borrowing practice when utilizing materials from the works of contemporary continental composers. Most often he borrowed notes, then added affect, imagery and expressive climax. But in Purcell's music more often it seems that the spirit of the passage caught his ear and that direct borrowings of musical material are less significant.

In building the chorus 'He spake the word' as a powerfully dramatic beginning for the epic plague sequence in *Israel in Egypt*, Handel took over Stradella's concerto-grosso structure intact – it was ideal for the double-chorus arrangement of the oratorio – along with all the themes, imitations, harmony and progressions.[5] First he added the choral text, 'He spake the word', which, when echoed in block chords by the second chorus and by various sections of the orchestra, produces an overall atmosphere of awe and mystery quite absent in the original. Handel did not merely fall back on the power of the words; he marshalled their power in a particularly imaginative and effective manner.

After conjuring up the flies, the 'lice in all their quarters', and the 'locusts without number', which of course are nowhere to be seen in Stradella's original *serenata*, Handel jettisoned the framework which had carried him thus far, composing new movements for the plagues of the frogs, 'blotches and blains', hail and brimstone (the fire running along the ground is Handel's own new feature in this scene), the great darkness, the waters turned into blood and, finally, the smiting of the first-born. In short, Handel added to the original notation his own vivid imagery, expressive affect, and dramatic climaxes – a process which may be seen also in the inspired reworkings of Italian duets in the 'duet choruses' of *Messiah*.

In borrowing from Purcell, Handel often seized upon a particular effect, working it into a quite different musical context to describe a quite different scene: thus in the after-strain of 'Sweet bird, that shun'st the noise of folly' from *L'Allegro ed il Penseroso*, he created a moonlit landscape from the barren, frozen waste which Purcell had described in musical terms for the Cold Genius and his people in *King Arthur*.[6]

The difference in Handel's procedures in these two instances is basic. In the latter he captured the atmosphere of the original by impressionistic means. In the former he borrowed notation, invention and scoring as a kind of trellis for his own expressive, dramatic or illustrative ends. The latter kind of borrowing is characteristic of his use of Purcellian material, while for the former he seems to have restricted himself to the compositions of continental composers, when he was not borrowing from himself.

5. See Sedley Taylor, *The Indebtedness of Handel to Works by Other Composers* (Cambridge 1906), pp. 47–163.
6. See F. B. Zimmerman, 'Musical Borrowings in the English Baroque', *Musical Quarterly* LII (1966), pp. 492–3.

Perhaps Handel felt safe in openly borrowing from continental music, since the insular English would not be so familiar with the originals. This argument, of course, overlooks the presence of a great many foreign artists in London, none of whom Handel would have wanted to ignore or offend. One wonders what Porpora or Veracini would have thought of Handel's frequent large-scale borrowings from their Italian contemporaries had they noticed (their silence on the subject seems to indicate they did not). On the other hand his very careful, indeed well-disguised, borrowings from Giovanni Bononcini's *Serse* in the formulation of his own opera *Xerxes*, as mentioned above, indicate that Handel was not afraid to take risks.

His careful avoidance of stolen goods from contemporary English composers (except from John Blow), along with evidence just cited, indicates that Handel may have been careful only to obey the Spartan law in these matters. Dent's abstract explanation of Handel's reluctance to borrow English material may now be strengthened with a more concrete explanation: Handel did not wish his pilferings to be easily identified. If, as Dent observes elsewhere,[7] Handel suffered from a kind of musical kleptomania, he certainly kept his malady fairly well under control, where English compositions were concerned, during his years in England.

However, there are a few clear-cut borrowings from Purcell's works, including a passage taken from the anthem 'O sing unto the Lord', a setting of Psalm 96 to which Handel apparently had turned in composing the earlier version of his Chandos Anthem on the same text. Setting all the text Purcell had used, plus a few more lines, Handel relied on his own invention throughout the first five movements. (In the second, his setting of the word 'who-le' as if it had two syllables reveals that his acquaintance with the English language was as yet slight, and that he had not studied Purcell's composition carefully for hints as to the best way to set the English language to music.) But in the sixth movement, after the solo entry, Handel modelled the entire choral setting of 'Let the whole earth stand in awe of him' after Purcell's. The two passages, which may be seen together in Ex. 1, are very similar in melody, rhythm, and text-setting, but not identical. Clearly, however, Handel had not turned to Purcell for guidance in proper accentuation. Again the word 'whole' is set as two syllables. Nor did he follow Purcell's example in setting the word 'stand' on a sustained note, although in Handel's setting the soloist achieves a similar effect, slightly later in the phrase, by sustaining the word 'awe' for seven beats.

Judging from Handel's finished product – and it is significant that he retained this Purcellian movement in the final version of this anthem[8] – it seems that his ear was caught by Purcell's energetic rhythmic declamation, which serves so nicely as a foil to the *sostenuto* solo line that connects the choruses. The rhythmic device

7. E. J. Dent, *Handel* (London 1947), pp. 100ff. See also F. B. Zimmerman, 'Handel's Purcellian Borrowings in His Later Operas and Oratorios' in *Festschrift Otto Erich Deutsch zum 80. Geburtstag* (Kassel 1966), pp. 20–30.

8. The two versions are published in Händel-Gesellschaft vols. 34 and 36 respectively.

Example 1
    (a) Purcell, 'O sing unto the Lord'
    (b) Handel, Chandos Anthem IV

Handel borrowed brought with it the ebullient feeling of Purcell's original, a kind of heavenly joy, and one suspects that this is precisely the quality which attracted Handel to the passage.

Joy also was the affect which Handel had sought in turning to other English compositions[9] and that which caused him to take possession of the key motif from Purcell's 'Rejoice in the Lord' (the 'Bell Anthem'). Handel's earliest use of this motif appears in his duet 'Beato in ver chi può', which he finished on 31 October 1712, shortly after he had arrived in England to stay (see Ex. 2). Only the forephrase of the opening section, which recurs steadily, belongs to Purcell: the rest is Handel's invention. So short a borrowing might seem coincidental, except that its forceful rhythmic pattern and melodic outline lend it a uniquely Purcellian character, as does the remarkable spirit of joy by which it is animated. The underlying affect in the duet, as in the anthem, is one of joy. Handel has expressed the joy of Horace's happy rustic, so fortunate as to be living on paternal soil, ploughing his own land. In Purcell's anthem it is the joy of a believer. For the entire first section of the duet, two of Handel's own motifs carry the composition forward: one is a short after-phrase, more or less tailored to Purcell's forephrase (see Ex. 2b), and the other is an accompanying contrapuntal figure, which serves

9. P. Robinson, 'Handel's Music-Paper with Other Notes', *Musical Times* LXIX (1928), pp. 509–10.

Example 2
  (a) Purcell, 'Rejoice in the Lord alway'
  (b) Handel, Duet 'Beato in ver'

(a)

Re - joice   in the   Lord al   -   way,   and a - gain

(b)

Be - a - to in __   ver chi   può   sol - car _____

to lighten and refine the texture. The allusion to Purcell is apt, and the borrowed affect imparts an extra exhilaration.

Handel borrowed the same motif for the dramatic oratorio *Hercules*, using it again as an allusion to joy – joy now tinged with irony. By this point in the drama – just before the end of Act II – Dejanira, wife of Hercules, is painfully aware that she has been put aside, and that her husband is in the grip of a new passion for his lovely captive, Iole. Dejanira's feelings about the admission of Iole as her husband's favourite in her own household are, to say the least, ambivalent. Iole, dissatisfied with her role as Hercules' concubine, resents the whole situation and makes her feelings known. She joins Dejanira in singing the duet 'Joys of freedom, joys of power'. Here Iole recalls the freedom and power she had enjoyed in another existence, even as Dejanira thinks back on happier days when she was Hercules' favourite (see Ex. 3). Succinctly, he presents the dramatic irony of both women's predicament, focusing the conflict of their feelings in a brief cadenza.[10]

Example 3. Handel, *Hercules*: 'Joys of freedom, joys of power'

and court thee __   to be   blest   and charm my __   soul to   rest

Handel began the composition on the long, winding 'plough' motif of the duet 'Beato in ver'. But this theme, even with its mellifluous imitation in thirds and tenths, would not generate the progressive, climactic peaks of joy which Handel had in mind. So he simply adopted – in quotation marks, as it were – Purcell's marvellous evocation of joy from one of the best-known and most popular anthems of the era. The manner in which Purcell brought in the recurrent theme of rejoicing grows more expressive with each return, and Handel has followed suit in one of the most delightful of all his borrowings.

A less conspicuous use of a variant of this same theme occurs in *Judas Maccabeus*,

10. See Winton Dean, *Handel's Dramatic Oratorios and Masques* (London 1959), p. 426.

as a key phrase in the trio 'Disdainful of danger we'll rush on the foe'. Here again Handel's purpose was allusive, although the dramatic point of Purcell's affect is not so clear as in *Hercules*. Reminiscing over his father's dying wish that the Israelites revenge past wrongs which they have suffered under long oppression, Judas Maccabeus issues a bold call to arms: 'Resolve, my sons, on liberty or death'. The Israelites rise to the call, singing the first phrase of the text to a bold syllabic motif which, through stretto imitation, develops the mounting battle fever to a climactic pitch. Then with the second phrase of text comes the allusion to Purcell's anthem, utilizing the end rather than the beginning of the phrase. The allusion is unmistakable, however; Handel even went so far as to retain Purcell's old-fashioned ensemble of alto, tenor and bass (see Ex. 4).[11] Presumably victory is intimated by the joy it brings, rising with the closing phrase 'that thy pow'r, O Jehovah, all nations shall know'.

Example 4. Handel, *Judas Maccabeus*: 'Disdainful of danger we'll rush on the foe'

thy pow'r, O Je - ho - vah, all na - tions shall know

One final, unmistakable allusion to Purcell's 'joy motif' occurs in *Theodora*, where Didimus in Act I scene 2 sings of the 'raptured soul' which 'defies the sword'. Here Handel varied the joy motif in a highly ornate version in 6/8 metre (see Ex. 5). The original stamp of Purcell's melody remains clearly discernible through the highly ornamented melodic web; but Purcell's style is represented less by the melody than by the atmosphere of elation which so expressively characterized the earlier use of this motif, going right back to Purcell's original. Again, the affect lends itself admirably to the dramatic situation: Valens, president of Antioch, has issued an anti-Christian decree whereby all citizens must sacrifice to Jupiter or be prosecuted. Didimus, a Roman officer newly won to Christianity, sings of the joy of Christian faith, whatever trials are met. The borrowed affect, like the ornate variation of the original theme, is altogether suitable at this point in the progress of the drama.

Example 5. Handel, *Theodora*: 'The raptur'd soul defies the sword'

11. This combination was already archaic in Handel's time. His purpose in presenting this musical fossil, which is so much at variance with his general style, remains unclear, unless he merely took the arrangement over directly from Purcell's original.

Another melodic fragment which Handel may have intended as a Purcellian allusion occurs in Cleopatra's second aria, 'How happy should we mortals prove', in *Alexander Balus*. The melodic outline and rhythmic organization of the main motif are precisely the same as for the motto of the Magnificat in Purcell's Service in B flat major (see Exs. 6, 7). Purcell's original phrase is a forceful theme, which not

Example 6. Purcell, Service in B flat: Magnificat

only unites various movements of the Service but also relates it to the 'motto anthem' 'O God, thou art my God'.[12] Handel's use of the scale motif might be coincidental, were it not for several other factors: the arresting quality of the music itself, the melodic progression of the bass, and the resemblance of Handel's after-phrase to the melody of Purcell's next phrase in the Magnificat, 'For he hath regarded the lowliness of his hand-maiden'. Furthermore, both the musical

Example 7. Handel, *Alexander Balus*: 'How happy should we mortals prove'

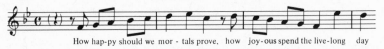

affect and the purport of the Magnificat text are appropriate to the dramatic development thus far in *Alexander Balus*. Cleopatra, who has already confessed that 'Subtle Love . . . plays around [her] captive heart', is on the verge of entering the king's presence for her first interview. Her feelings at this moment are revealed in her recitative,

> Aspasia, I know not what to call
> This interview. Grant, O ye pow'rs, it prove
> A happy one! but I am sick with doubt.
> Mark'd you the king, Aspasia? look'd he not
> A king indeed, while on his radiant brow,
> Deck'd with the rosy rays of youth, love seem'd
> To sit enthron'd and full of majesty.

Handel also turned to Purcell's music for inspiration in composing several melancholy passages; or so it seems in various instances where there are strong similarities between his settings and those of Purcell. E. D. Rendall[13] had remarked on some progressions in the closing section of the chorus 'Mourn all you

12. See F. B. Zimmerman, 'Purcell's "Service Anthem", *O God thou art my God*, and the B-flat-Major Service', *Musical Quarterly* XLIX/1 (January 1964).
13. 'The Influence of Henry Purcell on Handel, Traced in "Acis and Galatea"', *Musical Times* XXXVI (1895), pp. 293–6.

muses' from *Acis and Galatea*, which are strongly reminiscent of the closing phrases of the final chorus in Purcell's *Dido and Aeneas*. (Interestingly enough, E. J. Dent adds the Purcellian example 'Hush no more' from *The Fairy Queen*.)[14] Rendall also discusses other affective devices of this nature, ending with the suggestion that Handel had turned to Purcell not simply to study English declamation, but to learn techniques for forging more forceful dramatic expression in his music, and to find a nearer approach to the central current of his adopted country's native traditions of fine music and drama.

For another striking instance of this kind of veiled borrowing, one may turn to Purcell's 'Symphony for the God of Dreams' towards the end of the famous 'Conjuration Scene' in *The Indian Queen*, which obviously inspired Handel's introduction to the aria 'Behold a ghastly band' in *Alexander's Feast* (see Ex. 8). The other-worldly character of Purcell's symphony arises as much from his use of oboes and bassoons as from the antithesis of broken melodic lines, pitted against a rising bass. In Handel's symphony, this other-worldly atmosphere becomes downright macabre, as four bassoons provide a weird accompaniment to the solo line.

Example 8
   (a) Purcell, *The Indian Queen*: Symphony for the God of Dreams
   (b) Handel, *Alexander's Feast*: 'Behold a ghastly band'

(a)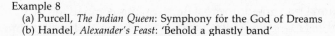

(b)

Despite the fleeting quality of such allusions or quotations, both context and considerable objective data rule out coincidence as a satisfactory explanation. More importantly, these examples bring us to a consideration of one of the most interesting aspects of the question of Purcell's influence on Handel. Virtually

14. 'Englische Einflüsse', p. 12.

every commentator on this subject has had to grapple with the elusive quality of various passages in Handel's works which sound 'Purcellian' but are difficult to identify and verify as definite borrowings. It would be otiose to enumerate all the commentaries of those who have noticed evidence of Handel's interest in characteristic dramatic passages from Purcell's late scores. So to 'truss up that long discourse' as Thomas Morley admonished,[15] let us turn to Charles Burney and Winton Dean, who represent the Alpha and Omega of literature based on comparisons of Purcell and Handel. Burney, in his *History*, did not go into a great deal of detail, being content to round out his comparison of Purcell with Carissimi, Stradella, A. Scarlatti, Keiser, Lully, Rameau, and Handel with the following paragraph:

> Handel, who flourished in a less barbarous age for his art, has been acknowledged his superior in many particulars; but in none more than the art and grandeur of his choruses, the harmony and texture of his organ fugues, as well as his great style of playing that instrument; the majesty of his hautbois and grand concertos, the ingenuity of the accompaniments to his songs and choruses, and even in the general melody of the airs themselves; yet in the accent, passion, and expression of *English words*, the vocal music of Purcell is, sometimes to my feelings, as superior to Handel's as an original poem to a translation.[16]

However, Winton Dean goes into great detail on this comparison in his *Handel's Dramatic Oratorios and Masques*. As for Burney's emphasis of Handel's superiority in the 'art and grandeur of his choruses', Dean points out that Handel's choral style expanded to the full only in England, suggesting 'that the precipitating agent was the genius of Purcell'.[17] Then, time after time, and especially in his commentary on masques or masque-like scenes in the oratorios, Dean points to passages demonstrating that the spirit of Purcell lived on in Handel's music, particularly in the dramatic oratorios.

Perhaps the clearest, simplest epithet we might apply to the Handel passages which have been the principal subject of this essay is that all are haunted, as it were, by the Purcellian spirit. Although this observation might seem flatly to contradict Dent's opinion regarding Handel's remoteness from the Purcellian age, it merely reminds us that all such broad generalizations are little more than half true. This fact permits another generalization, perhaps only slightly less than half true: contrary to received opinion, Handel was not more susceptible to Purcell's influence during the early part of his English sojourn than in later years; but, paradoxically, the more his genius took root in English musical soil, and the more he was able effectively to adapt to English musical needs, the more open he became to Purcell's musical influence. And thus may we understand why Purcellian passages seem so abundant in Handel's later works.

15. *A Plain and Easy Introduction to Practical Music*, ed. Alec R. Harman (London 1952), p. 214.
16. Charles Burney, *A General History of Music*, ed. Frank Mercer, 2 vols. (New York 1935, repr. New York 1957), vol. 2, p. 406.
17. Dean, *op. cit.*, p. 65.

'Or rather our musical Shakspeare': Charles Burney's Purcell

Richard Luckett

'We have now reached the prosaic period.' Thus, flatly, Henry Davey, a historian of music notable for his freedom from prejudice and his disinclination to acquiesce in received opinion, on contemplating the course of eighteenth-century English music, for which he also suggested an alternative designation: 'the period of patriotic songs'.[1] His view, expressed in 1895, was commonplace then and remains commonplace now, though the characteristic critical relativism of our own age does not favour so forthright a way of putting it.

It is, of course, a partial perception, dependent on the highly challengeable if surprisingly seldom challenged assumption that the music of a given epoch in a given country is to be defined by the products of native musicians, rather than of the musicians working in that country. It slights (such lists are necessarily facultative) Buononcini, Handel, Geminiani, J. C. Bach and Haydn. In another sense it slights Eccles, Weldon, Croft, Roseingrave, Boyce and Arne. It invites futile debate about the nationality of Storace, and ribaldry as to that of Gustav Holst, ironically prominent as a critic strident in his demands for 'Englishness'. It is frequently resolved (as, say, by Ernst Meyer in his *English Chamber Music* or Wilfred Mellers in *Harmonious Meeting*) by positing Marxian answers to a question which, if it is to be a serious one, depends on assent to the tenets of Herderian nationalism, tenets implicitly contradicted by the presuppositions of such a response.

Yet it remains a question which we can and do ask, and which was regularly asked in the eighteenth century. It usually contains two separate elements, which are more often than not confounded, for it is one thing to demand why there was no distinctively English music of any great excellence, another to inquire why there should have been a dearth of notable English composers. In the course of his elucidation of Roger North's remark that 'Mr H. Purcell, who unhappily began to

1. Davey, *History of English Music*, 2nd edn (1921), p. 336.

Plate 1. Daniel Purcell: drawing by Edward Francis Burney, after Closterman

Reproduced by permission of the Director, the Nottingham Castle Museum
This unfinished copy by Charles Burney's nephew is of a portrait by Closterman believed by Burney and his contemporaries to be of Henry, but now known to be of Daniel, Purcell. It was probably undertaken at the instigation of Charles, who was enthusiastic about portraits of Purcell, and who in 1793 attempted to persuade the members of the Musical Graduates Meeting to publish an engraving after a drawing (associated with the Kneller portrait of Henry) then in his possession and now in the British Museum; the proposal failed for lack of support.

shew his Great skill before the reform of musick al Italiana, and while he was warm in the pursuit of it, Dyed, but a greater musical genius England never had', Sir Jack Westrup cites Hawkins's conclusive retort to 'those, who, knowing nothing either of him of his works, assert that the music of Purcell is different from the Italian, and entirely English'.[2] Neither North nor Hawkins assumed that the music of a national master need be distinctively national; on the other hand North's contemporary Johann Mattheson did so (though in a confused way), and Hawkins's rebuttal would have been unnecessary had not some such presumption been current in the 1770s.

The purpose of this essay, however, is not to investigate the validity of the presumption or its relation to the heady concept of 'national song', nor to assess the extent to which a taste for 'English' music may depend on a palate too easily satisfied by a few simple flavourings such as the scotch snap and, in melody, descending intervals of the fourth and the fifth, but to inquire into the fate of Henry Purcell's works and reputation in the eighteenth century and in particular to consider the judgements arrived at by Charles Burney in *A General History of Music*. Burney, after all, believed in, and in a footnote to his account of Purcell specifically alluded to, that notion of a 'school of art' which his friend Sir Joshua Reynolds recalled when he said at the opening of his XIVth Discourse, delivered to the Royal Academy in 1788: 'If ever this nation should produce genius sufficient to acquire to us the honourable distinction of an English School, the name of Gainsborough will be transmitted to posterity, in the history of the Art, among the very first of that rising name.'[3] William Hayes, Professor of Music at Oxford, had in 1753 summarized his hopes for his profession in terms that have an evident common ground with Reynolds's: 'Suppose an ACADEMY formed under proper Regulation, in which no Author what ever should be studied, unless deemed truly *Classical*; might not this enable us in a few Years, to pay back with *Interest* what we have *borrowed* from foreign Countries at too large a *Praemium?*'[4]

The matter preoccupied others besides musicians; Oliver Goldsmith, in *The British Magazine* for February 1760, had spelled out what a 'school' of art properly signified ('that succession of artists which has learned the principles of the art from some eminent master, either by hearing his lessons or studying his works, and consequently who imitate his manner either through design or through habit') before going on to assert that in music

> The English school was first planned by Purcell: he attempted to unite the Italian manner that prevailed in his time with the ancient Celtic carol and the Scotch ballad, which probably had also its origin in Italy . . . But be that as it will, his manner was something peculiar to the English; and he might have continued as head of the English school, had not his merits been entirely eclipsed by Handel. Handel, though originally a German, yet adopted the English manner . . .[5]

2. Westrup, *Purcell* (1937), p. 241.
3. Burney, *A General History of Music*, ed. Frank Mercer, 2 vols. (1935), vol. 2, p. 399n; Sir Joshua Reynolds, *The Works*, ed. Edmond Malone. 3rd edn, corrected, 3 vols. (1801), vol. 2, p. 149.
4. [William Hayes], *Remarks on Mr. Avison's Essay on Musical Expression* (1753), 87.
5. Goldsmith, *The Bee and other Essays* (Oxford 1914), pp. 256–7.

In modern times Romain Rolland, followed by Winton Dean, has advanced what is broadly the same argument as Goldsmith's, and made more specific that notion of the assumption of Purcell into Handel which is dulled by the apparent conflict of 'eclipsed' and 'adopted' in Goldsmith's version.[6] Yet the proposition, despite its attractions, seems almost too neat, and makes it worth while to ask whether, in Hayes's terms, Purcell enjoyed, or could have enjoyed, 'Classical' status. A sketch of eighteenth-century views of the composer might help to test the case.

At the beginning of the century North's references are as tantalizing in their brevity as they are decisive in their substance. He is the 'devine Purcell', 'who hath given us patterns of all the graces musick can have'; and, in the consummately apt epithet by which Henry Playford chose to entitle the posthumous anthology which is in itself a unique (if tendentiously representative) monument to the composer, he is, inevitably, 'the Orfeus Brittanicus'.[7] The uniqueness of *Orpheus Britannicus* is a product of its size, its scope, its presentation, the implicit presumption that the contents are of classic standing: its components are as markedly conventional as the whole is novel. The prefatory collection of elegies follows a format employed for posthumous publications of all kinds which held sway from at least 1600 to 1750. The appellation of 'England's Orpheus' itself had previously appeared (in close conjunction with the word 'British') in one of the most popular of late-seventeenth-century elegies, John Oldham's *Bion, A Pastoral . . . bewailing the Death of the Earl of Rochester*, which was overtly imitated by more than one of Purcell's mourners. Dryden himself, whose magisterial 'our *Orpheus*' could well have given Playford his cue, in the ode that heads the collection drew extensively, though with brilliant economy, on *Bion*. The musical elegies, the words of two of which appear in *Orpheus Britannicus*, are in a long tradition, to which, in his lifetime, Purcell had made a notable contribution.[8] The significant factor, then, is not any inherent originality in the forms and language with which Purcell's contemporaries mourned him (Henry Lawes, in Horatio Moore's prefatory poem to the *Select Ayres and Dialogues, the Third Book*, had been, in anticipation of Dryden, 'Our Orpheus'; even Jeremiah Clarke's pastoral masque *On Henry Purcell's Death*, that remarkable staged tribute, could be argued to have a parallel in the lament for Rochester worked into Nathaneal Lee's *The Princess of Cleves*) but the way in which these commonplaces became definitive; the substance of what men felt was for once appropriate to, and indeed appropriative of, the available means of expression. Something similar had occurred with Shakespeare.

The *Orpheus Britannicus* poems are a far from complete collection of those on Purcell's death, but they make a fair representation of the commemorative spirit that the event had evoked, and their number was swelled when the second book

6. Rolland, *Handel*, trans. A. Eaglefield Hull (1916), pp. 58–60; Dean, *Handel's Dramatic Oratorios and Masques* (1959), pp. 20, 66–7.
7. *Roger North on Music*, ed. John Wilson (1959), pp. 349, 220 (*pace* Wilson, it is 'beauties' not 'ornaments' that North intends by 'graces' here), 307.
8. Cf. Vincent Duckles, 'The English Musical Elegy of the Late Renaissance' in *Aspects of Medieval and Renaissance Music*, ed. Jan LaRue (1967), pp. 134–53.

appeared in 1702. One poem not printed in *Orpheus Britannicus* deserves special attention, John Sheffield, Duke of Buckingham's *Ode on the Death of Henry Purcell, Set to Musick*. Sheffield's social position would in itself make his authorship of this poem remarkable, but he was also an acknowledged arbiter of taste and, beyond that, in an earlier prose essay had expressed the view that Britain had no native composer of consequence.[9] The poem, therefore, constitutes a claim for Purcell's classic stature, and it shared with Dryden's ode the distinction of being frequently reprinted in the eighteenth century. In 1700 John Blow's *Amphion Anglicus*, derivative of *Orpheus Britannicus* in title and format, paid a further and unusual tribute, in that three of its preliminary poems praised Blow through what, to a less unassuming man, might have appeared the odious device of comparison with his pupil. Tom Brown, in his *Letters from the Dead to the Living* (1702), employed the fiction of a correspondence between a translated Purcell and an untranslated Blow, which, despite its mockery of the monument to the composer that Lady Howard had set up in Westminster Abbey, is testimony to the unchallenged esteem in which the dead man was held.[10] The translator of the topically adapted 1704 edition of *Advertisements from Parnassus* (Boccalini's *I ragguali di Parnasso*), in portraying 'the great Count of Urania', introduced 'the famous *Purcel*' as his one named examplar of those 'Modern Musicians' who would entertain 'the Assembly with the Harmony of their excellent Performances'.[11] The painter Evert Collier adapted his musical *vanitas* formula to pay a tribute from another domain of art, whilst in Wych Street, Drury Lane, a finely executed *Purcell's Head* was set up as the sign of a music-house.[12] Playford offered for sale portrait engravings, framed or unframed; the other members of his pantheon were Dryden and Blow. During the first decade of the century Playford lost interest in music publishing and switched to prints, but the market for Purcell was strong enough for William Pearson to venture a 'second edition with large additions' (and some unacknowledged excisions) of *Orpheus Britannicus* Book I in 1706, and of the second book, 'with additions', in 1711.

Twenty years after his death Purcell's music was a staple of the concert rooms and the playhouses.[13] Theatre managers, having discovered that, as Lord Lansdowne put it in an epilogue (1701) to a production of *The Jew of Venice*,

9. John Sheffield, Duke of Buckingham, *The Works*, 3rd edn, corrected, 2 vols. (1740), vol. 2, p. 297.
10. Lady Howard was not (*pace* Franklin B. Zimmerman, *Henry Purcell . . . His Life and Times* (1967), p. 268) 'Lady Elizabeth Howard' but Annabella, Lady Howard, fourth wife of Sir Robert Howard. She was also the dedicatee of *Orpheus Britannicus*. Since Howard was Dryden's brother-in-law it is quite possible that, as Sir Walter Scott was inclined to believe (*Works of John Dryden*, 18 vols. (1808), vol. 11, p. 146), Dryden composed the epitaph.
11. Trajano Boccalini, *Advertisements from Parnassus . . . Newly done into English and Adapted to the Present Times*, 3 vols. (1704), vol. 3, p. 93.
12. The painting by Evert Collier was in the possession of the late Mr Edward Croft-Murray; for Purcell's Head, see Jacob Larwood and John Camden Hotten, *The History of Signboards*, 2nd edn (1866), p. 83.
13. I have drawn extensively on Michael Tilmouth, 'A Calendar of References to Music in Newspapers published in London and the Provinces (1660–1711)', *Royal Musical Association Research Chronicle* No. 1, rev. edn (1968).

> Shakespeares sublime in vain entic'd the Throng,
> Without the Charm of Purcels Syren Song . . . ,

were at pains to advertise their revivals as including 'all the music by . . . Henry Purcell'; the patentees of the Theatre Royal offered, in 1701, '20 guineas reward' to anyone who might bring forward the lost score, or a copy of the score, of *The Fairy Queen* (ten years later six guineas was a quite exceptional sum when floated for a 'Rich Gold Chast Scollop-sell Snuff Box', and 10s. generous for 'A brown and white Italian Greyhound Dog'); in 1705 it was worth claiming that a two-part song by Purcell to be given at the Ship Tavern, Greenwich, had been 'perform'd once only in Publick'; in 1711 a benefit concert consisted entirely in music from '*The Indian Queen, King Arthur, The Fairy Queen, Dioclesian, The Masque in Timon of Athens, The Pastorale in the Libertine*, and *St. Cecilia's Musick*'; in 1712 a concert performance of *Dioclesian* at Stationer's Hall was advertised as: 'Composed by the Immortal Henry Purcell, which for Beauty of Expression, Excellency of Harmony, and Grandeur of Contrivance, gives a first place to no Musical Opera in Europe'.[14]

Nevertheless, despite Purcell's national celebrity, and this at a period when Britain's intellectual and artistic achievements were beginning to attract continental attention, his reputation remained insular. His compatriots wished to believe that this was not so. Roger North, writing soon after Purcell's death, asserted that he had 'raised up operas and musick in the theatres to a credit, even of fame as farr as Italy, where Sig^r Purcell was courted no less than at home'.[15] A prefatory Pindaric to *Amphion Anglicus* claims, of Purcell, that

> His fam'd *Te Deum*, all the World admires,
> Perform'd in those Renown'd *Italian* Quires.

But the evidence is scant. A circumstantial account by Hawkins suggests that Dr Ralph Battel may have sent specimens of Purcell's and Blow's church compositions to Cardinal Howard at Rome, but affirms nothing beyond despatch.[16] In any case the contrafaction of the Latin texts necessary for Italian performances seems an improbable operation. The story that Corelli was so impressed by Purcell's music that he was travelling to England to see him when he heard the news of his death, and at once turned back, is flatly contradicted by the only contemporary evidence, a letter of 1699 from Addison, then in Paris, to Congreve, reporting that 'Corelli has a very mean opinion of Henry Purcell's works as a gentlemen told me that presented them to him, which I suppose Will be no Small Mortification to You Tramontane composers.'[17] It is revealing that when Addison's letter was re-

---

14. The prologue to Gildon's *Measure for Measure*, published the previous year, offers an interesting comparison with Lansdowne's lines:
    No more than this, We, for our Selves, need say,
    'Tis *Purcels* Musick, and 'tis *Shakespears* Play.
    The comparative rewards are from Lawrence Lewis, *The Advertisements of the Spectator* (1909), pp. 146–7.
15. *Roger North on Music*, p. 307n.
16. Sir John Hawkins, *A General History . . . of Music*, 5 vols. (1776), vol. 4, pp. 491–2.
17. John C. Hodges (comp.), *William Congreve: Letters and Documents* (1964), p. 203.

printed in *The Guardian* for 1712 this, the concluding sentence, was omitted. By 1775, according to Boswell, Thomas Davies was unabashedly retailing the anecdote to Dr Johnson, and even prefacing it with a reference to what seems likely to be its source, Pliny's account of the man who travelled from Spain to see Livy.[18] Mattheson in *Das Neu-Eröffnete Orchestre* (1713) includes the English amongst his four 'musical nations' but mentions no individual composer, maintaining that the English are limited to 'ploddingly' (*platterdings*) imitating the Italian style. He pursues the matter in *Critica Musica* (1725), where he mentions Purcell but betrays no awareness that he possessed particular genius and, with an accidental but apt irony, supposes him to be of French origin. J. G. Walther follows him in this in his *Musicalisches Lexicon* (1732), muddles Henry and Daniel, and offers no informed critical comment. Le Cerf's allusion in 1704 to those English who 'ont fait des sonates plus *sonates*, plus difficiles et plus bizarres que celles du cinquième opus de Corelli' is unspecific; if it does by any chance refer to Purcell its condemnation is comprehensive, and its indication of a general attitude to English music is sufficiently explicit.[19]

The merest handful of Purcell's works (and these, with the exception of one collection, of a trifling kind) seems to have reached the continent. The foreign publications of Henry Purcell appear to be limited to printings by Pointel of four dance-tune arrangements, by Estienne Roger of a scattering of recorder-duet arrangements in the *Airs Anglais* edited by George Bingham and, the sole substantial item, a piracy of the *Ayres for the Theatre* divided into two books. This is surprising in view of the quite extensive representation of works of English origin in Roger's catalogues, including a set of sonatas by Daniel Purcell.[20]

The decline of interest within England was gradual. When Arthur Bedford assaulted (in 1711) 'The Corruption of our Musick by mean Composures' he was concerned, above all, to make a point about the state of morals, and his book is a musical analogue of Jeremy Collier's attack on the profanity of stage plays (also the subject of a volume by Bedford). In claiming that 'Our *Purcel* was the Delight of the Nation, and the Wonder of the World', and inviting the reader to 'have some of our *Monthly Collections* perform'd at the same time with some of Mr. *Purcel's* . . .' and 'from his own Experience be sensible, how *Music* is of late declin'd', he assumes that Purcell's quality is immediately apparent.[21] The power Purcell's music held over Bedford himself is clear from the fundamental incoherence of his argument. The decline in the state of music, he maintains, is a direct consequence of the increase in the profanity of the words that composers set. But in alleging this he had to turn a blind eye to the nature of many of Purcell's

18. James Boswell, *The Life of Samuel Johnson* (Oxford Standard Authors), 2 vols. (1946), vol. 1, pp. 579–80.
19. J.-L. Le Cerf . . . de la Viéville, *Comparaison de la musique italienne et de la musique française*, 3 vols. (Brussels, 1704), vol. 2, p. 101.
20. The attribution of the *Ayres for the Theatre* to Daniel Purcell in François Lesure, *Bibliographie des éditions musicales publiées par Estienne Roger* . . . (Paris 1969), is erroneous; see Zimmerman, *Henry Purcell . . . An Analytical Catalogue* (1963), p. 522.
21. Arthur Bedford, *The Great Abuse of Musick* (1711), pp. 196, 201.

texts. Music, here, obviously triumphed over morals. Bedford's conflicting contentions, that modern music had lost its power, yet that modern music was powerfully furthering licence, reflected his own condition. Henry Carey, whose admiration of Purcell extended to the compliment of imitation, had a less contorted sense of the matter when, in a stanza written in or shortly before 1729, he registered a real fall in his reputation:

> Ev'n heaven-born Purcell now is held in scorn;
> Purcell, who did a brighter age adorn.
> That nobleness of soul, that martial fire
> Which did our British Orpheus once inspire
> To rouse us all to arms is all forgot;
> We aim at something . . . but we know not what.
> Effeminate in dress, in manners grown,
> We now despise whatever is our own.[22]

Though it is always easy to make too much of complaints of degeneracy, these lines perhaps have more substance than might at first be assumed. The young Dudley Ryder, on 22 March 1715/16, 'Went to see Mr. Skinner. There was his music-master with him who played upon the organ and sung to it "Genius of England", which is a noble song: there is something very grand and sublime in it and fit to inspire courage.'[23] What Ryder felt (one recalls, too, North's use of 'noble' in speaking of Purcell's sonatas) accords very precisely with what Carey felt but believed that most of his contemporaries did not feel.

There is other, less impressionistic evidence of change.[24] *Orpheus Britannicus* reached a 'third edition' in 1721; this in fact consisted of unsold sheets of the second edition, with a new title-page. The book had in any case become archaic in appearance, the typeset music showing very poorly (whatever their relative standards of accuracy might have been) against the engraved sheets of Walsh and his competitors. Indeed it was not long before Walsh produced *Mr Henr. Purcell's Favourite Songs out of his most celebrated Orpheus Britannicus and the rest of his Works the whole fairly Engraven* (?1724), but whilst this may be testimony to a market for Purcell, its comparative slenderness betokens a change in the nature of the interest and a reduction in the popular appetite. In 1745 Walsh issued another *Orpheus Britannicus*; this unimpressive work 'is merely a collection of single sheet songs engraved at different periods about the beginning of the 18th century'.[25] Walsh also seems to have acquired the remaining stock of the typeset editions: copies were still on his hands as late as *c.* 1747. John Johnson's *A Collection of Songs for Two & Three Voices taken from Orpheus Britannicus* (*c.* 1755) exhibits some originality of selection but fails to be anything like a satisfactory anthology.

22. Henry Carey, 'The Poet's Resentment' in *The Poems*, ed. Frederick T. Wood (1930), p. 102.
23. Dudley Ryder, *The Diary*, ed. William Matthews (1939), p. 203.
24. I am indebted for bibliographical material (though it should be noted that the accounts of *Orpheus Britannicus* are inaccurate and misleading) to Zimmerman, *Analytical Catalogue*, Appendix IV.
25. William C. Smith and Charles Humphries, *A Bibliography of . . . John Walsh 1721–1766* (1968), p. 280.

This is hardly surprising. Macky in 1722 had postulated the existence of an English school of music, yet as something under threat: '*Henry Purcell's* works . . . are esteem'd beyond *Lully's* every where; and [the English] have now a good many very eminent Masters; but the Taste of the Town being at this day all *Italian*, it is a great Discouragement to them.'[26] In 1728 it was Daniel Defoe in his *Augusta Triumphans* who took up the theme, indicating a still less satisfactory state of affairs, adducing Purcell as his crucial instance, and proposing a typically practical remedy:

> Not that we ought to disclaim all Obligations to *Italy*, the Mother of Musick, the nurse of *Corellie*, *Handel*, *Bononcini*, and *Geminiani*; but then we ought not to be so stupidly partial, to imagine our Selves too Brutal a part of Mankind, to make any Progress in the Science . . . We have already had a *Purcel*, and no doubt, there are now many latent Genius's, who only want proper Instruction, Application, and ENCOURAGEMENT, to become great Ornaments of the Science . . .[27]

Such grounding and assistance the establishment of a musical academy on *conservatorio* lines ought, in Defoe's opinion, readily to supply. This was to be an unrealized dream; English musical society would eventually organize itself sufficiently to offer, through the Royal Society of Musicians, some protection to its distressed members and their families, but it could not achieve the degree of structural rearrangement that Defoe envisaged. Defoe, moreover, was an elderly man in 1728, privileged to have lived through Purcell's heyday. The composer was a natural point of reference for Defoe, just as for Charles Gildon, who introduced '*Harry Purcell*' into his *The Complete Art of Poetry* (1718) as a paragon who 'seem'd to have the Genius of *Greek* Musick; he touch'd the Soul; he made his way to the Heart, and by that Means, left a Satisfaction in the Pleasure, when past'.[28] The Orpheus of the elegies has found his way into prose; but it has to be borne in mind that the author of the passage in question had, eighteen years previously, adapted *Measure for Measure* to accommodate *Dido and Aeneas*, performed as a masque within the play. Immediate and personal recollections, whether by a writer such as Gildon or by a musician such as Thomas Tudway, who had known Purcell 'perfectly well' and thought him 'confessedly the greatest Genius we ever had', could keep the candles at his shrine alight for a time, but not forever. We come to a period where silence is more significant than the things that are said.

What seems to have happened is not so much that Purcell disappeared from the repertoire as that the glamour vanished. At St Paul's, from 1713 onwards his Te Deum and Jubilate, hitherto in regular use, alternated with Handel's Utrecht settings, until in 1743 the Dettingen Te Deum superseded both, though the Corporation of the Sons of the Clergy, at its annual meetings, reverted to Purcell on abandoning the Utrecht version, and the Dublin Philharmonic Society is to be

26. [John Macky], *A Journey through England in Familiar Letters*, 2 vols (1722), vol. 1, p. 171.
27. Daniel Defoe, *Selected Poetry and Prose*, ed. Michael F. Shingrue (New York 1968), pp. 316–17.
28. Charles Gildon, *The Complete Art of Poetry* in *Critical Essays of the Eighteenth Century*, ed. W. H. Durham (New Haven 1915), p. 31.

found giving Purcell's 'Grand *Te Deum*' 'for the first time in this Kingdom' in 1750.[29] But these were untypical happenings: in the issue of 13 November 1752 Boddely's *Bath Journal* unabashedly referred to Handel as 'our British Orpheus' (more than a straw in the wind), and the general position was summed up by Burney when he wrote of the Te Deum in 1789 that since 1743 'Purcell's composition has been but seldom executed, even at the triennial meetings . . .' (yet one notes the three consecutive years when it was performed at the Three Choirs Meeting in 1755–7, though not without the benefit of 'Dr. Boyce's additions', and Hawkins claimed that 'the Te Deum and Jubilate of Purcell are well known to all persons conversant in cathedral music').[30] Burney also reports Purcell's *Ayres . . . for the Theatre*, extensively used in the playhouses for overtures and act tunes, as being superseded by Handel's oboe concertos and overtures; this must have occurred in the 1720s. When the unavailability of a score of *Theodosius* prompted Arne to provide new music for a Dublin performance in 1744, the customary diet of Purcell was further diminished; but a reduced ration should not be equated with famine.[31]

There were still bastions where Purcell was customary fare, the cathedrals and the popular playhouses: in the context, that is, of the vernacular liturgy and the vernacular theatre. When John Robinson opened the enlarged Westminster Abbey organ in 1730 he did so with Purcell's 'O give thanks'. The Charterhouse does not seem to have abandoned 'Blessed is the man' as its Founder's Day piece; different choirs stayed true to their particular selections of the anthems. In 1789 Burney noted ten as still performed in the King's Chapel, nearly twenty as still used at York. On the other hand Boyce's *Cathedral Music* (1760), despite a fair representation of Purcell, prints more works by Blow, and Purcell achieves pride of place in no single category of composition, whether services, full anthems or verse anthems. In the theatre, *King Arthur* was several times successfully revived (London 1735, 1770; Dublin 1750), but its success was not seen by contemporaries as a direct consequence of musical excellence. This had earlier applied equally to *Dioclesian*; Dudley Ryder and the Lancashire Squire, Nicholas Blundell, who both attended a 1715–16 revival at the New Exchange, both gave non-committal accounts of their visits which do not mention Purcell.[32] Thomas Gray was enthusiastic when he attended the Goodman's Fields revival of *King Arthur* (as *Merlin or the British Enchanter*) in December 1735, but his long account of it in a letter to Walpole is principally devoted to the staging and scenery.[33] He considered that

29. Brian Boydell, 'The Dublin Musical Scene 1749–50', *Proceedings of the Royal Musical Association* cv (1978–9), p. 86.
30. Burney, *History*, vol. 2, p. 388; Otto Erich Deutsch, *Handel: A Documentary Biography* (1955), pp. 765, 777; Hawkins, *History*, vol. 4, p. 501. Evidence for a local (but qualified) admiration for Purcell at Worcester is to be found in William Hughes, *The Efficacy and Importance of Musick* (Worcester 1749), and *Remarks upon Church Musick* (Worcester 1758).
31. Roger Fiske, *English Theatre Music in the Eighteenth Century* (1973), p. 116.
32. Ryder, *Diary*, p. 166; Blundell, *Diary and Letter Book 1702–1728*, ed. Margaret Blundell (Liverpool 1952), p. 154.
33. Thomas Gray, *Collected Correspondence*, ed. Paget Toynbee and Leonard Whibley, 3 vols. (Oxford 1971), vol. 1, p. 37.

'the finest song in the Play' was sung by the Genius of Winter in the Frost scene, but held that 'the Songs are all Church-musick . . .' Gray evidently enjoyed himself; nevertheless the production chiefly appealed to that aspect of his nature which delighted in the Gothick and in grottoes, and for him the chief merit of the music seems to have been that it conformed to that taste, perhaps by a happy accident of time. In other circumstances Gray could be a precise commentator on musical matters; he does not seem to have found Purcell's achievement remarkable. When Garrick restaged the play in 1770, Arne 'thought it necessary', as he put it, to lay before him 'a true state of the merits and demerits of the Musical Performance, you are about to exhibit in King Arthur'. Arne had 'not only, with the utmost care and candor, inspected the score of Purcell's composition; but attended two rehearsals of it'.[34] The highest praise that he could give to any of its constituent parts was 'tolerable': otherwise he complained of a 'dull, tedious, antiquated suite of chorus' and thought that of the solo songs all but 'Come if you dare' (in which, nevertheless, Purcell had failed to match the inspiration of Dryden) were 'infamously bad; so very bad, that they are privately the objects of sneer and ridicule to the musicians . . .' After Garrick had made it clear to Arne that he would not give him the job of recomposing it, Arne relented, admitting that 'Purcell's music . . . (though excellent in its kind) was Cathedral, and not to the taste of a modern theatrical audience'. Gray had found it to his taste thirty-five years earlier, but it is noteworthy that both men described the style of the music in just the same way. When in 1758 *The Prophetess; or, the History of Dioclesian* had been revived ('Not acted these 30 years') at Covent Garden, the announcements mentioned only the new songs by Arne and were mute as to the part played by Purcell.

The same characterization is suggested by one of the breathtaking (if tacit) dismissals that mark the mid-century. Mainwaring, in his *Memoirs of the Life of . . . Handel*, encouragingly promises 'a word or two on the state of Music at his [Handel's] first coming into England' but then goes on to maintain that at that date, 'Excepting a few good compositions in the church style, and of a very old date, I am afraid there was little to boast of, which we could call our own.'[35] Purcell is not accorded a mention, and his name is as conspicuously absent from the pages of Avison's *An Essay on Musical Expression* (1752): if the English have a national school, and Avison is inclined to doubt that they do, then the 'original they have chose to imitate' is presumed to be Handel, and Avison's query is not as to whether there might be some fitter native master but as to whether even Handel is an adequate model. William Hayes, in his forceful if understandably intemperate riposte, affirmed the existence of an English school: 'the Ancients' (Gibbons, Morley, Byrd, Tallis); the 'great' Purcell; Croft. But his account is virtually restricted to church music and, whilst he assumes Purcell's excellence, he fails to make out any reasoned case for it; yet this at least marks an advance on writing as if Purcell never was.

34. W. H. Cummings, *Dr. Arne & Rule Britannia* (1912), p. 68.
35. [J. Mainwaring], *Memoirs of the Life of the late George Frederic Handel* (1760), p. 76.

The pertinent defence of Purcell between 1740 and 1770 was more a matter of what was said and done than of what was written. Dr Pepusch praised him to Wesley, and enshrined him in the repertoire of the Academy of Ancient Musick. In 1750 Thomas Reinhold sang Purcell at Sadler's Wells. 'From rosie bow'rs' was a standard concert piece. 'From silent shades and the elysian groves' ('Mad Bess') enjoyed equal popularity and afforded Sir Francis Eyles Stiles, lecturing to the Royal Society on Ancient Greek modes in 1759, a convenient and familiar instance of the effect of a sudden change of modulation.[36] The popularity of these two songs is alluded to by Burney, and continued throughout the century: Madame Mara frequently gave 'From rosie bow'rs' 'by request' and on at least one occasion with exceptionally distinguished assistance, since Joseph Haydn recorded, on 1 June 1792, that 'I accompanied her, all by myself at the pianoforte, in a very difficult aria by Purcell'.[37] In the theatre 'Britons strike home' never failed to please, particularly in periods of national crisis. Arne included pieces by Purcell in his 1768 concert of glees and catches at Drury Lane, and even admitted to the 'extream pretty design, in the music', of 'Jack, thou'rt a toper'; the catches also found their way into plays and pasticcios.[38]

Before turning to Burney's assessment, we need to consider the view offered by Sir John Hawkins, and not merely because Hawkins's chronological priority in the field of musical history was at once such an influence upon, and such an embarrassment to, his competitor. From what is known of Hawkins's tastes, his conservatism, his patriotism, even his quixotic tendencies, we might reasonably expect a defiantly unfashionable eulogy of Purcell, a determined assertion of his classic status. But this is not at all what Hawkins provides. He describes the Te Deum and Jubilate as 'that sublime composition', proposes 'What shall I do to shew how much I love her', 'If love's a sweet passion', and 'No, no, poor suff'ring heart' as 'perhaps the finest [ballads] ever made', and avers that the instrumental compositions 'are greatly superior to any of the kind published before his time'.[39] He praises several of the anthems as 'in a style so truly pathetic and devout, that they can never be heard without rapture by those who are sensible of the powers of harmony'.[40] Yet he seems to hesitate in his final judgement: 'Of the Golden sonata', he writes, 'the reputation is not yet extinct; there are some now living who can scarce speak of it without rapture . . .'[41] He prints the sonata so that the reader may form his own conclusion, but ventures nothing conclusive himself; and when he comes to make what could well have been the definitively affirmative statement he qualifies it drastically and damagingly by putting it in the past tense: 'so finely were his harmonies and melodies adapted to the general sense of mankind, that all who heard were enamoured of them'.[42] 'Rapture' is indeed a word that Hawkins finds appropriate to Purcell; but 'modified rapture' more accurately describes the tenor of his account.

36. Burney, History, vol. 1, p. 59.
37. H. C. Robbins Landon, Haydn in England 1791–1795 (1976), p. 171.
38. Cummings, Dr. Arne, pp. 64–6; Fiske, English Theatre Music, pp. 437, 540, 603.
39. Hawkins, History, vol. 4, p. 521, 524, 526.
40. Ibid., p. 522.   41. Ibid., p. 527.   42. Ibid., p. 522.

If Hawkins promises more than he performs, the converse is the case with Burney. His criticism of Purcell is disorganized, repetitious and contradictory. It shows every sign of having been written under the pressure of work so vividly recorded for us by his daughter. It is nevertheless a wholly remarkable piece – its virtues an object lesson in what 'the strengths of its weaknesses' may mean. For Burney's mechanical and often flatulent diction is redeemed by the empirical nature of his approach, by the fact that he does indeed endeavour to 'acquaint the musical reader in what manner I have been affected by some of these productions, in a late attentive perusal of them' – affected, as it proves, beyond the scope of the presuppositions with which his perusal was undertaken.[43]

Burney commenced his reconsideration of Purcell for the *General History* as a professed Handelian who had publicly maintained that the master's works 'were so long the models of perfection in this country, that they may be said to have formed our national taste'.[44] In his *Account of the . . . Commemoration of Handel* (1785), when he came to establish the 'Character of Handel as a Composer' by demonstrating his superiority over his rivals in each separate class of composition, Purcell achieved only a glancing mention. In the same work Burney also expressed his suspicion of musical chauvinism: 'Purcell's *Te Deum*, in design, and expression of the words, is, perhaps, superior to all others; but in grandeur and richness of accompaniment, nothing but national partiality can deny HANDEL the preference.'[45] Handel had 'arrived among us at a barbarous period for almost every kind of music, except that of the church', and if it was the case that in English cathedrals 'harmony, and the ancient choral style' had been preserved free from 'corruption and decay', this merely made Handel's manifestly superior achievements in that field the more remarkable.[46]

The *History* alters the emphasis; and then the emphasis alters even in the course of the *History* account. Burney is haunted by the transitoriness of musical fashion, by the spectre of the process which replaces Purcell's theatre music by Handel's, Handel's by Boyce's and Arne's, Boyce's and Arne's by van Maldere's and Stamitz's: '*Sic transit gloria Musicorum*'.[47] He regarded his subject as building his fame 'with such perishable materials, that his worth and works are daily diminishing', his celebrity 'so much . . . already consigned to tradition, that it will soon be as difficult to find his songs, or, at least to *hear* them, as those of his predecessors Orpheus and Amphion . . .'[48] At points his account threatens to become hedged with Hawkinsian prevarications; just as according to Hawkins the merits of the sonatas will be apparent only to those aware of 'the state of instrumental music in [Purcell's] time, which was hardly above mediocrity', so for Burney, at times at least, 'the superior genius of Purcell can be fairly estimated only by those who make themselves acquainted with the state of music previous

43. Burney, *History*, vol. 2, p. 383.
44. Charles Burney, *An Account of the Musical Performances in . . . Commemoration of Handel* (1785), p. iii.
45. *Ibid.*, p. 11.   46. *Ibid.*, p. v.
47. Burney, *History*, vol. 2, p. 389.   48. *Ibid.*, p. 380.

to the time in which he flourished . . .'; and Burney seems uncomfortably close to his predecessor when he remarks that in Purcell's own time 'his songs seem[ed] to contain whatever the ear could then wish, or heart could feel', restricting this bold claim for an universal appeal to a past when the composing of, say, songs on a ground bass did not appear, as it appears to him, a 'Gothic' practice.[49]

That is on the one hand. On the other there is a quite contrary awareness that though

> Exclusive admirers of modern symmetry and elegance may call Purcell's taste barbarous [as indeed Burney himself has done]; yet in spite of superior cultivation and refinement, in spite of all the vicissitudes of fashion, through all his rudeness and barbarism, original genius, feeling, and passion, are, and ever will be, discoverable in his works, by candid and competent judges of the art.

When he writes in this vein Burney abandons the notion that the admirer of Purcell is necessarily versed in the music of a vanished epoch. Rather, 'if ever it could with truth be said of a composer, that he had *devancé son siècle*, Purcell is entitled to that praise . . .'[50] In 'From rosie bow'rs',

> The variety of movement, the artful, yet touching modulation, and above all, the exquisite expression of the words, render it one of the most affecting compositions extant to *every Englishman* who regards Music not merely as an agreeable arrangement and combination of sounds, but as the vehicle of sentiment, and voice and passion.[51]

The reader begins to appreciate why, at the commencement of his account, Burney could confess to 'a particular pleasure in being arrived at that period of my labours which allows me to speak of HENRY PURCELL, who is as much the pride of an Englishman in Music, as Shakspeare in productions for the stage, Milton in epic poetry, Lock in metaphysics or Sir Isaac Newton in philosophy and mathematics'.[52] His sense of musical fashion compels him to report that the Te Deum 'is only now performed occasionally, as an antique curiosity, even in the country'; his sense of something quite other prompts him to the claim that 'in the choruses and disposition of the whole work . . . Purcell is still admirable, and will continue so among Englishment, as long as the present language of this hymn shall remain intelligible'.[53]

The patient peruser of Burney's engagement with Purcell will have his rewards. He will have to endure the Doctor's opportunistic mode of procedure as he goes through the available works in the often haphazard and illogical forms imposed by the randomness of unsystematic publication; he will have to tolerate the reiterated rehearsal of an unrepentantly evolutionary reading of musical history. He will become aware of Burney's uneasy consciousness of a public to whom 'the name and productions of our British Orpheus, or rather our musical Shakspeare, are alike indifferent'.[54] But beyond those things he will sense the response that

---

49. Hawkins, *History*, vol. 4, p. 526; Burney, *History*, vol. 2, pp. 385, 383, 394.
50. *Ibid.*, pp. 390, 392.   51. *Ibid.*, p. 393.   52. *Ibid.*, p. 380.
53. *Ibid.*, p. 387.   54. *Ibid.*, p. 396.

Burney – almost, it would seem, against his better judgement – could not repress, that Purcell was the only native musical genius, since whose time nothing has been able to 'secure success to an English composer, but dexterity at imitation', that 'when a Carissimi, a Stradella, a Purcell, or a Handel writes a fugue on any subject, it becomes interesting to every master and judge of good composition', that Purcell was 'truly a national composer', that here was genius transcending the erosions of time and vicissitudes of taste.[55]

If Burney had commanded the opportunity and possessed the inclination he might conceivably have reorganized his criticisms in a more consequent form. A logical starting point for such a process would have been his comment that 'You twice ten hundred deities' 'opens with what seems to me the best piece of recitative in our language . . .', which makes it fair to inquire whether he thought that Purcell's achievement was in the field of music or of poetry. At first glance the question would seem to violate every critical canon to which Burney might have subscribed, but in fact he had only to cast back to 1786 for an impeccable precedent. In his XIIIth Discourse Sir Joshua Reynolds had pronounced a noteworthy eulogy of Vanbrugh, the more effective because unfashionable and unexpected, and dependent on the assumption that it was reasonable to treat of Vanbrugh as a painter (or even a poet) rather than an architect. Vanbrugh's buildings could not be brought into accord with the rules of architectural taste prevailing at the close of the eighteenth century: Reynolds resolved the problem at a stroke by assimilating him to his own profession: 'I can pretend to no skill in the detail of Architecture. I judge now of the art, merely as a Painter. When I speak of Vanbrugh, I mean to speak of him in the language of our art.'[56] Burney lacked Reynolds's boldness and perhaps his authority, yet he could not avoid the conclusion, when asserting the superiority of Handel over Purcell in 'many particulars', that 'in the accent, passion, and expression of *English words*, the vocal music of Purcell is, sometimes to my feelings, as superior to Handel's as an original poem to a translation'.[57]

Burney's difficulty was in being constant to his feelings or allowing them the weight they deserved, yet it is his great merit that he could not disguise what he felt. In this sense it is enlightening to view him as a 'pre-Romantic', in touch with the emotional impetus of the Romantic movement but debarred from its intellectual liberations. His dilemma is apparent both later in the *History* and in his subsequent writings. Of Arne he writes that

> though this composer . . . had formed a new style of his own, there did not appear that fertility of ideas, original grandeur of thought, or those resources upon all occasions, which are discoverable in the works of his predecessor, Purcell . . . yet, in secular Music, he must be allowed to have surpassed him in ease, grace, and variety . . .

In his *Verses on the Arrival of Haydn in England* (1791) he again exhibited his inability to reconcile his perceptions:

55. *Ibid.*, pp. 399n., 579, 404. 56. Reynolds, *Works*, pp. 440–1.
57. Burney, *History*, vol. 2, p. 406.

> Our *Tallis, Bird* and matchless *Purcell*, still
> Each sacred dome with sounds seraphic fill;
> But grace and elegance, to them unknown . . .
> From foreign fields we are ever forc'd to glean.[58]

Just such a tentativeness can also be discerned in the opinions of Burney's friend William Mason, the poet, critic and musician whom literary historians have treated as something approaching a definitive pre-Romantic. He maintained that Purcell was 'the greatest genuine, English Composer . . .' and held that his 'sublime Strains' proved 'the powers, which Vocal Music might have upon the mind, when so managed, that sound might be subservient, or rather assistant to sense'.[59] It is once again a defence in terms of poetry, but if we pursue Mason's correspondence with Thomas Gray and others we find no evidence that Purcell had quite that quotidian significance for him that the references in his *Essays . . . in English Church Musick* might be taken to imply.

A useful indication of the general popularity and estimation of Purcell's works in the years adjacent to the publication of the *General History* is provided by the failure of Benjamin Goodison's proposed 'complete, correct and elegant Edition of the whole of them', which has been examined and summarized by Alec Hyatt King.[60] Goodison was a lawyer by profession, and it is not clear why he ventured into music publishing, as he did in the late 1780s. He was evidently seized by the ambition of producing a collected Purcell, a project which he thought 'due to the Memory of our excellent Country Man' and from which he hoped that 'some Degree of national Credit may result'. He presumed that such an edition would not be 'unacceptable to [Purcell's] numerous Admirers', but the 105 subscribers whom he in due course attracted did not make up the total of 150 which he eventually decided that the venture required. It was a modest target: as Hyatt King observes, Arnold's edition of Handel failed despite attracting nearly 380 subscribers. But for all the lustre of many of the names on his list Goodison was forced to abandon his project.

What Goodison's attempt seems to demonstrate is that by the last quarter of the eighteenth century Purcell had become a composer of considerable interest to a small but far from insignificant number of people. This is confirmed by other evidence. When *Bonduca* was revived at the Haymarket on 30 July 1778, Purcell's music was treated by the management as a probable attraction. On 26 February 1779 a performance of *Acis and Galatea* was filled out with 'Songs, Chorusses, etc., selected from the Works of the late Henry Purcell', a combination that was apparently successful, since it was repeated. Philip Hayes gave a bust of Purcell (along with one of King Alfred and another of William Hayes!) to the Oxford Music School, where the composer had hitherto been unrepresented in the gallery of English musicians. The name of Purcell became firmly attached to *The*

58. *Ibid.*, p. 1016; Robbins Landon, *Haydn in England*, p. 33.
59. William Mason, *Essays Historical and Critical on English Church Music* (York 1795), pp. 72, 131.
60. A. Hyatt King, 'The First "Complete Edition of Purcell" ', *Monthly Musical Record* LXXXI (March–April 1951), pp. 63–9.

Tempest, evidence at least that what was generally agreed to be good music was felt plausibly to match the reputation of a man generally held to be a good composer. Purcell began to be collected, notably by William Shield (who drew on him in his pasticcios) and Viscount Fitzwilliam.

Yet there was no abrupt revival. At the beginning of the new century John Christmas Beckwith could tell his pupils that 'the longer you live, and the more you study Purcell, the more you will admire his music',[61] but they would have been hard put to it to equip themselves to do so in any systematic manner, nor, from Beckwith's time to ours, has the question of an adequate edition been satisfactorily resolved. What is significant, however, is the extent to which, by 1800, the climate of opinion had changed. The way was clear for the work of Vincent Novello and for the foundation of the Purcell Club. Purcell could convincingly be presumed to have a standing that had hitherto eluded him, even if real knowledge of his work remained very limited. It is, in any case, easy to exaggerate the significance of the extent of knowledge of an artist, rather than the intensity with which that which is known is apprehended. In 1833 Coleridge, whose musical sensibility has been so inexplicably ignored, would aver that 'Some music is above me; most music is beneath me. I like Beethoven and Mozart – or else some of the aërial compositions of the elder Italians, as Palestrina and Carissimi. – And I love Purcell.'[62]

It is the affirmation appropriate to the paradox of Purcell's reputation. In the age of Authority Augustan taste, for all its patriotic proclivities, never elevated Purcell to the status of a British Worthy. The Augustan in Burney legislated against Purcell; the lurking Romantic responded with an entirely contradictory series of reactions, quite at variance with the conceptual frame of the *History*. This may be felt to be too easy an imposition of the generalizations of literary history on to a musical matter, but I believe the case to be otherwise. Swift, Pope and Addison mocked at music – in different ways and for different reasons, but the cumulative effect is unmistakable. We can only speculate as to the part played by personal factors, but the main point of attack is clear enough: the art of music insufficiently involved the intellectual faculties, and necessarily lacked the vital cultural elements of literature. Its weaknesses were demonstrated, with exquisite appositeness, by the spectacle of musical life in the capital dominated by castrated foreigners singing manifest absurdities in a tongue incomprehensible to most of their auditors. It was, besides, an art proficiency in which demanded more time than a gentleman could properly spare from more serious matters.[63] Minor Augustans such as Arbuthnot might have musical talent and judgement, but these dismissive attitudes were nevertheless taken for granted in the circles most influential in critical consideration of artistic matters, and they were vividly

61. J. S. Bumpus, *A History of English Cathedral Music 1549–1889*, 2 vols. (1908), vol. 2, p. 355.
62. S. T. Coleridge, *The Table Talk and Omniana*, ed. T. Ashe (1905), pp. 240–1. His *Lines to W[illiam] L[inley] while he sang a song to Purcell's Music* (1797) are also germane.
63. Cf., for instance, *The Memoirs of Martinus Scriblerus* in Alexander Pope, *Works*, ed. Bishop Warburton, 9 vols. (1764), vol. 6, pp. 145–8; *The Spectator* Nos. 5, 13, 18 and 29; Matthew Prior, *Dialogues of the Dead*, ed. A. R. Waller (Cambridge 1907), pp. 187–8.

represented in Burney's time by his friend and admiration, Samuel Johnson. To Boswell Johnson alleged that he was 'very insensible to the power of musick', yet in an unguarded moment he confessed that 'if he had learnt musick, he should have been afraid he would have done nothing else but play', and on the one occasion when he did admit to being moved by musical sounds (french horns at a Masonic funeral at Rochester) he also voiced his suspicion of the merely emotive, suspicion to which he had previously given memorable expression when Boswell confessed the extent to which music affected him, and Johnson responded: 'Sir, I should never hear it, if it made me such a fool.'[64] It was such a climate of opinion that impelled Burney to define music, in the Preface to the *History*, as 'an innocent luxury, unnecessary indeed to our existence, but a great improvement and gratification of the sense of hearing'. If a historian and practitioner of the art could be made so cautious (and Burney's belief that fashion must rule in music is a direct consequence of this attitude), it is hardly surprising that a composer of a past epoch, once his initial celebrity had dimmed, should have been nationally un-appreciated, and the position would obviously be the more acute to the extent that a composer made demands on a *literary* sensitivity – the point which is central to Burney's claims for Purcell. In short, there is a case for applying to Purcell, though in a less particular sense, the words that Reynolds used of Vanbrugh who, according to Sir Joshua, 'was defrauded of the due reward of his merit by the Wits of his time'. For as Vanbrugh was directly, so Purcell became indirectly, 'the object of petulant sarcasms of factious men of letters', though these sarcasms, in the musical instance, were directed at the art, not the artist.[65]

The Augustan deprecation of music marched with a hardly less marked, though less ostentatiously deployed, deprecation of theatre. Purcell, whose compositions were so often designed for a dramatic context, was thus doubly dis-advantaged. Winton Dean, in taking up John Mainwaring's plea for staging Handel's oratorios, pays what is perhaps undue attention to the influence of the 'Puritan anti-theatrical party' in shaping the circumstances of the form.[66] If Handel had written staged works on secular topics in the vernacular, it is still probable that they would have met with sarcasm and neglect in the most influential literary circles. As it was Handel could achieve the audiences attracted by scriptural subjects only at the price of adherence (conveniently economical, as it happened) to the supposed scriptural inhibitions on theatrical performance. The musical drama was an intellectually unrespectable form, which is why attempts to reinstate it retrospectively have about them such a pungent odour of unauthenticity: the works in question cannot be made to flout the conditions that created them. When Thomas Gray reports to his literary friends the operatic excursions which he so greatly enjoyed, he does not attempt to disguise that, in one sense, he has been slumming.

The suggestion that Purcell failed to achieve classic status until the nineteenth

64. James Boswell, *The Journal of a Tour to the Hebrides* (Everyman's Library) (1948), p. 261, and *Life of Johnson*, vol. 2, pp. 348, 151.
65. Reynolds, *Works*, pp. 141–2.   66. Dean, *Handel's Dramatic Oratorios*, p. 123.

century, and that this was to a large extent a consequence of the Augustan distrust of music, cannot comprehend the whole truth. It is, of course, intensely relevant that he founded his instrumental writing on the school of Torelli, Cazzati and Vitali, rather than that of Corelli which superseded it. It is equally relevant that so many of his works, designed with particular occasions or functions in mind, should inspire in his successors an emulation that led to his own works being replaced. There is no denying that he was in many ways eclipsed by Handel, though that this eclipse should have been accomplished by so comparatively inferior a word-setter is a demonstration of the dimming of literary sensibility in the musical arena to which this essay has been pointing. It equally cannot be denied that Purcell, amongst composers, may be a special case: the love that Coleridge so spontaneously professed can be matched by the remarkable tributes of Robert Bridges and, above all, Gerard Manley Hopkins. Burney's achievement as a critic was that, despite himself, he responded to and came some way to describing the poetry of Purcell. But he had a precursor (who happens also to have been one of his oldest friends) whose homage supports my contention in several ways.

Christopher Smart is arguably the greatest English poet between Pope and Wordsworth. His relation to the orthodoxies of his time is illustrated at its most strained by his eventual incarceration in a madhouse. He left his fellowship at Cambridge for the world of London journalism and the popular theatre. He satirized, with some elaboration, the Italianate musical establishment. In 1746, sufficiently long after the praise of Purcell had ceased to be a poetic commonplace to leave no doubt that sentiment, not convention, dictated what he wrote, he published his *Ode on St Cecilia's Day*, which concluded with a stanza interlacing praise of the saint with a panegyric on Purcell:

> Mellifluous, yet manly too,
>   He pours his strains along,
> As from the lyon Sampson slew,
>   Comes sweetness from the strong.
> Not like the soft *Italian* swains,
>   He trills the weak enervate strains,
>   Where sense and musick are at strife;
> His vigorous notes with meaning teem,
>   With fire, with force explain the theme,
>   And sing the subject into life.[67]

If this is the language of Romanticism uttered in the accents of Augustanism (and the 'enervate strains' neatly link Addison's reiterated complaints with Coleridge's *Lines composed in a Concert Room*), it is nonetheless a demonstration, in its congruence with later judgements and its apparent incongruity with its own time (when minor poets praised Handel, and major poets no musician at all), of the way in which apathy in just those quarters where we might most have expected sympathy – quarters literary rather than musical; but that is the crux – retarded Purcell's fame.

67. Smart, *The Collected Poems*, ed. Norman Callan, 2 vols. (1949), vol. 1, p. 141.

Walsh's editions of Handel's Opera 1–5: the texts and their sources

Donald Burrows

The printed editions of Handel's music which were published during the composer's lifetime were often very inaccurate, and comparison with his autographs usually reveals a substantial number of corrupt readings. Where there are no reliable alternative sources to compare with the printed texts, editorial decisions have to be made as to where wrong notes, defective passages or misplaced movements occur. There must inevitably be a subjective element in the editorial treatment of these texts, both in the choice of passages for correction and in the 'restored' versions which are presented in their places. No correspondence between Handel and his publishers survives, nor have any printed copies with the composer's corrections come to light. It is therefore difficult to know how responsibility for the texts of the printed editions should be apportioned between composer and publisher. Deficiencies in the printed texts published by the Walsh house point to the conclusion that Handel did not correct the proofs: either he never saw them or he was a very inefficient proofreader. It seems most likely that Handel's involvement in the publications extended only up to the moment when Walsh paid him for music copy: after that it was up to the publisher to make what he could from the raw material with which he was provided. The composer's main interest in music publishing may have been the negative one of limiting the amount of his recent music which fell into the hands of publishers.

Cluer seems to have been Handel's favoured publisher in the 1720s, and we cannot be certain that Handel had any official arrangement with Walsh until the late 1730s.[1] The editions of his instrumental music which Walsh published as Opera 1–5 during the 1730s appeared in two groups. Op. 4 and Op. 5, published

---

1. See William C. Smith and Charles Humphries, *Handel: A Descriptive Catalogue of the Early Editions*, 2nd edn (Oxford 1970), pp. xiv–xv. The best evidence for Handel's business arrangements with Walsh is the document purporting to be a leaf from Walsh's Cash-Book (reprinted in Otto Erich Deutsch, *Handel: A Documentary Biography* (London 1955, repr. New York 1974), p. 468) which records payments during the period 1721–38. There are no entries relating to Opera 1, 2 and 3.

at the end of the decade, were certainly produced with some sort of co-operation from the composer, but there is no such certainty about the earlier sets. Between 1730 and 1734 the Walsh house was reorganized, probably under the influence of John Walsh the younger: the catalogue of current publications was extended considerably, and technical modifications, such as the addition of plate numbers to the title-pages, were introduced. Handel may have been attracted by the forward-looking appearance of the revitalized Walsh organization; alternatively, he may have been driven to an arrangement with Walsh because of the success of the latter's piracy. The thinness of some of Walsh's publications from the critical period 1730–5 may or may not be a sign that these were pirated.[2] The interests of the composer and the publisher wers radically different at this time. Handel had only a limited interest in the instrumental music which was such a popular part of the publisher's market, while Walsh was interested in Handel's theatre works only in so far as they contained material which could be turned into commercially viable collections of songs.

Op. 1 – Op. 3

Walsh's editions of Handel's *Solos*, Op. 1, *Trio Sonatas*, Op. 2, and *Concerti Grossi*, Op. 3 all include some works for which there are no other more reliable sources, and also some music which appears in a different guise from that found in the composer's autographs. Each of these publications has been investigated in the course of individual studies,[3] but although the music texts have been subjected to minute scrutiny, very little attention has hitherto been paid to the work of Walsh's engravers. A more detailed study of the idiosyncrasies of the engravers may suggest ways of assessing the accuracy of their work. The clef and notation forms used by the engravers changed from time to time, and they can be subjected to the same sort of analysis as that already employed for the identification of copyists' hands in musical manuscripts. Because of the widespread use of punches for musical symbols the engraving styles are rather less individual than musical handwritings. Nevertheless each style has consistent characteristics, and it seems likely that each engraver worked with his own punches, which he probably had to make as part of his trade. Unfortunately, very little seems to be known about the industrial organization of eighteenth-century music publishing, though it seems unlikely that more than a handful of engravers were active at any time. We do know that Cluer's substantial volume of Handel's *Radamisto* was the work of a single engraver, and that the work was delayed until he had finished another publication.[4] Walsh probably had no more than two or three music engravers at

2. See, for example, *The Most Celebrated Songs in the Oratorio Call'd Deborah*, described by Winton Dean, *Handel's Dramatic Oratorios and Masques* (Oxford 1959), p. 239.

3. For Op. 1, see Terence Best, 'Handel's Solo Sonatas', *Music & Letters*, LVII/4 (October 1977), pp. 430–8; for Op. 2, see the edition with introduction by Basil Lam, published by Eulenburg, nos. 1364–5 (London 1978); for Op. 3, see Hallische Händel-Ausgabe (HHA) Ser. IV, vol. 11, ed. Frederick Hudson (Kassel: Notenband 1959, Kritischer Bericht 1963).

4. The advertisement partially quoted by Deutsch, *Handel*, pp. 118–19, includes the publisher's

work simultaneously. A complete change of engraving style in a series of publications probably indicates a change of personnel. For the present purpose, I shall assume that each consistent style represents the work of a separate engraver.

Observation of changes in engraving styles can obviously provide information which helps to establish the date at which the plates were prepared. An interesting transformation can be seen taking place between the first and second volumes of Croft's *Musica Sacra*, prepared by Walsh in 1724–6.[5] Three consistent styles are found. One engraver made substantial contributions to both volumes, the work of another is found in vol. 1 but not vol. 2, and the third is represented in vol. 2 but hardly at all in vol. 1.[6] Comparison with other Walsh publications of the period reveals that the change was a general one: one style faded out and another one appeared in its place. The two engravers who prepared vol. 2 of *Musica Sacra* were also jointly responsible for Handel's Opera 1–3. I have designated them A and B (see Plates 1 and 2, pp. 84–5 below). The precise form of style B which occurs in the Handel publications does not, to my knowledge, appear in any of Walsh's productions prior to the autumn of 1726. This suggests that a revision must be made to the commonly accepted date for the publication of Op. 1 and Op. 2.

The preparation of Op. 3 can be dated with some certainty to late 1733 or early 1734, on account of the reference to the royal wedding on the first state of the title-page.[7] It has been generally presumed, from the existence of copies carrying the imprint of Jeanne Roger on the title, that Op. 1 and Op. 2 were published about ten years earlier.[8] Close examination of the 'Roger' versions reveals that the music pages are completely the work of the Walsh house and that the 'Roger' title-pages are deliberate spuriosities.[9] The situation is somewhat confused by the fact that there does seem to have been a genuine Walsh/Roger Handel publication about the year 1720: the *Pièces à un & Deux Clavecins* were engraved in the current Walsh style (very different from that of Opera 1–3), marketed with Roger title-

reassurance that the engraver would proceed to finish Corelli's Opera 1–4, on which work had been interrupted by the preparation of *Radamisto*. Meares's statement that it was 'thought necessary that the same Workman who began them should finish the whole' leaves no doubt that only one engraver was involved with the music text.

5. The chronology for the preparation of *Musica Sacra* can be traced through newspaper advertisements:

    Vol. 1: *The Post-Boy*, 2–4 April 1724: 'Next week will be published proposals for printing by subscription' *idem*, 14–16 January 1724/5: 'Just published'

    Vol. 2: *idem*, 22–25 January 1725/6: 'Next week will be published'

    The Privilege included in vol. 1 is dated 30 October 1724.

6. It is tempting to associate the second style with the name of John Hare, one of Walsh's publishing associates, who died in September 1725.

7. The wedding took place on 14 March 1734, but it had originally been planned for the previous November. See Hudson's Op. 3 edition (HHA IV/11), Kritischer Bericht, pp. 12–24.

8. Smith and Humphries, *Handel: A Descriptive Catalogue*, pp. 242, 244; see also Lam's Op. 2 edition (Eulenburg), introduction.

9. The results of the discoveries which I made in 1977 concerning the 'Roger' editions and Walsh's engraving styles were communicated to Terence Best; his subsequent examination of the same evidence confirmed my findings exactly. In what follows I have, as far as possible, avoided repeating the information included by Mr Best in a letter published in *Music & Letters* LX/1 (January 1979), p. 121.

pages, and listed with the correct plate number in the Roger/Le Cène catalogue of 1722.[10] The 'Roger' title-pages of Op. 1 and Op. 2, on the other hand, include plate numbers which conflict with those of genuine publications from the Roger/Le Cène publishing house, and it is significant that all of the known 'Roger' copies are of English provenance. The forgery was cleverly done. The general format of a 'Roger' title-page was carefully copied, and only the details of the letter forms and serifs give away the fact that they are not genuine 'Roger' titles. They may have been the work of engraver A. Op. 1 and Op. 2 cannot have been prepared before 1726: my guess is that they date from c. 1730–3 – just before Op. 3 – and that Walsh quickly replaced the first editions with others bearing his own title-pages.[11] Why Walsh should want to put out a publication with a spurious air of antiquity in the first place, bogus plate number and all, is something of a mystery. It may have something to do with Handel's Privilege (which did not run out until 1734),[12] or it may be that Walsh suspected that competition was in the wind. Handel's chamber music was an evident lacuna in what was available in print in England, and in January 1733 Benjamin Cooke was beginning to offer genuine Witvogel editions of various keyboard pieces for sale.[13] Perhaps Walsh was trying to make sure, in a rather extravagant way, that no one could claim a more 'original' publication of the music.

10. A copy of this catalogue is in the Library of Durham Cathedral. It is not dated, but it can be assigned to 1722 on internal evidence (the latest date in the annual sequence of *Airs Serieux et à Boire*). The Handel volume is listed on p. 71: '490 Pièces pour le Clavessin de Mr. Handel'. 490 is the plate number which appears on the *Pièces à un & Deux Clavecins*; the highest number in the catalogue is 523. It is noteworthy that Walsh later used the plate number 490 for his republication of Handel's first set of keyboard *Suites* (Smith and Humphries, p. 249, no. 5).

11. The advertisements for other publications which appeared on the Walsh title-pages seem to indicate the following ranges of dates:

    Op. 1: April 1731–March 1732   Op. 2: February 1733–February 1734

    The first newspaper advertisement to refer to the publications by their opus numbers did not appear until December 1734. There are some earlier advertisements (for example, that in the *Craftsman, or County Journal* dated 4 July 1730) which refer to Walsh's publications of instrumental music in general terms that might include Op. 1 and Op. 2, though there is always the possibility that references to 'Handel's Solos' relate to the *Six Solos* (Smith and Humphries, p. 241) rather than to Op. 1. The situation is further confused by the fact that there was not simply a sudden transition from the 'Roger' to the 'Walsh' versions. Two pieces of evidence illustrate that Walsh was constantly making alterations to the early copies. Gerald Coke's collection included exemplars of both Op. 1 and Op. 2 with Walsh labels stuck over the 'Roger' titles: the list of music included on these labels is basically the same as that found on the 'Walsh' edition of Op. 1, but there are two typographical variations in the layout of the list. Sets of parts for Op. 2 in the collection at the Bodleian Library, Oxford, (Mus. 175.c.36 and Mus. 175.c.25) have Walsh title-pages, but the music text of Sonata 3 includes three readings which Lam (Op. 2, Eulenburg edn no. 1364, p. VII) lists as being characteristic of the 'Roger' version: second movement, bars 27 and 63, and third movement, bar 18.

12. The Privilege is reprinted in Deutsch, *Handel*, pp. 105–6.

13. Cooke's advertisement is quoted by Smith and Humphries, p. 217. It is possible that the Witvogel editions were reissues of music inherited from Roger and Le Cène. When Cooke issued his own edition of Op. 2 (Smith and Humphries, p. 245) he imitated the style of the Roger/Walsh title-pages. Arnold's curious title to Op. 2, 'First published in Amsterdam 1731', is probably based on hazy guesswork, half a century later, about the source of Cooke's edition.

The editions of Op. 1 and Op. 2 with 'Walsh' title-pages stated that they were 'more correct than the former edition'. Some improvements were indeed made to the music text, though other errors remained, and the two new sonatas inserted into Op. 1 as Nos. 10 and 12 are no more likely to be by Handel than the ones they replaced. The new plates inserted into Op. 1 were mainly the work of engraver A. The music texts engraved by A and B are readily distinguishable from each other in Opera 1–3 (see Plates 1 and 2). This is true also of the letter forms in the titles to the sonatas or concertos, but the other printed words, particularly in Op. 3, are in a variety of styles: it looks as if the plates were subjected to 'topping and tailing' with the addition of extra speed indications, 'Volti', 'Fine', and the like, after the basic music text had been completed. A and B must have worked in close co-operation and agreed on a division of labour as the work proceeded. In Op. 1, A was responsible for Sonatas 1, 2, 3, 6, 8, 9, 10 and 12, and B for the rest; in Op. 2 and Op. 3 the two men shared the work on the parts. It will be noticed that the two dubious sonatas in Op. 1 (and their replacements) were the work of A, and it is my impression that A was responsible for a certain type of mistake involving bars omitted or inserted, or whole sections miscopied, rather than just the odd wrong note here and there. We cannot be certain that all of the mistakes are the fault of the engraver, since he may have had to work from defective sources, but the characteristic errors in the A style are of a suspiciously consistent type.

To begin with a couple of examples where there can be no doubt of the defectiveness of A's work. The edition of Op. 2 with the 'Roger' title-page contained a major howler in the last movement of No. 6 (Chrysander No. 7) which was corrected in the subsequent 'Walsh' issue. In Op. 2, A was responsible for the first violin part, B for the second violin and basso continuo parts: they presumably worked from a score. A began the first violin part of the last movement of No. 6 correctly, but accidently went over the second violin part in the middle of the second bar and followed it for a further five bars before going back to the correct part (see Ex. 1). Perhaps the start of a new system of staves in the score put him back on the right track at bar 7. The correction of this error in the 'Walsh' edition involved squashing in quite a few extra notes in the first violin part, making that part of the page rather crowded. Similar crowding at other places in the Walsh texts should perhaps alert us to the possibility that a correction has been made.

In the third movement of Op. 3 No. 3, A made a botched job of the flute/oboe part. Except in the special case of No. 6, I think it likely that the first violin parts of Op. 3 were engraved before the others.[14] In No. 3, A was responsible for all of the parts except the second violin part. The first violin part of the Adagio and the rest of the string parts were engraved correctly, but when A prepared the obbligato wind part he skipped a bar at bar 2: here he was probably bemused by the visual

14. The first violin part was by way of a 'master' copy and normally included, below the title, the specification of instruments required for each concerto. Engraver A was responsible for the first violin parts throughout, including that for the 'wrong' concerto No. 4b. When he replaced this with the correct No. 4 he forgot to include the instrumental specification, presumably because he was working under pressure.

Plate 1. Engraving style A in the 'Roger' edition of Op. 1

Reproduced by permission of the Bodleian Library, Oxford

Plate 2. Engraving style B in the 'Roger' edition of Op. 1
Reproduced by permission of the Bodleian Library, Oxford

Example 1. Op. 2 No. 6, fourth movement
(a) 'correct' form of violin parts, as found in the 'Walsh' edition
(b) first violin part, as found in the 'Roger' edition

similarity of bars 2, 3 and 4. In this instance, probably because the string parts had already been finished, A had to compose his way out by adding an extra bar at the end. The total number of bars was thus correct, though purchasers of Op. 3 would have been surprised by the sound of bars 3–6 when they performed from the parts (see Ex. 2). The correct text can be restored from its source in the 'Chandos' Te Deum.[15] This restored text still awaits publication, though two modern editions have texts which come close to it.[16] It was known to T. W. Bourne, who wrote it into his copy of the first edition of the parts.[17]

Only Nos. 1, 2 and 4 of Op. 3 seem to have had an existence as separate integral works before Walsh's publication: the rest were put together from other sources, mainly the Chandos Anthems. Handel may have given his general consent to the

15. Händel-Gesellschaft (HG) vol. 37, p. 76.
16. Ed. Stanley Sadie, Eulenburg edn no. 379 (London 1959); ed. Hudson, HHA iv/11.
17. Bodleian Library, Oxford, Mus. 183.c.22. Bourne died in 1948, but most of his work as a Handel scholar seems to have been done before 1910.

overall form of the publication, though there is no reason for believing that he took an active interest in its publication. I am disposed to attribute most of the errors in the last movement of Op. 3 No. 3 to a defective source rather to A's misguided creative genius. One bar is missed out in all parts in this movement and, although it is possible that A engraved the first violin wrongly and then fiddled with the other parts to make them fit, the nature of the omission seems to point to an error in a source score. There is certainly no reason to credit (if that is the word) Handel with this movement as it stands in the Walsh parts: it is full of errors which extend beyond the minutiae of the text. The music is arranged from a keyboard fugue, and the orchestral arrangement is so clumsily done that it is

Example 2. Op. 3 No. 3, third movement

Ex. 2 (contd)

surely not Handel's work.[18] It was probably sketched out in score by a copyist before the parts were engraved. A textual mistake at bars 78–9 reveals that the arranger was working from a copy of the keyboard fugue in which the upper staff was written in the soprano clef, as in the composer's autograph (see Ex. 3).[19] It is difficult to put this passage right in the concerto without rewriting the surrounding bars of the upper parts completely. My own solution, which also takes in the omitted bar 81, is given as Ex. 3c. We would do Handel no disservice by rethinking the whole of the movement again from the keyboard fugue.

Example 3
    (a) No. 2 of *Six Fuges*, as in Handel's autograph (R.M. 20.g.14, fol. 31v)
    (b) Op. 3 No. 3, last movement
    (c) one possible version of the passage

(a)

18. Among the musical infelicities are entries which tack a redundant note on to the beginning of a subject (flute/oboe, bars 53/83) and clumsy phrase-endings (second violin, bar 35). The added part-writing is uninteresting and, in one instance, incompetent: the second violin part in bar 85 moves in octaves with the bass. There are also consecutive fifths between flute/oboe and first violin at bar 92. (Bar-number references are to the HHA edition.)
19. A similar mistake occurred at bar 86 of the first violin part.

Ex. 3 (contd)

(b)

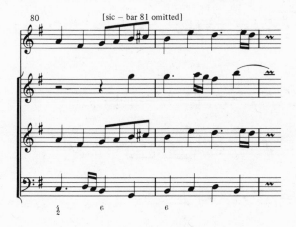

Ex. 3 (contd)

A number of interesting textual points arise concerning the last movement of Op. 3 No. 6. This music was published again by Walsh after Handel's death in a slightly different form, as the last movement of the Organ Concerto Op. 7 No. 4. Although the composer's autograph for the movement is not extant, it is possible to assess the accuracy of the text by comparing the two Walsh editions, and by comparing these with the British Library R.M. 18.c.6, fols. 5–8, a manuscript in the hand of the copyist of S3, whose activities were approximately contemporary with the publication of Op. 3.[20] Walsh's source for the version found in Op. 7 No. 4 is not known;[21] however, where Op. 7 No. 4 and R.M. 18.c.6 agree but are in conflict with Op. 3 No. 6 we may reasonably treat the text of the latter with some suspicion. Although B prepared most of the parts of Op. 3 No. 6, the 'master' parts for keyboard and first violin are the work of A: the 'Organo e Clavecin'[22] was obviously the most important part, and A probably began with that one. He missed out a bar 14 bars from the end of the movement, with the result that a cramped correction had to be made: a first hint of 'business as usual' with A's particular genius. The agreement of Op. 7 No. 4 and R.M. 18.c.6 at bar 16 suggests that A misunderstood the accidentals in the left hand, engraved them wrongly and treated all parallel passages in the same way. It is with the passage beginning at bar 48 that A really comes into his own, however. Comparison with the other sources suggests some dittography in bars 50–1, producing an additional bar (see Ex. 4).[23] The defective passage occurs at the turn of the page, and it is not impossible that A was trying to be helpful: he may have realized that he was

20. See Hans Dieter Clausen, *Händels Direktionspartituren* (Hamburg 1972), p. 269.
21. It was almost certainly not R.M. 18.c.6.
22. This specification is rather curious. It may be an accurate transcription of a source copy which indicated Handel's use of some form of claviorganum (see Dean, *Handel's Dramatic Oratorios and Masques*, pp. 109–10), or it may simply be a mistake by the engraver. Walsh sometimes named an alternative instrument, presumably with an eye to increasing sales: the Op. 4 concertos were for 'Harpsicord or Organ', and the obbligato wind part in Op. 3 No. 3 is for 'Flauto Traversa or Hautboy'. R.M. 18.c.6, which is a more reliable source for the movement, labels the solo part simply 'Organo'. The history of the movement, which is Handel's first published organ concerto, is not known, though I suspect that it originated from Handel's Oxford performances in 1733. Burney ('Sketch of the Life of Handel' in *An Account of the Musical Performances in Westminster-Abbey* (1785), p. 23) seems to imply that Handel first performed organ concertos in the London oratorio performances of 1732–3, but organ concertos are not mentioned in the advertisements for his London performances until 1735. Burney's story about Handel playing organ solos in *Athalia* at Oxford in 1733, on the other hand, seems more straightforward. The organ concerto movement from Op. 3 No. 6 could have been performed appropriately during either interval at a performance of *Athalia*, the final choruses of Part I and Part II in this work both being in D minor.
    We need not assume that the two movements of Op. 3 No. 6 were coupled on any authority from the composer. The first movement is associated with *Ottone*, which was in the repertoire in Autumn 1733. The paper characteristics of the autograph of this movement (British Library R.M. 20.g.13, fols. 1–4) suggest that it was composed for the original (1723) production, and that it belongs with the Adagio and Allegro found later in the same manuscript (fols. 30–32). These fragments together make up a complete three-movement orchestral concerto.
23. Useful comparison can also be made with the similar passage in a movement from the overture to *Pastor Fido*, printed in HG vol. 59, p. 12. There is also a version of this movement with the solo parts transcribed for 'Cembalo', a copy of which is found (in the hand of

giving the performer an impossible page-turn and resorted to composing his own crazy 'one-handed' solution. Unless some new evidence appears, I have no hesitation in believing that A mauled the text here and then adapted the other parts in his source before they were engraved.

Example 4
    (a) reading of R.M. 18.c.6
    (b) reading of Op. 7 No. 4, last movement
    (c) as printed in Op. 3 No. 6, second movement

(a)

copyist S5) in the 'Miscellanies' volume from the Barrett Lennard Collection, Fitzwilliam Museum, Cambridge, MS Mus.798. This version seems to be connected with the 1734–5 performances of *Pastor Fido* and its prologue *Terpsichore*, and therefore postdates Op. 3.

The movement from Handel's third Keyboard Suite of the First Collection (HG vol. 2, p. 21), although based on the same theme, does not provide exact parallels.

Ex. 4 (contd)

Knowing A's weaknesses, it may be possible to make some reasonable critical guesses about other places where his text may be wrong, though it cannot be proved to be so on account of the absence of authoritative sources for comparison. One example which suggests itself is a passage from the 'Walsh' Op. 1 No. 12 (Chrysander Op. 1 No. 12). This is one of the sonatas of dubious authenticity, but it is popular with the violinists and is played sufficiently often for comments on its text to be useful to performers. The angular harmonic movement of some sections of the final Allegro is rather tricky to bring off in performance, and on more than one occasion, both as listener and as performer, I have felt that the music was unnaturally cross-grained. There are usually problems of ensemble, especially in the passage following bar 33. Some of the problems may arise from the music text supplied by A's print, the only source. I suggest that he indulged in some dittography parallel to that found in Op. 3 No. 6, introducing an extra bar: the echo dynamics[24] do not make sense as they stand, and this feature reinforces suspicions of a garbled music text. In the succeeding bars the harmony does not seem to scan properly, and my guess is that A accidentally or deliberately recomposed the bass line, adding a beat and then making the sequence conform. The Walsh text is in HHA iv/4; Ex. 5 gives my suggestion for a 'restored' text. Some may feel that I have departed too far from the original here, and that Walsh's text should be performed as it stands; but it is worth reflecting on the results of this argument if applied to the Walsh text of Ex. 2. The combination of error and recomposition on A's part which is suggested in Ex. 5 is in keeping with his efforts elsewhere. It is perhaps worth noting that, here as elsewhere, he seems to have made worse errors as he progressed further into the music, as if he became more careless as he finished the job. The nature of his mistakes, and of his 'solutions' to them, suggests that A was clumsy and careless, but not ignorant of the musical notation which he engraved.

Op. 4 and Op. 5

By 1738 Walsh's engraving styles has undergone another change. Engraver A may have been involved in the preparation of Op. 4 and Op. 5, but I have not found any examples of textual howlers in these publications which are on the same scale as those quoted above. During the period between the publication of Op. 3 and Op. 4, John Walsh junior must have made some agreement with Handel which included obtaining the composer's authorization for his publications.[25] The title-page of Op. 4 carried the following note:

24. These dynamics are not reproduced by Chrysander in HG vol. 27, p. 46, but they can be found in the modern Urtext editions edited by Johann Philipp Hinnenthal, HHA iv/4 (Kassel 1955), and Stanley Sadie (Munich and Duisburg, 1971).
25. It is difficult to resist the conclusion that Handel's previous dealings with the Walsh house were in some way clouded by his relationship with John Walsh senior. Walsh's death in March 1736 seems to have removed old obstacles, and a new series of substantial Handel publications, which eventually included a 'complete' Alexander's Feast as well as Op. 4 and Op. 5, began in May 1736 with an advertisement for Atalanta 'Corrected by the Author'.

Example 5. Op. 1 No. 12, 'Walsh' edition, last movement: conjectural 'original' of bars 33–43

These Six Concertos were published by Mr. Walsh from my own Copy Corrected by my Self, and to Him only have I given my Right therein. George Frideric Handel.[26]

This statement can be taken at its face value. The phrase 'my own Copy' does not necessarily indicate that Walsh worked from the composer's autographs, and indeed this seems very unlikely.[27] The autograph of Op. 4 No. 2 includes some

26. Smith and Humphries, p. 224. The 'spurious and incorrect Edition' against which this note was partly directed has never been traced. Walsh himself had published Op. 4 No. 2 only a month previously in *The Ladies Entertainment 5th Book*.
27. No copies of Handel's music have yet come to light which can be regarded with certainty as copy texts for Walsh's editions. Burney ('List of Handel's Works' as part of the 'Sketch of the Life of Handel', p. 44) refers to a collection of scores made for Walsh which were in the possession of Walsh's successor, Wright, in 1785. I believe that the collection to which he refers is now to be found, at least in part, within the Barrett Lennard collection. My study of the text of 'Let God arise' (Anthem XIB) has convinced me that the Lennard manuscript of this anthem was the copy text for Wright's publication of 1784. I have not yet found any firm evidence that Walsh's own editions were based on the Lennard sources. See also note 44, below.

pencil markings which appear to be directions in German to an engraver:[28] it is difficult to make sense of them, they are not necessarily in Handel's hand, and they may not relate to the Walsh publication. The 'Copy' which Handel supplied to the publisher may have been a collection of partial copies marked up with the appropriate cues rather than a complete score. If so, Walsh may not have interpreted Handel's cues correctly in some details, though there is good general agreement between the surviving autographs and the published versions of Op. 4. The autographs include two revisions in the composer's hand which might have been made in connection with the preparation of copy for Walsh's edition.

Op. 4 No. 4 was originally composed to lead into a choral Alleluja and was used, with the choral movement, to conclude the 1735 performances of *Athalia*.[29] The last movement of the concerto is based on the subject material of the choral movement, but the instrumental section is substantial in its own right. It would not have been sensible for Walsh to publish one concerto in the set with a choral finale, and Op. 4 No. 4 appeared in print with an adapted ending, closing the concerto just before the choral entry. This adaptation was made by Handel himself, who squashed the revised ending on to the unused staves at the appropriate point in the autograph.[30] Although it is possible that the adaptation was made when Handel wanted to detach the concerto from the chorus so that he could use the concerto separately in one of his oratorio performances, it is equally likely that he made the revision for use in the Op. 4 publication. Between 1735 and 1738 Handel is known to have used the Alleluja in one other context – at the conclusion of the 1737 revival of *Il Trionfo del Tempo*. Since this performance was advertised as including 'Concertos on the Organ, and other Instruments', it seems most likely that the concerto and chorus remained coupled for that occasion.[31]

The autograph of Op. 4 No. 3 includes many revisions in Handel's hand, not all of them necessarily made at the same time. In its original form this concerto had an obvious drawback for inclusion in a published set of organ concertos: only one movement (the second) gave an extensive solo role to the organ. Handel re-worked the music of the last movement into organ concerto form. He may have done this originally for use in his own performances. The paper on which the revised form of the movement was written is identical with that of the rest of the

28. British Library, King's MS 317, fols. 1–10. This manuscript contains Op. 4 Nos. 2, 3 and 4. R.M. 20.g.12 contains the autograph of No. 6 and part of No. 1; R.M. 20.g.13 has a copy of No. 6 with Handel's amendments. For No. 5, see p. 99 and note 38, below.
29. The autograph of the concerto and chorus is dated 25 March 1735; *Athalia* was performed on 1 April. By ending *Athalia* with an Alleluja chorus, Handel was apparently following a hint from the original 1733 wordbook (see Dean, *Handel's Dramatic Oratorios and Masques*, p. 263). The concerto was cued into the conducting score (Clausen, *Händels Direktionspartituren*, p. 119); Op. 4 No. 4 was presumably the 'new' concerto mentioned in the advertisement (Deutsch, *Handel*, p. 385)
30. The relevant page of the autograph has been reproduced in facsimile: Ernst Roth (ed.), *Composers' Autographs* (London 1968), vol. 1, plate 38.
31. Deutsch, *Handel*, p. 431. The 1739 performance carried a similar advertisement (*ibid.*, p. 477), though the Alleluja was performed without the concerto at some stage in 1737 or 1739: see Clausen *op. cit.*, p. 244.

concerto, which suggests that this revision was made almost immediately.[32] Two movements (the first and third) then remained in which the solo parts were taken by violin and cello rather than organ. In a later thorough revision of the concerto Handel dealt with this situation by cutting the third movement completely and cueing the first movement in pencil to show that the organ should take over the solo string parts. Stanley Sadie has suggested that the revision to the first movement was made in 1740, when an organ with pedals was available which could cope with the three-part texture of the solo passages.[33] This is very plausible, but it is also possible that Handel made this alteration when preparing the concerto for Walsh. He wrote 'org' in pencil next to the upper solo parts in bars 3–4 and also wrote something, now illegible, against the continuo part which included a reference to 'organo' as part of the original specification. Perhaps Handel intended the organ to take the upper two parts while continuo instruments maintained the bass line. If so, Handel's intention did not reach Walsh (or was ignored by him), for the concerto was published in its hybrid form with two movements for organ solo and two movements with string soloists.

Because the alterations to both Op. 4 No. 3 and Op. 4 No. 4 may have been made either in 1738 in connection with the preparation of copy for the Walsh publication or at some other time to meet the demands of Handel's performances, we cannot be certain that the preparation of Op. 4 received much attention from the composer. In the case of Op. 5, on the other hand, there is definite evidence from Handel's autographs that he was active in the early stages of preparations for the publication. If the evidence of Walsh's account-book is to be believed, Handel delivered the copy for Op. 5 in Autumn 1738 within a fortnight of that for Op. 4.[34] Presumably Handel received at some stage a specific request from Walsh for material for a set of trio sonatas. He seems to have decided that four sonatas could be worked up from pre-existing music, mainly the overtures to the Chandos Anthems. He needed two more sonatas to make up the set, and these he then composed. Handel headed the autographs of these new sonatas 'Sonata 5' and 'Sonata 6',[35] so the conclusion is inescapable that he had planned out a complete set. We do not know whether Walsh followed Handel's plan exactly, though circumstantial evidence suggests that perhaps he did not.

The autographs of the Chandos Anthems carry alterations and annotations connected with Handel's ideas for the first four sonatas of Op. 5. He evidently decided not to re-use any of the movements which had already been commandeered for Op. 3, and this limited the number of movements still available. He made three significant revisions on the autographs:[36]

32. The paper characteristics of all three concertos in King's MS 317 are identical, and it seems very likely that the other two (Op. 4 Nos. 2 and 3) were the 'two new Concertos' for Handel's performance of *Esther* on 5 March 1735.
33. Stanley Sadie, *Handel Concertos* (London 1972), p. 26, 56.
34. The dates given in the account, which are presumably the dates on which payments were made after the delivery of music copy, are 28 September (Op. 4) and 7 October (Op. 5).
35. British Library, R.M. 20.g.14, fols. 1 and 6.
36. The following comments should be read in conjunction with a forthcoming article by Graydon Beeks, 'Handel's Chandos Anthems: More "Extra" Movements'.

(1) *Chandos Anthem I* (R.M. 20.d.8, fol. 103v). Handel rewrote the closing bars of the Allegro movement of the Sinfonia, replacing the final imperfect cadence with a tonic ending. The revised bars, written in ink, partially obliterate the instruction 'Segue O be joyfull' and this suggests that the alteration was made after the anthem had passed out of use. The imperfect-cadence ending is presumably the one designed for the anthem, though some later secondary sources, including the one which Chrysander worked from when preparing the text for the collected edition,[37] have the later ending. The perfect-cadence ending was used for the second movement of Op. 5 No. 2, and the alteration was probably made in 1738.

(2) *Chandos Anthem VIA* (R.M. 20.d.6, fols. 1–2). The first movement was shortened and amended in pencil by Handel to bring it to the form found in the first movement of Op. 5 No. 3. Secondary sources support the idea that the uncut version is the correct one for use in the anthem. Handel also shortened the movement when he adapted it for use as the Sinfonia of Anthem VIB in the 1720s. An additional amendment to the first violin part at bar 50 shows that Handel's pencil marks in the autograph of Anthem VIA relate to Op. 5 and not to Anthem VIB.

(3) *Chandos Anthem XIA* (RM 20.d.6). The anthem originally began with the 'second' movement of the overture (HG vol. 35, p. 212), which carries Handel's heading naming Psalm 68 as the source for the text of the anthem (fol. 51). The preceding movement (fols. 43, 50) was connected up with this later. The headings to the two movements have been subjected to many alterations by Handel. Two facts are clear:

(a) The Larghetto movement dates from the Chandos period, even if it was not originally connected with the anthem. This is proved by the paper characteristics of the autograph.

(b) The final pencil alterations to the speed indications for both movements conform to those found in the printed texts of Op. 5 No. 7.

The latest pencil amendments, including Handel's cue marks 'N1' and 'N2', appear to be contemporary with the alterations to Anthem VIA noted above. Handel's heading to the Larghetto (fol. 43) 'to be played before the Symphony of the Anthem Let God arise' does not necessarily indicate that it was to be used in connection with the anthem itself. If such was Handel's intention, the expression of his instruction was unusually clumsy. It seems more likely that the name of the anthem was merely used for identification. The earliest secondary sources for the anthem do not include the Larghetto movement. The evidence, taken as a whole, seems to point to the conclusion that the two movements were put

37. The volumes which Chrysander used as the working sources for his edition (now Hamburg, Staats- und Universitätsbibliothek, MA/177) do not include a copy of Chandos Anthem I. My suspicion, which seems to be confirmed by the preface to HG vol. 34, is that Chrysander prepared this anthem from Arnold's edition. Arnold's 'Symphony to the Jubilate' has the perfect-cadence ending.

together, and the speed indications modified, in connection with the preparation of Op. 5.

One curious feature common to each of the alterations noted above is that they make no attempt to modify the texture of the movements. Handel's Chandos Anthem overtures were composed for a four-part ensemble, with an oboe in addition to the two violin parts and the cello/continuo part. The alterations retain the four-part layout, and indeed there are no markings in any of the autographs which can be interpreted as instructions for the reduction of texture required for trio sonatas. It may well be that Handel was thinking in the first instance of working up the anthem movements into another set of concertos, and was only informed later that trio sonatas were the next step in Walsh's planned publication programme. It is even possible that Walsh suggested to him that concertos should be delayed until Op. 6, for which a new set of works should be written on a musical level which would invite obvious reference to and comparison with Corelli's famous Op. 6: in that case, an artistically suitable filler would have been required for Op. 5. The adaptation of the Chandos movements into trio sonatas presented no great technical difficulties. A certain amount of doubling between the violin and oboe parts was inherent in Handel's technique in the anthem overtures, and their rearrangement as trio sonatas could easily have been accomplished by an intelligent copyist. The rearrangements in Op. 5 are skilfully done, and there is no sign of the activity of the wayward genius who mangled the last movement of Op. 3 No. 3.

Since Handel headed the original sonatas of Op. 5 'Sonata 5' and 'Sonata 6' it is rather disappointing to find that the Chandos Anthem autographs which formed the source for the opening movements of other sonatas from Op. 5 do not carry similarly numbered headings. Having selected the music for each sonata, Handel may have left the task of putting everything in order to the copyist who was responsible for preparing the score for the publisher. A plausible reconstruction of how composer and copyist co-operated in the preparation of such a score can be made on the basis of a surviving fragment of the Organ Concerto Op. 4 No. 5.[38] This concerto was composed by rearranging the Recorder Sonata in F (Chrysander Op. 1 No. 11). J. C. Smith copied out the sonata (solo and bass) as an organ part, presumably on Handel's instructions, and Handel added the additional parts for the orchestral ritornellos. The concerto was probably put together for use in oratorio performances, rather than as a filler for the Op. 4 set, but Handel could have adopted the same procedure when rearranging music for Walsh. Handel presumably decided on the pattern and content of the first four sonatas of Op. 5 and then gave instructions to a copyist to arrange the music suitably in a trio-sonata format. If the copyist did the arrangement well, Handel needed only to give the result a cursory glance and, perhaps, add titles to the sonatas. The new Sonatas 5 and 6 could then be added, and the complete set bundled off to the publisher. As with Op. 4, it is possible that there was not just one copy score but a

38. Fitzwilliam Museum, Cambridge, MS Mus. 264, pp. 25–7.

collection of copy texts with cues to indicate the continuity. If Handel did indeed work in this way, the only marks which we would expect to find on the autographs would refer to the very first stage of the operation, when Handel was deciding for himself which movements he would use and what major textual alterations would be necessary.

Although we do not find the numbering of the intended Op.5 sonatas added to the appropriate movements of the Chandos Anthem autographs, Handel's titles deserve further examination. Four of the anthems carry a heading to the opening instrumental movement. They are as follows:

Anthem I, R.M. 20.d.8, fol. 102: Sinfonia [this title may have been added some
    time after the completion of the anthem]
Anthem VIA, R.M. 20.d.6, fol. 1: Sonata
Anthem VIII, R.M. 20.d.8, fol. 60: Sonata
Anthem X, R.M. 20.d.7, fol. 24: Sinfonia [this appears to be the original heading]

Handel almost certainly added the headings to Anthems VIA and VIII when he was selecting the music for Op. 5. The title 'Sonata' does not appear above the copies of the anthems in Tenbury, MSS 881–3, which originate before 1739, and it is significant that when the copyist added a title of his own it was 'Sinfonia', not 'Sonata'.[39] The heading to Anthem VIII poses something of a problem, since the music involved does not appear in Walsh's Op. 5 at all. Either Handel changed his mind, or the copyist who prepared the Op. 5 source misunderstood his directions, or Walsh rearranged what Handel sent him to suit himself. I am inclined to think that Walsh took some liberties with what he received. The number of sonatas comprising the Op. 5 set is unusual: we would expect six works, as in Opera 2–4, instead of the seven which Walsh published. The entry in the Walsh account-book, furthermore, refers to payment to Handel for 'six new sonatas'. The advertisements for subscriptions for Op. 5, which appeared in January 1739, said that the sonatas would be 'corrected by the Author'.[40] This need not be taken too literally and might in practice only mean that Walsh was claiming to work from authentic copy, but perhaps Handel discovered what Walsh was up to before the publication appeared and insisted that at least one more sonata – that based on the movements of Anthem XIA (cf. p. 98 above) – should go in, with the

39. These copies were the work of J. C. Smith senior and two other scribes. Smith's main
     associate added the title 'Sinfonia' to the anthems for which he was responsible (VA, VII,
     VIII and X), and Smith added the same title to his copy of Anthem II. It will be noted that
     Anthem VIII is therefore headed 'Sinfonia'; if the word 'Sonata' had been present on the
     autograph it would surely have been transmitted to the copyist. There is no heading to
     Anthem VIA. The watermarks of the manuscript include a type (D1) which seems to suggest
     a date before 1720 for this source.
        Another early set of copies of the Chandos Anthems, British Library Add. MSS 29417-26
     (main watermark Cb, probable date c. 1720–30) presents a little difficulty. In this collection,
     Anthem VIA (Add. 29423) is headed 'Simphonia', but Anthem VIII (Add. 29420) is headed
     'Sonata'. I am inclined to believe that the latter heading, which is in a different style of
     handwriting from the remainder of these two manuscripts, is a later addition. Another early
     copy of Anthem VIII (York Minster Library, M 113) carries the heading 'Simphony'.
40. Deutsch, *Handel*, p. 474.

result that it had to be added to the six that Walsh had already prepared. Looking back over the first four sonatas of the set for an 'odd man out', the most likely one to suggest itself is No. 4, whose more extended movements are based on music which originally included a genuine, if rather uninspired, viola part.[41] Handel may have intended Op. 5 No. 7 to stand as No. 4, which would have given Op. 5 three sonatas in sharp keys and three in flat keys. This still does not explain what became of the movements from Chandos Anthem VIII, which Handel appears to have intended to use somewhere. The most likely explanation seems to be that he planned Op. 5 No. 1 in a rather different form. The Oboe Concerto published by Walsh in 1740 in the Fourth Collection of *Select Harmony*,[42] which consists of the two movements from Chandos Anthem VIII followed by two from Anthem VA, may reflect the scheme which Handel intended for Op. 5 No. 1.

The suggested pre-publication revision of this sonata involves a radical change in its musical content. Strikingly similar revisions can be found if the autographs of the two original sonatas of Op. 5 are compared with the published versions. The autograph of No. 5 contains just the first four movements: there are three unused staves at the end, but no cues or any signs to indicate that there should be any more movements to the sonata. No. 6 has the first four movements as in the printed edition, but then ends with the Andante/Variatio movement instead of the Menuet printed by Walsh;[43] there can be no doubt about Handel's original plan for this sonata since he wrote 'Fine' after the end of the Variatio. Whether the alterations and additions found in the printed editions of these sonatas were the responsibility of Handel or Walsh cannot be established with certainty, but the alterations are of a consistent character. Handel's autograph versions of Op. 5 Nos. 5 and 6 are composed to the 'Italian' plan of four movements in a slow–fast–slow–fast sequence. The last movement of No. 6 is an addition which does not seriously disturb this scheme. The plan was not only the time-honoured one for trio-sonata composers attempting a 'just imitation of the most fam'd Italian Masters' in the generations after Purcell and Corelli: it was also the plan generally followed by Handel himself in Op. 1 and Op. 2. The published versions of the trio sonatas in Op. 5, on the other hand, follow a much more 'French' scheme. Every one of the sonatas concludes with at least one dance-rhythm movement, and in Nos. 2 and 3 the Chandos movements that begin each sonata serve mainly to introduce a short suite of dance movements. My suspicion is that Walsh was

41. The first two movements were derived from orchestral music which Handel shuffled around between the overtures of *Athalia* and *Il Parnasso in Festa*. The 'Passacaille' is a shortened version of the Chaconne from the *Terpsichore/Pastor Fido* music. The Chaconne and its accompanying Gigue both included viola parts in their original form: I thank Anthony Hicks for drawing my attention to the fact that the Chaconne was probably first composed for inclusion in *Radamisto*.

42. HG vol. 21, pp. 91–7. See Smith and Humphries, p. 240.

43. The conclusion of the incomplete autograph of Sonata 6 in R.M. 20.g.14 is found in Fitzwilliam Museum MS Mus. 263, pp. 43–5. Neither Chrysander nor Siegfried Flesch, the editor of Op. 5 for HHA, discovered this. The autograph version of the conclusion to the sonata was nevertheless printed by both from secondary sources: HG vol. 27, pp. 193–4, ending 'A'; HHA IV/10 pt 2, Anhang pp. 92–4.

responsible for the change in the character of the sonatas: either he suggested to Handel that the market demanded something lighter than the traditional Italian form, or he took the law into his own hands and altered out of all recognition the copy texts which Handel supplied. Fortunately, Handel's association with Marie Sallé's company of dancers during the 1734–5 opera season had provided a number of movements which could be pressed into service with only slight adaptation once a suite-type pattern for the Op. 5 sonatas had been decided upon.[44] If the stimulus to revise Op. 5 before publications came from Walsh, it nevertheless probably coincided with a trend in Handel's own thinking. The *Grand Concertos*, Op. 6, which Handel composed later in 1739, contain a more equal mixture of 'Italian' and 'French' elements than is found in his previous sets of instrumental music. Whether or not the published versions of Op. 5 turned out as Handel intended, the individual sonatas are on the whole successful musical entities. Nos. 2, 3, 4 and 7 are suspiciously shackled to the tonic throughout, and this may indicate the hand of the publisher rather than the composer; on the other hand, Handel's shortening of the first movement of No. 3 is appropriate to the movement's new role in the sonata as published. Unfortunately very few of Handel's autographs or working copies of the dance movements used in Op. 5 are extant. I have not been able to find any markings comparable to the cues and revisions found in the Chandos Anthem autographs which might establish Handel's authority for their use in the trio sonatas. There must remain a strong possibility that the arrangement of the movements in Op. 5 owes something to the taste, commercial sense or even whims of the publisher.

44. The 'Miscellanies' volume from the Barrett Lennard Collection, Fitzwilliam Museum MS Mus. 789, includes a number of shorter movements from Op. 5 in the hand of Smith senior, (fols. 158v–161v). This collection of movements, later given the title 'Sinfonie Diverse', was printed by Chrysander in HG vol. 48, pp. 140–3. An earlier section of the volume contains copies of Op. 5 Nos. 5 and 6 (versions as in the autograph) and the third and fourth movements from Op. 5 No. 1, all in the hand of copyist S1, It is possible that these two manuscripts are fair copies of sources which were used in the preparation of Op. 5.

The recovery of Handel's operas

Winton Dean

The story of the gradual transposition of Handel's operas from the obscurity of the library shelf back to the footlights is fascinating in itself and raises many important issues, historical, aesthetic, theoretical and practical. Some of it has been told before, but it will bear repetition; and certain aspects have never been subjected to a synoptic examination, if only because evidence is still accumulating.

It is no longer paradoxical to maintain that Handel's operas, like those of Monteverdi but of no other composer before Gluck, represent one of the peaks of that complex art. The total eclipse of the operas of both masters until the present century was due not to any intrinsic defect but to changes in public taste and the consequent rejection of their conventions as primitive, obsolete and no longer capable of artistic communication. Monteverdi's operas were virtually unknown before 1900, although he published one of them himself. Handel's were in slightly better case; but apart from the five included in Arnold's collected edition of 1787–97 none was printed complete for more than a century after his death. The contemporary scores issued by Walsh, Cluer and others could not be used for performance since they lacked nearly all the recitatives and a great part of the orchestration. Chrysander, who published the thirty-nine surviving operas between 1868 and 1894, performed an invaluable service, even if some of his editions are incomplete or misleading owing to his use of defective sources. For all but three of the operas Chrysander's are still the only available full scores. But – apart from three performances of the Hamburg opera *Almira* inspired by local piety between 1878 and 1885 and reduced to a fragment in a triple bill – they did not lead to stage productions. They supplied concert singers with choice titbits, but otherwise remained in the library till long after the editor's death. No one thought of Handel as a viable proposition for the theatre.

We should not be surprised. That was the age of the sophisticated music dramas of Wagner and the vernacular operas of Verdi and their successors, two traditions palatable to post-Romantic taste but quite remote from eighteenth-

103

century *opera seria*. The honour of restoring Handel to the stage belongs to Germany, and specifically to the city of Göttingen, which inaugurated a long series of Handel festivals with a production of *Rodelinda* in 1920 – the first revival of a Handel opera anywhere (apart from those of *Almira* mentioned above) since 1754. (The so-called *Giulio Cesare* of 1787 was a pasticcio put together by Arnold to please George III.) The Göttingen *Rodelinda*, like its immediate successors, was very much a compromise between what Handel wrote and what Oskar Hagen and his colleagues thought a German audience nourished on Wagner and Strauss could be induced to swallow without digestive disorder. Although these versions remained current in Germany till after the last war and some were published in vocal score, no one finds them acceptable today. Nevertheless they won great popularity for Handel and even assumed the dimensions of a craze. Hagen's arrangements of *Giulio Cesare* and *Rodelinda* in particular were staged repeatedly all over Germany; *Giulio Cesare* had 222 performances in thirty-four different cities in less than five years. Other German towns followed Göttingen's lead, and by the outbreak of war in 1939 nineteen of the thirty-nine operas had been restored to the theatre.

Of course they were cut, rescored, padded out with all manner of extraneous insertions, their plots rewritten, and the high male parts transposed down an octave. But at least they were seen in the theatre. Faint echoes of this enterprise reached England and the United States. The three operas most successful in Germany, *Giulio Cesare, Serse* and *Rodelinda*, were produced in both countries (the United States first), but in isolated performances outside the commercial theatre. The Germans also set about staging the dramatic oratorios. Here their example was taken up with enthusiasm and no little success in England; the first stage production anywhere of *Semele*, perhaps the greatest opera ever written to English words (although Handel performed it 'in the manner of an oratorio'), took place at Cambridge in 1925.

After the war the Germans continued with occasional productions, adding one or two fresh operas to the repertory but allowing others to fall back into obscurity. The movement received a considerable boost from the establishment in 1952 of a regular series of annual festivals at Halle, Handel's birthplace. But until 1955, just over two centuries after the last revival of a Handel opera in London (*Admeto* in 1754), Germany stood alone; apart from a few radio performances, sometimes of single acts, in the BBC Third Programme, the English-speaking countries had done nothing. Then two events, one of them almost a pure accident, changed the whole situation, at least in Britain. The first was the Handel Opera Society's production of *Deidamia* at St Pancras Town Hall in 1955. This was a somewhat Irish occasion, for the Society did not then exist: it was the consequence of the production, not its cause. The instigator was that great scholar Edward J. Dent, who translated Handel's last opera (one of the weakest, but chosen because it required a chorus) for the Board of Trade Choir and its young conductor Charles Farncombe. It received a single insecure and not very stylish performance; but it aroused enthusiasm and launched the Society on its courageous albeit financially precarious career, which has resulted in the staging of one or more of Handel's dramatic works in every subsequent year.

The second event was the bicentenary of Handel's death in 1959, celebrated by a substantial festival in London (with productions of *Rodelinda* and *Semele* by the Handel Opera Society, now at Sadler's Wells, and *Samson* by the Royal Opera at Covent Garden) and similar if smaller enterprises elsewhere. Unlike many revivals stimulated by anniversaries, these were not allowed to lapse. Anthony Lewis, then Professor of Music at Birmingham University (who had been responsible for most of the Third Programme broadcasts), inaugurated one new series of opera productions – not confined to Handel, though he featured prominently – at the Barber Institute of Fine Arts, and Alan and Frances Kitching another in the tiny Unicorn Theatre at Abingdon. The latter has since been discontinued through lack of funds, but its truly remarkable record included one opera (*Agrippina*) in a British première and four others (*Floridante, Giustino, Sosarme* and *Lotario*) that had never been staged anywhere since Handel himself gave them in London. Since 1959 theatrical productions of his operas have cropped up in the most surprising places, not only in Britain and Germany (where of course the bicentenary received prominent attention) but in the United States, South America, many European countries (including the Soviet Union) and even Japan.

An important element in this rebirth was the *Zeitgeist*: not simply the peculiar modern urge to disinter the past, but a radical change in the artistic climate, not confined to opera. With the reaction against the bloated post-Romanticism that followed Wagner and the revival of interest in music before Beethoven (of which Stravinsky's neo-classicism was another manifestation), attention was bound to be focused in due course on the great masters of the Baroque. Bach had been sanctified long before, thanks to the efforts of Mendelssohn and his generation; it was now the turn of Monteverdi and Handel – and many lesser figures, not all of whom have stood the test. Their operas must be revived and tried out; but how?

Here we encounter a whole complex of problems, centred not simply on the abstract concept of 'authenticity', however that may be interpreted, but on the nature of *opera seria*, the presumed intentions of the composers, how they performed their operas, and how we ought to tackle the task in the changed conditions of today. If we glance at what has happened, it becomes apparent that we were inadequately equipped, erratic in our aims, and weak in practical scholarship; impractical scholarship in matters of performance is apt to be a hindrance rather than a help. There was bound to be a great deal of the blind leading the blind; all too many experiments have illustrated the words so genially set by Handel: 'All we like sheep have gone astray'.

The situation in Germany was and is quite distinct from that in England. The old Hagen editions were gradually discarded, but a tradition had been established which has something in common with that of oratorio performance in Victorian England. While Handel's scoring for instruments was increasingly respected, his treatment of the voices was not. With very few exceptions, including one or two Göttingen productions where an English countertenor was imported to sing a castrato part, the high male roles are still automatically put down an octave, presumably because soprano and alto voices are regarded as incompatible with the German conception of the *Held* or hero. In other words the operas are judged not in their own right but by the extent to which they can be made palatable to *a priori* assumptions about modern taste. This has also involved rearrangement of the plots and the order of movements. Two quite different versions of *Radamisto* have been staged at Halle, in 1955 and 1977 (the former was published in vocal score); neither came within measurable distance of doing justice to that great opera. A feature of German productions has been the care devoted to the dramatic side, both scenically and in clarifying the complex librettos for a non-specialist audience. The aim is a worthy one; but the manner of its execution has crippled the music, with the deliberate pace of the recitatives and the frequent intervals to change the sets bringing all forward dramatic momentum to a halt. This is far too high a price to pay. The problem of reconciling the spectacle of Handel's theatre with the pace of his music needs to be tackled from quite a different angle. It is a cardinal issue, and it has presented one of the most awkward hurdles in the whole recovery programme.

One obvious difference between the German and English approaches needs further stress. In Germany, and elsewhere on the European continent, most productions have been fully professional affairs in commercial opera houses; Handel has had to take his chance in the general repertory. With a very few exceptions this has not been the case in Britain or the United States. Here the initiative came from small bodies of enthusiasts, university music departments and amateur societies operating on shoestring budgets. They employed professional singers in the principal parts, but inevitably the visual side received short shrift. Tiny stages like those of the Barber Institute or the Abingdon Unicorn could offer no equivalent for the lavish spectacle of Handel's London productions, especially in magic and grand heroic operas. When more facilities were available, as in the Handel Opera Society productions at Sadler's Wells, there were not enough funds to make proper use of them. For the same reason the musical side, even when conceived on sensible lines, was liable to be weakened by insufficient rehearsal. In the better productions the opera, by the last performance of a short run, showed signs of knitting together into something impressive, only to be cut off before promise could expand into fulfilment.

British productions have made plenty of avoidable blunders, but they have shown greater willingness to experiment than their counterparts in Germany and have paid more attention to recent scholarship. Octave transposition of high male parts would be unthinkable today, and other malpractices are gradually being eliminated. Even so, allowances have still to be made for inadequacies of performance, and there is too much evidence of our national habit of muddling through. If British Handelians can accuse the Germans of standing still or following an obsolete tradition, the Germans are entitled to reply that British productions lack professionalism and our national bodies do not take Handel seriously (otherwise his operas would be in the repertory). There is justification on both sides. What is needed is a combination of the better qualities of both.

The best way to view the problem in perspective is to approach it from the opposite direction, beginning not with the modern audience and its preconceptions but with the operas themselves. It should be axiomatic that if we propose to revive a work in an unfamiliar idiom whose traditions of performance have been completely lost, we must study the aims of its creator and his methods of realizing them, even if we have to employ substitutes or equivalents. The difficulty with Handel's operas is that until very recently our acquaintance with this whole domain was superficial and undermined by prejudice. We are still making major discoveries, and those made yesterday have scarcely begun to penetrate the realm of practical realization. It is best to leave theoretical matters on one side and plunge *in medias res*.

The most important feature of Handel's operas, and the most difficult to grasp (perhaps no one in our time ever grasped it without first floundering into error), is that they are complex and sophisticated unities involving not only music (voices and instruments) but verbal drama, scenic action, spectacle and sometimes dancing. To put it another way, the greatest of them – they are of course unequal in merit, like the works of any artist – are among the supreme masterpieces of opera. In a form that outwardly comprises little more than long strings of secco recitatives and da capo arias, with an occasional orchestral sinfonia, a rare duet or other concerted movement (often only one to an opera, and sometimes not even that), and an apparently perfunctory final ensemble in which the characters celebrate an obligatory happy end, this may seem a bold claim. So it is; but it has been validated by experience. Handel was not only a great composer with almost unlimited powers of invention but an immensely practical man of the theatre. If the demonstrations have not been as frequent or conclusive as with Mozart and Verdi, the cause had been defective or misguided methods of performance, which have seldom given the operas a fair chance.

The elements in Handel's success can be isolated, always provided we remember to put them together again; it is their interaction that raises the operas to their full stature. One of the most crucial is the staging, the manner in which musico-dramatic effects were created in the eighteenth-century theatre. Unless we grasp this and apply our knowledge (and we very seldom do), the opera misses its target and disintegrates into a concert in costume. The modern theatre is so liberally endowed with gadgets and machinery of every kind that we can easily reproduce Handel's effects even if we use different means. There is no need to construct special buildings; all that is required is understanding. In Handel's day the music within each act was continuous. The house curtain rose at the beginning of the opera (Handel often achieved a brilliant *coup de théâtre* by raising it during the overture, converting the last movement of the latter into the first of the action and precipitating the audience into the story); it fell at the end of the last act. Handel allowed for this in the few bars of coda that conclude nearly all his final ensembles. The curtain was not lowered between acts, although there were intervals, sometimes filled with dancing. In the first (unpublished) version of *Radamisto* produced in April 1720 Handel composed his own entr'acte ballets. When the scenery was changed during an act (there are at least two scene changes in almost every act of a Handel opera), the operation was executed in full view of the audience: wings, sliding in grooves on either side of the stage (there were five sets in the King's Theatre in the Haymarket), borders and backflats were changed simultaneously and very rapidly by means of a windlass in the basement of the theatre. These visible scene changes were one of the major attractions in an eighteenth-century opera. Handel regularly wrote them into the score by jumping at the same time to a remote key, and at least once (in *Teseo*) by ending one scene with a descriptive recitative and beginning the next with a presentation of the action described. As the scenery changed the audience witnessed what the character was talking about.

It follows that in modern productions the house curtain should never be lowered during the course of an act. To do so snaps the musical as well as the dramatic thread, encourages the audience to chatter, and chops the opera into a series of disconnected episodes, reinforcing the traditional heresy that that is just what it is. Old theatres with their original machinery for scene-changing (now worked by electricity instead of by hand) survive at Drottningholm and at Bad Lauchstädt just outside Halle. Handel operas have been staged in both. At Bad Lauchstädt, at one and the same performance, some scenes have been changed by machinery in the eighteenth-century manner, with marvellous effect, yet at other points the curtain has been lowered, throwing away all the advantage gained. An equivalent to the Drottningholm practice, with revolving wings, was adopted in the Stockholm Opera's production of *Il Pastor Fido* at the 1974 Edinburgh Festival and worked perfectly.

A second potential stumbling-block – though a purely imaginary one – is the pitch of the voices, already mentioned. Everyone knows that the heroic male roles in all serious operas of Handel's time were written for high voices, sopranos or altos. Tenors and basses were confined to tyrants, old men, and occasional comic characters or servants. The high parts were not necessarily taken by castratos; many of them, including heroes, generals and emperors (Radamisto, Goffredo in *Rinaldo*, Valentiniano in *Ezio*) were written for women. A number of female singers specialized in breeches roles and seldom played any others (in Italy, especially in Rome where the Pope banned women from the stage, castratos played female roles). Handel regarded pitch, not sex, as all-important, and used castratos and women interchangeably. He showed a strong preference for altos in these parts (nearly all his leading castratos were altos), and never transposed any of them down an octave for baritones or basses. To do so today is to destroy not only the texture of the music (Handel was a master of balance in this respect) and sometimes its structure (by taking the vocal line below the instrumental bass) but the characterization as well, turning young heroes into rumbling tyrants and even buffoons. A comparison between even an indifferent alto and a first-rate bass singing the same passage in the wrong octave is so conclusive that it is a matter for amazement that the lesson has not been learned in Germany – until we remember that not so long ago basses had their defenders here. Some listeners find the countertenor voice objectionable, but there is no obligation to use it; there must be as many mezzos capable of playing male roles in our day as there were in Handel's.

A third problem, less commonly recognized but of decisive importance, is the performance of the recitatives, especially those accompanied by continuo alone. The sight of a couple of pages of secco recitative is liable to make a score-reader blaspheme and jump to the next aria. But it is the recitative that generates drama by motivating the aria; and Handel's recitatives are nearly always carefully adjusted, in melodic shape, rhythm and movement (especially harmonic movement), to express not just the meaning of the text but the predicament of the characters and the emotion that impels them to give tongue in the arias. In Handel's day recitatives were enunciated (rather than sung) rapidly, flexibly, and without regard to bar-lines; their pace and articulation were conditioned by the sense of the words. Above all, the cadences – except very rarely for a particular effect – were elided or foreshortened, the dominant chord coinciding with the last accented syllable of the voice, not following it.[1] They were always written thus; on the rare occasions when Handel wanted a delayed cadence, he put in a rest. Editors, from Chrysander onwards, almost invariably print them incorrectly, following the usage of Mozart's and later ages, not Handel's (the practice changed about 1750). The difference that the correct method makes in the theatre is incalculable, quite apart from the time it saves. Nearly all modern performances take the recitatives too slowly, pay too much attention to bar-lines and not enough to appoggiaturas, and conclude them with that egregious thump-thump that brings forward movement to a standstill and interposes a deadly pause between recitative and aria. One might as well place a colon between an adjective and the noun it qualifies. (The same principle applies to cadences within sections of recitative.) The aria should follow instantly; and (except briefly at scene changes) the next recitative, often motivated by the previous aria, should likewise be attacked at once. An audience will regard a pause here as an invitation to applaud; and although Handel's singers may have played for applause – as modern singers sometimes do in operas of every school, even in the most inappropriate places – we cannot afford to place the drama second. In fact most of Handel's brilliant arias, the natural invitations to applause, are carefully placed at the end of scenes, where the interruption is less serious; but even there, as we have seen, it should not be so long as to disperse concentration.

A thornier problem is the ornamentation that singers were expected to add to their written parts, especially (but not exclusively) in da capo repeats. The difficulty today arises from at least three causes. Since ornamentation involves the notoriously variable element of taste – that of the singer and that of the listener – opinions are bound to differ. What one singer or listener admires another may

1. Winton Dean, 'The Performance of Recitative in Late Baroque Opera', *Music and Letters* LVIII (1977), p. 389.

loathe, and – within reason – no one can say him nay. Secondly, since the ornaments were improvised (at least in theory) and probably not sung in identical fashion at every performance, they were seldom written down. Thirdly, at least until very recently, modern singers were not trained to improvise in the style of Handel and his contemporaries; nor for that matter were conductors or editors. What we know for certain, from the famous singing-teacher Tosi (whose book was published in 1723) and many others, is that ornamentation was regarded not merely as a custom but as an obligation. One or two scholars have suggested cutting the gordian knot by eschewing vocal decoration, except perhaps for the occasional cadential trill, on the ground that it offends modern taste and spoils our enjoyment of the music. Jens Peter Larsen believes that Handel himself disliked the practice and would have stopped it if he could, a conjecture for which there is no evidence. But this is to shirk the issue; and it is a solution that manifestly does not work. An entire opera performed without ornamentation is a recipe for mechanical monotony, as anyone can discover by playing the complete Deutsche Grammophon recording of *Giulio Cesare* conducted by Karl Richter, where the thirty da capos are virtually all dead-literal repeats. On the other hand there is no doubt that obtrusive ornamentation, especially when it contradicts the affect of an aria or deviates beyond the style of Handel's age, can do hideous damage to an opera.

Granted the variable of taste, the problem is not insoluble, though it is easier to point to bad solutions than good ones. Of course we can never know exactly what Handel's singers did with their da capos. Their taste may have been as erratic as that of singers in any age, though we know that he took a strong line over their misdemeanours in other respects and we can be sure that they did not improvise in the style of Mozart or Bellini. We should be wary of the exorbitant cadenzas cited by Burney and others from the repertoires of a few great castratos, which by their very nature can hardly have been typical. But, in addition to the general and particular remarks to be found in works of contemporary theorists and teachers like Tosi, a number of copies of operas and single arias survive with manuscript ornaments written in, though very few of them have been published. Sometimes the singer and even the date can be identified, and occasionally a composer's autograph, including several of Handel's. By far the most important of these is a Smith copy in the Bodleian Library containing the arias of the soprano part of Teofane in *Ottone*, transposed down for a mezzo.[2] Handel himself added copious ornamentation to three of them and the opening bar of a fourth, presumably for an inexperienced English singer since a trained Italian would have scorned such help. It is just possible that they were intended for the young Susanna Arne, later Mrs Cibber, in an abortive revival planned for the spring of 1733, when the prima donna Strada was ill. The production was cancelled, and Handel never finished the ornaments; had he done so and brought them into use, he would undoubtedly have made a few modifications to the string parts.

2. MS Don.c.69, fol. 6; published in *G. F. Handel: Three Ornamented Arias*, ed. Winton Dean (Oxford 1976).

These ornaments are of great importance, both for themselves and as a model of the type of decoration Handel recommended and approved. They differ radically from what we usually hear today. While they offer the singer ample opportunity to display her technical skill, it is the flexibility of the voice and its expressive power, not its range, that Handel exploits. The compass is virtually confined to that of the arias as first composed, extended upwards by a tone at very rare climaxes (not more than one in each aria). There are no concessions to showmanship or vapid pyrotechnics, and above all no infringement of the affect of the music; this is virtuosity at the service of art. Although the original line is floridly decorated, it is never obscured or distorted beyond recognition. The ornaments are often bold and unexpected but are directed always towards intensifying the emotion behind the notes.

The *Ottone* ornaments are not the only ones supplied by Handel. The Fitzwilliam Museum contains an aria in *Amadigi* (the only autograph material to survive from that opera) decorated in a similar but less elaborate style, probably for a performance with continuo alone,[3] and the British Library another from *Floridante*, an autograph arrangement for harpsichord with vocal and instrumental cues noted.[4] The ornaments, again very expressive, may have been intended for the keyboard, but their compass and disposition make them equally suited to the voice. In addition several public and private collections contain Handel manuscripts with eighteenth-century ornaments not written by the composer but conforming to his practice as described here.[5]

The lessons to be deduced are obvious but are seldom applied. In many modern revivals the licence to decorate seems to have gone to the head of the singers, or less forgivably the conductor: they twist the line out of shape, add rocketing top notes regardless of the affect, transpose whole sections into a higher register, and in addition to marring the eloquence of the music sometimes make mincemeat of Handel's style. We know that the object of vocal decoration was twofold, to increase the expressiveness of the music and to allow the singer to demonstrate how well he could do this. The two aims are not incompatible: there is no need for one to frustrate the other, provided we follow Handel's guidance.

Another issue that has lately come to the fore, especially in recorded performances, is the use of Baroque instruments, originals or reproductions. Until a few years ago this was an academic matter: not many players possessed the skill, experience or historical knowledge to give a satisfactory account of the music. Moreover there has been, and to some extent still is, considerable debate as to what eighteenth-century orchestras sounded like and how they played the works

3. MS Mus. 256, fol. 41; see Winton Dean, 'Vocal Embellishment in a Handel Aria' in *Studies in Eighteenth-Century Music, A Tribute to Karl Geiringer* (New York and London 1970), p. 71.
4. MS R.M. 18.c.2, fol. 28; see Terence Best, 'An Example of Handel Embellishment', *Musical Times* cx (1969), p. 933.
5. Many examples in the Barrett Lennard collection in the Fitzwilliam Museum, Cambridge; one, from *Radamisto*, published by J. Merrill Knapp, 'Handel, the Royal Academy of Music, and its First Opera Season in London (1720)', *Musical Quarterly* xlv (1959), p. 145. Other examples in the collections of Gerald Coke and the Earl of Malmesbury.

of particular composers. It is recognized that French and Italian music employed different conventions of performance; everyone knows the story of Corelli refusing to play a Handel piece written in the French style, which he professed not to understand. Handel was a thorough cosmopolitan, familiar with German and English as well as French and Italian styles, both of composition and performance, and he made use of everything that came to hand. In so doing he laid traps for modern performance. Certain features of the French style – overdotting, *notes inégales*, silences of articulation and so on – while manifestly applicable to his overtures and many instrumental works, are not necessarily appropriate for arias that are Italian in style as well as language. Some conductors, confronted with pairs of quavers, are tempted to dot the first almost as a matter of course, breaking the flow of the long melodies characteristic of Handel's lyric style into a series of hops and jerks. Other disturbing habits sometimes practised in the name of authenticity are an exaggerated emphasis on the first beat of the bar and a tendency to lean on sustained notes, especially in string parts, so that each receives an inbuilt crescendo and diminuendo. This produces an intolerably mannered performance, the note emphasized at the expense of the phrase, the phrase at the expense of the melody, and the part at the expense of the whole.

That is doubtless an oversimplification; there are plenty of tricky details to be sorted out and inconsistencies of notation to be reconciled – although one recent study maintains that they are deliberate and should not be regularized. But it is impossible to believe that Handel countenanced a manner of performance that contradicted the flow of the music, especially in his vocal melodies. Fortunately not all performances with Baroque instruments aiming at an authentic style fall into these traps.

Authenticity is a worthy aim, provided it does not degenerate into preciousness, especially in such a virile composer as Handel. A musical performance with modern instruments is preferable to an unmusical one cluttered with Baroque impedimenta. In the last resort absolute authenticity is a chimera – and would probably not be welcome if it could be achieved. The theatres for which Handel wrote do not survive; their construction and acoustics were not those of today. We should scarcely appreciate the habits of Handel's audiences: the nobility sitting on stools at the side of the stage and interfering with the performance, dripping candles (for following the libretto) in listeners' hands, constant chatter and interruptions, orange peel and less salubrious secretions descending from the gallery into the pit, not to mention prima donnas coming to blows on the stage. One exceptional instance of authenticity in a modern performance is worthy of mention. The occasion was Kent Opera's production of *Atalanta* at Hintlesham in 1970, the first anywhere since Handel's Covent Garden revival of November 1736. The opera was written to celebrate the marriage of the Prince of Wales, and concluded with a series of choruses and instrumental movements accompanied by spectacular transformations, fireworks and bonfires on the stage. The Lord Chamberlain would surely assume a reactionary stance if Covent Garden chose to revive the opera today. But Hintlesham had an open-air stage, and the proceedings culminated in the appropriate climax, though the fireworks did not always go off on the beat.

Leaving such frivolities aside, it is undeniable that few modern productions of Handel's operas have even approached the limits of what is practicable and desirable. Some reasons for this have been mentioned. We have been feeling our way by trial and error, applying lessons from scholarship as they have been discovered – or not applying them. In England there is another reason, the reluctance of our national opera houses to admit Handel to the repertory. Their record has been deplorable, in omission and commission. The few productions have been so ham-handed that they have reinforced the standing prejudice against Handel as a dramatic composer. Covent Garden has seen two productions of *Alcina*, one in a corrupt pre-war edition imported from Stockholm, the other in a version that butchered a great opera to make a vacuous entertainment for a set of courtiers planted on the stage. The dramatic oratorios *Samson* (Covent Garden, 1958) and *Jephtha* (Glyndebourne, 1966) and the English opera *Semele* (Coliseum, 1970) received such perverse treatment that no idea of their musical or dramatic stature could emerge. The New York City Opera *Giulio Cesare* (1966, subsequently recorded) was no better. The English National Opera production of the same opera (1979) met some of the requirements and certainly attracted the public; but it missed opportunities and in one respect betrayed Handel. The conductor chose to regard the ornaments in the Bodleian manuscript as spurious, although they are unmistakably autograph, and indulged in a type of extravagant decoration that defaced the music and fell into all manner of stylistic solecism. The result was not so much a musical drama as a series of show-stoppers.

One further point is worth making. If Handel's operas are great dramas, what is to be done about cuts? Most of them are longer than the run of repertory operas today, though not nearly so long as common report has it. The decision to cut becomes a reflex action. In fact Handel's greatest operas – perhaps ten or a dozen of them – can scarcely be cut at all without palpable damage to the fabric. A clumsily cut performance makes the opera seem longer, not shorter, because it destroys the balance of an organic whole. This emerged clearly from the uncut *Giulio Cesare* at Birmingham in 1977 – the first complete stage production since Handel's original run in 1724. The rapid pacing of the recitative and avoidance of pauses in the action saved much time (the Deutsche Grammophon recording is half an hour longer); but the relative saving was far greater, since the audience was gripped by the drama. Other Handel operas could benefit from similar treatment. If we can stomach more than five hours of Wagner, why should we shrink from less than four of Handel? The moment for that cannot be delayed indefinitely.

Intellectual contexts of Handel's English oratorios

Ruth Smith

Taken as a whole, modern criticism of Handel's oratorios lacks coherence. They have been explained as a social phenomenon, their late-eighteenth-century reception as a religious one; they have been placed in Handel's oeuvre; their musical origins have been traced in Germany and Italy; but we still have no satisfying reasons, only excuses, for what critics have reluctantly identified as their unevenness of structure and content, still less for their frequent, perhaps overall, peculiarity and inaccessibility. Showing that much in them can be appreciated as drama in the conventional modern sense has revealed much that cannot, and has led critics to write regretfully of passages that seem boring in even the most exciting works, to dismiss whole oratorios as failures and to recommend cuts which will redeem the 'essential structure' in compositions classed as masterpieces. The major attempt to explain the oratorios by categorization was weakened by the number of qualifications it entailed;[1] and we have not discovered why our estimate is often contrary to that of Handel's audience.[2]

A new understanding could be gained by examining Handel's raw material – the librettos – and the intellectual contexts that produced them: the literary, religious and political commonplaces of the mid eighteenth century. The contexts of the librettos seem to me a richer and more apposite field of enquiry than the identity of the librettists, who were mostly minor men of letters adapting major sources, and whose ideas are likely to have been drawn from a contemporary common fund. Nevertheless, any complete study of this topic would require research into their lives and other writings.[3] What follows is an outline of work

1. J. P. Larsen, *Handel's 'Messiah'* (1957), pp. 1–29; criticized by P. H. Lang, *George Frideric Handel* (1967), p. 360.
2. Contrast the number of performances in Handel's lifetime of *Esther* and *Judas Maccabaeus* (many) and of *Semele*, *Hercules* and *Belshazzar* (few), listed in W. Dean, *Handel's Dramatic Oratorios and Masques* (1959), pp. 631–7, with Dean's evaluations of these works.
3. For Hamilton, whose *Samson* is used as a pilot example in this essay, see R. Loewenthal [Smith], 'Handel and Newburgh Hamilton: New References in the Strafford Papers', *Musical Times* cxii (1971), pp. 1063–6.

begun under Charles Cudworth's supervision and sustained by his characteristically generous interest and encouragement. Though the conclusions I draw here are provisional, it is apparent that by setting the librettos in the light of current ideas we can identify common themes in oratorios which have previously seemed widely diverse in subject and quality. This yields a more satisfactory description of the genre than we have hitherto achieved – establishes it, in fact, *as* a genre, on the grounds of consistency of ideas and their expression, and shows it to be not a thing apart but a signal repository of the intellectual generalizations of its time. The next step is to compare the musical with the verbal realization – to see what Handel made of his librettists' formulas – in the light of contemporary aesthetic doctrine and practice; but that requires a separate study.[4]

Samson makes a good starting point. Though always popular, it has been faulted by modern critics, chiefly on a point to which Handel's audience apparently made no objection: for most of the first half nothing happens. The hero is passive, the tone is uniform. We can elucidate the origins of this by comparing the text with its sources; such a comparison is necessary, in exhaustive detail, for an understanding of any of the librettos. Hamilton's fidelity to Milton has been variously appraised, but close reading shows that he eliminated from *Samson Agonistes* all the areas in which the hero displays vitality: spiritual conflict; political debate; and moral criticism and self-criticism. Most transformingly, he relieved Samson of almost all responsibility for his plight. He was right to drop 'Agonistes' from the title, for he jettisoned Milton's 'plot' of spiritual regeneration. This leaves Samson as merely pitiable in Act i, an impression which Hamilton heightened by his additions: the juxtaposition of the solitary, helpless captive first with his jubilant enemies and then with his compassionate friends, whose sympathy is purged of the criticism and disagreements against which Milton's Samson asserts himself.

But though pathos is the predominant mood, it is not so continuous as critics have suggested: the scenes that have been found tedious actually progress (in sharp contradistinction to the source) by abrupt fluctuations of mood. We are swung between Samson's recurrent despair and unanswered prayers (the

---

4. Only summary references are possible here. 'The librettos' means the full texts of the first editions. For convenience the term 'oratorio' is extended to cover *Acis and Galatea*, *Semele* and *Hercules*. 'Modern critics' means those already cited and E. Bredenfoerder, *Die Texte der Händel-Oratorien* (Leipzig 1934); C. Cudworth, *Handel* (1972); J. Herbage, 'The Oratorios' and 'The Secular Oratorios and Cantatas' in *Handel, a Symposium*, ed. G. Abraham (1954), pp. 66–131, 132–55; R. M. Myers, *Handel's Messiah* (New York 1948); S. Sadie, *Handel* (1962); H. E. Smither, 'Handel and the English Oratorio' in *A History of the Oratorio*, ii: *The Oratorio in the Baroque Era* (Chapel Hill, N.C. 1977), pp. 175–360; P. Young, *The Oratorios of Handel* (1949).

   Dean's chapter 'The Oratorio and English Taste' concerns late-eighteenth- and early-nineteenth-century responses to the oratorios rather than the early- and mid-eighteenth-century climate that produced them, and constitutes social rather than intellectual history. No study of the oratorios has yet applied a historical perspective other than social, or concentrated on the librettos independently of their musical settings, though Dean called for such a study in his preface.

Chorus, Samson), a vision of God's wrath (Samson), confident optimism (the Chorus), pity (the Chorus, Manoa), self-pity (Samson, Manoa) and rapturous anticipation of heavenly bliss (the Chorus); and receive, where it seems hardest to accept, a lesson in stoical faith ('All is best', wrenched out of its Miltonic context). Emotional logic is replaced by a series of emotional tableaux; the audience's attention is engaged, if at all, not by the action (still less by the interaction) of character, but by the episodic presentation of units of feeling.

Nor are the characters of a kind to involve or complicate our feelings. 'Shakespearian' characterization – complex but finally comprehensible – is evidently not Hamilton's intention; he omits, even from recitative, the passages of debate, judgement and choice that form the sinews of *Samson Agonistes* and explain motive and behaviour. His characters are therefore much simpler than Milton's, especially Dalila and Harapha. In their scenes we do see action and reaction, but of the most external kind, for the pattern is one of appeal-and-rebuff or challenge-and-rebuff rather than an interplay of emotion and argument. The simplification of character allows individuals to be representatives, and this is most obviously the case for Samson: in less complex treatments than Milton's he has always been identified as simply the national hero, and here it is as such, not as a multi-faceted person, that we are concerned for him.

In *Samson Agonistes* the hero gradually regains the glorious isolation of the elect; in the libretto he suffers the dismal isolation of the afflicted. Hamilton's hero, unlike Milton's, is unalterably human: more pitiable and pitied; more directly exposed to, and more sensitive to, his enemies' scorn; self-pitying, without incurring any of the reproof meted to self-pity in *Samson Agonistes*; and, immediately after his heroic triumph, mourned in an extended elegy (which Milton wrote for the Marchioness of Winchester), a concession to suffering humanity expressly vetoed as irrelevant in *Samson Agonistes*. He is also frequently prayed for, and this both unites him with his fellows and emphasizes that his distance from them is a deprivation. He is their saviour, but they evidently have to intercede for him; they find God more accessible than Samson does, constantly describing, invoking and even directly petitioning Him – whereas Milton dramatizes the hero's achievement of unique intimacy with God. Hamilton's main theme is God's championship of His chosen people, of whom Samson is only the figurehead. He is not God's arch-betrayer but a vulnerable man arbitrarily singled out by fate to exemplify the pitfalls open to any of us; and his shame as a fallen hero is externalized and becomes a shared national anxiety, as in the centrally placed 'Return, O God of Hosts'.

Furthermore, Hamilton omits those of Milton's political references that would impair his portrayal of Israelite unity and strength, and instead selects other Miltonic texts to express the interdependence of Samson and the nation. But while the Israelites have greater corporate identity and confidence, they also have greater fear. Milton purges terror and pity, but Hamilton evokes them, largely with the threat of destruction by the national enemy (again drawn chiefly from other Milton poems) – a threat made more real by the presence of the Philistine nation and the suspense inherent in Hamilton's real 'plot': will God intervene in time? As in the Old Testament, confidence that God will eventually defeat the ungodly is combined with uncertainty about the immediate future. Hamilton's God is more hidden and miraculous than Milton's (whose working in Samson is so consonant with human psychological response that some readers have been able to ignore it). The difference is most striking at the final crisis. In *Samson Agonistes* Samson has passed beyond his friends' comprehension; at the same point in *Samson* they make their most urgent appeal for him ('With thunder arm'd'), immediately after which he feels the operation of the divine spirit for the first time. And since the Chorus has annexed Samson's role as God's elect, his sudden acquisition of superhuman power seems miraculous.

It is a commonplace of Handel criticism that the Chorus is not hindered by its role as protagonist from filling its classical role as commentator. Hamilton so valued its provision of sententious observation that he invented a character through whom to extend its scope. But Micah is not only a bystander, he is also a warmly sympathizing friend – like the whole Chorus, which is alternately outside the action and immersed in it. This flexibility is especially convenient to Hamilton's finale, which requires the Chorus to be halfway between its roles as God's nation and moral commentator, voicing the feelings appropriate to the audience at the end of a sacred concert. The difference between Hamilton's closing chorus and its source shows him concerned to secularize: the reference to an angelic chorus was originally framed by the expression of a hope that we might soon be admitted to its ranks. But in *Samson* the area of struggle has been shifted from the life of the individual in eternity to the temporal welfare of the nation.

There are several distinctive characteristics here, all representing changes of emphasis from the source: an insistence on pathos; the use of contrast; the presentation of emotion rather than action; the extended use of the Chorus for unqualified commentary; the centrality of the virtuous nation rather than the sympathetic individual; and the championship of that nation by an accessible yet miraculous God. And when we look at the other librettos, we find to an astonishing degree that these initiatives are consistently repeated; they are the essential features of the Handelian libretto.

The pathos of isolation from one's fellows is given a further dimension in *Jephtha*, in that the hero's downfall coincides with the nation's triumph, and another in *Saul*, where the hero's isolation is made complete by the nation's total withdrawal of sympathy and support (he is not thus isolated in the biblical account). In *Acis and Galatea* and *Semele* the chief anguish of loneliness is caused by distance from one person rather than many – by the separation, through absence or inequality, of lovers or relations; but there is also a poignant difference between the intense yearning of the lovers and the 'free and gay' integration of the Chorus in nature and society. The librettist of *Susanna* introduces the same emotive device (in the Apocrypha Joachim does not go away); and this text is a fine example of varied emotions, in this instance all touching or pathetic, evoked in tableaux rather than provoked by action or issuing in action. We are presented in turn with connubial, parental and filial love, parting, absence, the death of the beloved, compassion and – the culminating interest – imperilled integrity, imperilled less by physical assault than by unsuspected hypocrisy, and involving a wholly innocent victim. Unmerited suffering is also visited on the central characters of *Alexander Balus*, *Acis and Galatea* and *Theodora*; and suffering disproportionate to the degree of responsibility, like Samson's, is the fate of Jephtha. In *Hercules* we have the fascinating spectacle of a librettist attracted to a source by its emphasis on unmerited suffering, characters isolated from each other, and the evocation and expression of pity, but so repelled by its power to shock that he alters it almost out of recognition. (So sweeping are Broughton's changes, and so strenuously do they avoid tragedy and nourish pathos, that I can see no other reasons for his selection of a play that explicitly denies the belief in God's protection of His creatures which he elsewhere publicly defended and to which as a Church of England divine he must have subscribed.)

The liking for variety in the sense of contrast appears at its simplest in those librettos which alternate, but do not mix, the concerns of love and war (and for this reason are deplored by modern critics), such as *Joshua* and *Alexander Balus*; and it can be seen shaping characterization in *Semele*, *Athalia* and *Hercules*, where fierce and gentle women are juxtaposed. In *Hercules* this juxtaposition is part of a larger variety – the reactions of characters to situations and to each other. The central scenes (I.4–II.5) exhibit Hercules' bearing to Iole and Dejanira; Iole's to Hercules, Dejanira and Hyllus; Hyllus' to Iole; and Dejanira's to Hercules and Iole. But at the end of all this their situations are exactly what they were to start with, and the only initiative, Hyllus' proposal, has been thwarted. Such focus on feeling instead of action is objected to by modern critics who require 'motivation', and has provoked complaints about lack of plot and characterization in (for example) *Esther*, *Deborah*, *Samson*, *Joseph*, *Judas Maccabaeus*, *Alexander Balus* and *Joshua*. In some of these (e.g. *Deborah* and *Judas Maccabaeus*) the place of action is supplied not by emotion but by declaration, by asseverations of confidence and faith – which modern critics have also deplored, both for their brash aggressiveness and for their tendency to 'hold up the action'. This latter offence is perpetrated mainly, of course, by the Chorus.

Choric moral commentary tends to punctuate every episode, in secular and religious texts alike. The librettist of *Hercules* uses the Chorus to generalize the individual's emotion, to place it in a framework of universal human feeling and desirable human behaviour. The Chorus praises Hyllus' 'filial piety', advises against despair and denounces jealousy as a 'tyrant of the human breast' (that is, as a failing to which all are susceptible and which thus seems the less reprehensible in Dejanira). Like the Chorus in *Samson*, and even more like the Choruses in the other secular librettos, it is more knowing than the individual. The Chorus in the religious works is superior by virtue of its closer relation to God; that in the secular works by its possession of a mind unclouded by passion. Broughton has the best of both worlds in making his Chorus, like that of the religious works, intercede with the deity – with Love and Hymen, on behalf of 'the hero and the fair'. Lichas, Micah's counterpart, comments on Dejanira's indulgence of grief, on her abrupt change to joy, and on the delights of reconciliation; and Broughton's need for a proper comment at every juncture is evident in his introduction of a '1 Trachinian' to fill Lichas' place when he is acting as herald.

If we respond to *Hercules* as domestic melodrama we are bound to ask why a chorus haunts the palace (in *Trachiniae* it is more plausible, being outside and consisting of Dejanira's friends); but at least Broughton does not try to make it both commentator and participant, like the Chorus of *Susanna* (whose inconsistent role has been much criticized), *Saul* and *Jephtha*. While such a dichotomy can be traced to Greek tragedy, the effect in the oratorios is more powerful because of the far greater authority of the Chorus. Not only is it given dramatic prominence at the expense of the individual, it has greater moral stature. In the librettos society not only knows better than the individual, it *is* better, even when it is in the thick of the action. In *Saul* its conspicuously high standards of behaviour and emotional sensibility and generosity counterpoint the king's degeneracy; and it scarcely need be said that the moral gap is Jennens's creation. Critics have noticed that the moral excellence of an oratorio character frequently results from alteration of the source: for instance Rahab (in *Joshua*) is not described as a harlot, and her betrayal of Jericho is passed over in an unexplained order to spare her life; Jael does not kill Sisera out of personal hatred; ignoble feelings are mitigated in the main characters of *Semele*. But invoking high moral standards can also have the effect of blackening the character of an individual (never of the Chorus), as in the cases of Saul and Dejanira. *Saul* is a peculiarly interesting example of the moralizing tendency, since it involves an alteration of God's morals as well as man's. In the Bible God persecutes Saul because he has made a mistake, but the librettist makes Saul an irredeemable criminal so that God's destruction of him is justifiable in terms of human ethics. Even when Jennens refers to the Amalekite incident for the first time (near the end of the oratorio), he imputes to Saul a morally culpable motive – greed – of which he is innocent in the Bible. The librettos give ample scope to unmerited suffering, but exclude unmerited destruction.

In effect God, like His hero-nation, is virtuous. The terrifying and mysterious Jehovah is replaced by a humanitarian, paternal, available God. Nor is the alteration confined to the religious oratorios. The gods of *Hercules* are genial versions of the remote and pitiless scourges of *Trachiniae*; the whole libretto is characterized by Broughton's excision of terror, most noticeably, of course, in his conversion of the awesome demigod hero into an affable retired general. The service of God in the librettos is seldom so demanding as in *Jephtha*. In Racine's *Athalie* it is a burden to which no human being is equal; in *Athalia* it is a social pleasure, a delight ratified by its very easiness (see also *Messiah*). At the grave crisis when Racine's Chorus describes God as hidden and mysterious, Humphreys's affirms confidence in His protection. The alteration is even more pronounced in the character of the High Priest. Racine's Joïada refuses to tolerate any human frailty: he rejoices in violence as an attribute of his God, and reflects it in his own bullying of everyone in the play. But Humphreys's Joad has all the warmth of the protective father, husband and lover; the oratorio ends with a love duet for him and his wife. As in *Samson*, the issue is much simplified by the wholesale omission of the political matter in the source, here with the result (perhaps intentional) that God is not implicated in actions that fall below human moral standards – whereas this paradox is essential to Racine's God. And yet, as in *Samson*, so in *Athalia* and in all the Old Testament librettos the action is firmly located in human history, and is therefore fraught with uncertainty. Accounts of military campaigns do not provide ideal material for treatment as unstaged drama, but more obviously suitable Old Testament scenes – episodes of spiritual triumph such as Elijah's on Mt Carmel (noted as a possible subject by Handel), or of spiritual agony and enlightenment such as Job's – did not attract the librettists. They constantly returned either to corporate victories over a human enemy, with the aid of divine intervention, or to scenes exemplifying moral virtues rather than religious faith (courage and friendship in *Saul*, right government in *Belshazzar*, peace in *Solomon*, justice in *Susanna*, obedience in *Jephtha*). The relation of man to God is temporal, corporate and of immediate importance. Confidence in His ultimate triumph over the heathen coexists with fear for the survival not of the soul in eternity but of the nation now. The question at the crisis is not Does God exist and will He overcome evil, but Does God care for us and will He enable us to defeat the Philistines?

Not that there is ever any serious doubt of God's faithfulness; He is trusted to save His people in the end (His partisanship is taken for granted, although He is constantly hymned as the author of all); but they must supplicate Him for aid. That aid is often miraculous, and where the biblical source provides no miracle the librettist is liable to introduce one, or more: in *Jephtha* the episodes of the defeat of the Ammonites by flaming ministers and the final visitation by the angel are imported by Morell from an intermediary source, and he also transforms the Bible's passing historical reference to the crossing of the Red Sea into an extended account of it as an instance of divine intervention. But just as the hero and the nation are mutually dependent, so are God and His people. And the nation of the librettos frequently contributes more to the victory than its biblical counterpart (e.g. in *Joshua*). It is not tested spiritually (once it has renounced false gods), but on its own terms of moral and physical courage it has to earn a miracle – which is thus not wholly miraculous.

The librettos and contemporary literature

Having identified the distinctive qualities of the librettos, we are likely to ask: Why are they as they are? and are they idiosyncratic, or do they reflect current concerns? Previous work has provided some answers, musical and social. The use of contrast clearly has one origin in the norms of contemporary musical, especially vocal dramatic, composition. It also has a wider background in current aesthetic theory: writers on music, diction, literary taste, the drama and art all recommend this kind of variety.[5] A full consideration of mid-eighteenth-century aesthetic theory is highly necessary to an increased understanding of Handel's oratorios; their reception has been much better studied than the relevant prescriptions.

But there are other areas, less obviously related to the oratorios as music but more specifically relevant to the librettos themselves, which provide illumination. Of these the closest to the librettos is contemporary opinion of the sources. Does it concur with the librettists' adaptations? To take *Samson* again as an example: mid-eighteenth-century criticism of *Samson Agonistes* simplifies it as drastically as Hamilton does, and in much the same way. The poem is read as an autobiographical outpouring unevenly mixed with political propaganda. Commentators seek to extract from it the maximum of pathos and the minimum of argument: they avoid grappling with its religious philosophy, which they regard as a weakening intrusion, and ignore Milton's continuous measuring of the hero's spiritual achievement. They equate Samson with Milton and maintain unqualified sympathy for him throughout. Manoa's fondness (which the modern reader is likely to see as one of the most insidious threats to Samson's fulfilment) is particularly, and unreservedly, admired. The theme is taken to be the resurgence of a nation's hero against its oppressor. The poem is not imagined to be a useful example to dramatic authors, and the reason given (e.g. by Mason) is instructive: it is too intellectual; its emotional effect is encumbered by its argument.[6]

This whole response is symptomatic of mid-eighteenth-century dramatic taste, and if we widen our frame of reference to consider this we find further parallels with the librettos.

To excite pity was the chief ambition of the dramatist of this period;[7] the sensation was found to be particularly gratifying because it permitted the spectator to be conscious both of his own security and of his own refined moral and emotional sensibility.[8] The favourite eighteenth-century pathetic tragedies (e.g. Rowe's *Jane Shore* and *The Fair Penitent*), like the librettos, focus sympathy on

5. C. Avison, *An Essay on Musical Expression* (1752); S. Say, *An Essay on the Harmony, Variety and Power of Numbers* (1745); A. Blackwall, *A New Introduction to the Classics* (1718); J. Brown, *A Dissertation . . . on Poetry and Music* (1763); W. Hogarth, *The Analysis of Beauty* (1753).

6. S. Johnson, *Rambler* No. 139 (16 July 1751); W. Mason, prefatory letters to *Elfrida* (1752), repr. *Works* (1811), vol. 2, pp. 180–2; T. Newton, *Paradise Regain'd . . . to which is added Samson Agonistes . . . a New Edition, with Notes of Various Authors* (1752); J. Toland, *The Life of John Milton* (1696); J. Upton, *Critical Observations on Shakespeare* (1746).

7. See e.g. J. Addison, *Spectator* No. 40 (16 April 1711); Brown, *Dissertation*; P. Brumoy, 'Discourse upon the Theatre of the Greeks' in *The Greek Theatre* (1759); A. Dacier, *Aristotle's Art of Poetry* (1705); [C. Gildon], 'An Essay on the Art, Rise and Progress of the Stage' in *The Works of Mr William Shakespeare*, ed. N. Rowe, vol. 7 (1725); R. Hurd, *Q. Horatii Flacci, Ars Poetica*, 3rd edn (Cambridge 1757); H. Pemberton, *Observations on Poetry, especially the Epic* (1738); [B. West], *Hecuba* (1726).

8. See e.g. Addison, *Spectator* No. 418 (30 June 1712); M. Akenside, *The Pleasures of Imagination* (1744); J. B. du Bos, *Critical Reflections on Poetry and Painting* (1719); G. Campbell, *The Philosophy of Rhetoric* (1776); [attrib.] T. Hanmer, *Some Remarks on the Tragedy of Hamlet, Prince of Denmark* (1736); D. Hume, 'Of Tragedy' in *Four Dissertations* (1757); Hurd, *Ars Poetica*; Lord Kames, *Elements of Criticism*, 3rd edn (Edinburgh 1765); R. Steele rev., A Philips, *The Distrest Mother, Spectator* No. 290 (1 February 1712); Lord Shaftesbury, 'Soliloquy, or Advice to an Author' in *Characteristicks*, 4th edn (1727); J. Trapp, *Lectures on Poetry* (1742).

suffering individuals, isolated from the community to which they belonged and given special anguish through that loneliness. They are either innocent of any crime, or are barely responsible for their present misery, or are racked by remorse for a momentary lapse, little enjoyed and muted by distance (like Samson and Dejanira). Modern commentators on pathetic tragedy[9] have traced the philosophical basis of its insistence on compassion to belief in a benevolent God, who implanted active feelings of sympathy in men as a way of directing them to virtue, and have noted that as a result, in formulas for life as for dramatic writing, rational choice came to be deemed inferior to spontaneous emotional responsiveness. Thus Steele's suggestions of subjects for tragedy[10] ignore all ideas of the function of responsibility and inevitability in the drama and show no interest whatever in characterization, or in a connection between character and action. The same concentration on emotion is observable in pathetic tragedy and sentimental comedy as in the librettos, and takes the same form of tableaux illustrative of feeling.

There are other parallels for the librettos in contemporary drama, both among the devices used to generate emotion and in the kinds of emotion generated. The plays extol the ties of private life that promote security. Old age is regarded with loving respect for its powerful wisdom, not (as for example in Dryden's heroic dramas) with contempt for its impotent decay. The librettos' catalogue of worthy elder relations illustrates this theme: Manoa, Celsias, Cadmus, Caleb, Mordecai and Jacob may be inactive, but they never lose their status as representatives of essential moral standards. Warm, enduring friendships are of central importance, and in the librettos the relationships of David and Jonathan, Didymus and Septimius, Jonathan and Alexander, Ino and Semele are exemplary instances. Conversely hypocrisy or treachery, between friends or in general, is a peculiarly abhorrent crime: so it is in Saul, in the deception of Semele by Juno, in the betrayal of Alexander, and in the assault on Susanna. That only virtuous happiness is true happiness is a doctrine as firmly conveyed in the drama as in (for example) the opening scenes of *Susanna*, and an especial joy attaches to the happiness of increased virtue – a joy which often springs from reconciliation, through resolution of misunderstanding or absolution of the abased transgressor. The choric commentator in *Hercules* calls 'bliss from reconcilement flowing' 'love's sublime repast'; and Joseph's magnanimous forgiveness of his brothers, balanced between reproof and sympathy and swayed by love, coupled with the unrestrained remorse and gratitude of the brothers, is close in tone as well as content to the reconciliation of Bevil and Myrtle in Steele's *Conscious Lovers*. In both texts the superiority of one person over another, in both tactics and virtue, colours the emotional release. It is not surprising that *Joseph and His Brethren* was liked better

9. E.g. I. Donaldson, 'Cato in Tears: Stoical Guises of the Man of Feeling' in *Studies in the Eighteenth Century*, ed. R. F. Brissenden, vol. 2 (Canberra 1973), pp. 377–95; N. S. Fiering, 'Irresistible Compassion: An Aspect of Eighteenth-Century Sympathy and Humanitarianism', *Journal of the History of Ideas* xxxvii (1976), pp. 195–218; P. Parnell, 'The Sentimental Mask', *Publications of the Modern Language Association* lxxviii (1963), pp. 529–35.
10. *Tatler* No. 82 (18 October 1709).

in Handel's day than since: it is a model sentimental drama, delicately balanced (as Parnell describes the true sentimentalist – spectator, protagonist or author – to be) between hypocrisy and sincerity. By summarizing the plot in the Advertisement, Miller leaves himself free to dwell on emotions, in tableaux linked by suspense which together comprise a pattern of the genre. All the favourite situations and sensations are there: gratitude and ingratitude, humility, solitary distress, remorse, fraternal, filial, conjugal and parental love, innocence, jealousy, misunderstanding, unjust accusation, treachery, magnanimity and, above all, faith, truth, patience and falsehood tested with the aid of silence, disguise and deceit, the whole culminating in a reconciliation which heightens the moral standing of all concerned. However, not all dramas of the period end with universal self-congratulation; some provide a scapegoat whose monstrously unethical behaviour puts them beyond the range even of the divine quality of pity (man's and God's) and allows them to be hated and destroyed (e.g. Millwood in Lillo's *George Barnwell*). The Philistines of the librettos are in an interestingly parallel position.

As in the librettos, so in the plays, the demonstration of character revealed in action which results from choice was replaced by the description of character revealed in reaction to past or inevitable events. The Aristotelian prescription was abandoned in eighteenth-century practice and given idiosyncratic interpretation in eighteenth-century theory. Handelian oratorio has been compared to Greek tragedy, *Samson Agonistes* was modelled on Greek tragedy, and eighteenth-century critics paid lip-service to Aristotle; but these same critics actually thought either that Athenian tragedies were shocking, because they lacked decorum (princesses should not be seen to kill their mothers, nor gods to ratify homicide), or that they provided worthy if simple-minded moral lessons (*Oedipus Tyrannus* warns us against anger, *Trachiniae* – as in Broughton's version – against jealousy). The critics' pained and sometimes confused debate about poetic justice, their uneasy arguments against the implications of a blind or malevolent destiny, are direct pointers to the librettists' handling of their sources in *Hercules, Semele* and *Athalia*; and the real parallel with *Hercules* is not Sophocles' *Trachiniae*, but James Thomson's *Agamemnon* (1738).[11]

Those who valued Greek tragedies for the moral lessons they found there particularly approved of what they considered the chief moral mouthpiece, the Chorus; and an animated debate lasting several decades explored the possibilities of reintroducing a Chorus of the Athenian kind, complete with music, to the British stage.[12] Modern critics have dismissed this discussion as insignificant

11. See, besides the authorities cited in note 7 above, G. Adams, *The Tragedies of Sophocles* (1729); J. Collier, *A Short View of the Immorality and Profaneness of the English Stage* (1698); C. M. de St Evremond, 'Of Ancient and Modern Tragedies' and 'Upon Tragedies' in *Works* (1700–5); B. le B. de Fontenelle, *Reflections on the Poetic Art* (1742); C. Gildon, *The Laws of Poetry* (1720); E. N. Hooker, ed., *The Critical Works of John Dennis* (Baltimore, 1939–42); C. Johnson, *Medaea* (1731); T. Morell, *Prometheus in Chains* (1773); L. Theobald, *Censor* No. 36 (12 January 1717).
12. See Adams, *Sophocles*; Brumoy, 'Discourse'; Dacier, *Aristotle*; Hooker, ed., *Dennis*; Hurd, *Ars Poetica*, Kames, *Elements*; Trapp, *Lectures*; and J. Beattie, 'An Essay on Poetry and Music, as

because it had no practical result;[13] they have not related it to Handel, although at least one contemporary (Henry Fielding) did. The prominence of his Chorus has seemed fortuitous in origin, the lucky by-product of the use of Racine's *Esther* as a source; but perhaps *Esther* was chosen in part precisely for the sake of its Chorus, in response to the stimulus of the current literary debate.[14] One of the chief advocates of a revived Chorus, Mason, argued that it afforded the audience the pleasure of identifying with bystanders who were responding to the spectacle of affliction with laudable sensibility; which is exactly how the oratorio Chorus behaves, for long stretches of time, in (for example) *Samson*.

Eighteenth-century biblical commentary and religious debate

Beyond *Samson Agonistes* lies the Bible, and Hamilton made more use of the Book of Judges than Milton did. But though his Samson is (like that of Judges and unlike that of Milton) closely identified with his nation, he is also (very unlike the biblical hero) moral and humane. Contemporary biblical commentators similarly tried to exonerate Samson from the amorality of his actions and reduce him from the level of 'a person separate to God' (Milton) to that of the ordinary man occasionally raised above himself (as in the libretto), on whom pity can be lavished when his external supports are withdrawn (as in the libretto).[15] The commentators' attempts to show Samson as intermittently divinely inspired, but at the same time to show the miraculous elements in his life as reconcilable with reason, are a picture in little of the dilemma in which orthodox theologians were being placed by the deist controversy.

This debate was not confined to Church circles; the reviews and lists of new publications in the literary magazines of the day suggest the huge volume of print and the breadth and intensity of interest it generated. For instance, the *Monthly Chronicle*'s Register of Books for August 1728 lists nineteen books published in the

they Affect the Mind' (1762) in *Essays* (Edinburgh 1776); H. Blair, *Lectures on Rhetoric and Belles Lettres* (Dublin 1783); H. Fielding, *Covent Garden Journal* No. 2 (16 September 1752); T. Francklin, 'Dissertation' in *Tragedies of Sophocles*, 2nd edn (1766); [attrib.] C. Gildon, *A Comparison between the Two Stages* (1702); T. Gray, *Correspondence*, ed. P. Toynbee and L. Whibley (Oxford 1935) (replies to Mason's *Elfrida* and *Caractacus* (1759)); E. Phillips, *Theatrum Poetarum* (1675); R. Potter, *The Tragedies of Aeschylus* (Norwich 1777); [attrib.] N. Rowe, *The Ajax of Sophocles* (1714); T. Rymer, *A Short View of Tragedy* (1693).

13. Hooker, ed., *Dennis*; C. C. Green, *The Neo-Classic Theory of Tragedy in England during the Eighteenth Century* (Cambridge, Mass. 1934).

14. *Esther* and *Athalie* are referred to by nearly every contributor to the debate; for contemporary views of them as admirably didactic see T. Brereton, *Esther* (1715); W. Duncombe, *Athalie* (1728).

15. See e.g. W. Dodd, *A Commentary on the Books of the Old and New Testament* (1770); R. G[ough], *History of the Bible* (1747); M. Henry, *An Exposition of the Historical Books of the Old Testament* (1707), vol. 2; S. Humphreys, *The Sacred Books of the Old and New Testament* (1735); W. Lowth et al., *A Critical Commentary and Paraphrase on the Old and New Testament and Apocrypha* (1844), vol. 2; J. Marchant, *An Exposition of the Books of the Old Testament* (1745); S. Patrick, *A Commentary upon the Books of Joshua, Judges, and Ruth* (1702); T. Pyle, *A Paraphrase with Short and Useful Notes on the Books of the Old Testament* (1725); E. Wells, *A Help for the More Easy . . . Understanding of the Holy Scriptures* (Oxford 1724–8).

previous seven months relating to just one deist tract; of twenty-three theological works listed for the month of November 1729, eleven concern a single aspect of the debate. In other words, it was impossible to be an oratorio librettist and not know about it.[16]

The deist attack on orthodox Christianity was levelled at the ideas of a paternal, partisan God and a personal, divine redeemer; its chief target was the history of the Jews in the Old Testament. It aimed to discredit prophecies, miracles and the Mosaic law, by pointing out the implausibility of a personal God revealing Himself and His precepts for mankind to an obscure member of a degraded tribe of ex-slaves wandering in the desert on a small planet. Defenders of the established Church accepted the challenge on its own terms of reasoned argument, so both sides wrote books with titles like *The Evidence of Christianity*. The orthodox response involved attesting that God could aid men with miracles; that He had thus aided the Israelites, whose leaders were brave, noble, wise and sensitive (favourite examples being the oratorio heroes David, Joseph, Samson, Jephtha, Joshua and the Maccabees); and that Jesus fulfilled the Old Testament prophecies of the Messiah. The startling parallels here with the librettos look even more like influence than coincidence when we note the correspondence in date: 1735–51 is the period both of the major religious oratorios and of the strongest Anglican rebuttals of deist attacks. While there is no external evidence (to my knowledge) that Handel's oratorios were an organized section of the defence, the similarity of subject-matter at least suggests that they were strongly influenced by, and perhaps implied reference to, the orthodox position. All the religious oratorios from *Saul* to *Jephtha*, except *Theodora*, draw on the Old Testament and Apocrypha, at the

16. The two accounts I have found most helpful are L. Stephen, *History of English Thought in the Eighteenth Century* (1876) and R. N. Stromberg, *Religious Liberalism in Eighteenth-Century England* (1954). Relevant specimens of the orthodox defence include: T. Broughton, *Christianity Distinct from the Religion of Nature* (1732); T. Bullock, *The Reasoning of Christ and His Apostles Vindicated* (1728); J. Butler, *The Analogy of Religion* (1736); D. A. Calmet, *Antiquities . . . or . . . Dissertations on the Old and New Testament* (1724); E. Chandler, *A Defence of Christianity* (1725); S. Chandler, *A Vindication of Daniel's Prophecies* (1728); *idem*, 'A Defence of the Prime Ministry and Character of Joseph' in *A Vindication of the History of the Old Testament* (1743); J. Chapman, *A Discourse of the Nature and Use of Miracles* (1725); *idem*, *Eusebius or the True Christian's Defense* (1739–41); S. Clarke, *Works* (1738); R. Clayton, *An Impartial Enquiry into the Time of the Coming of the Messiah* (1751); D. Collyer, *The Sacred Interpreter* (1732); P. Delany, *An Historical Account of the Life and Reign of David King of Israel* (1740–2); J. Entick, *The Evidence of Christianity* (1729); J. Green, *Letters* (1726); J. Hallet, jnr, *An Essay on the Nature and Use of Miracles* (1730); *idem*, *The Immorality of the Moral Philosopher* [i.e. T. Morgan] (1737); W. Harris, *Practical Discourses on the Principal Representations of the Messiah throughout the Old Testament* (1724); R. Kidder, *A Demonstration of the Messias* (1726); J. Leland, *The Divine Authority of the Old and New Testament*, 2nd edn (1739); [C. Leslie], *A Short and Easie Method with the Jews*, 6th corr. edn (1726); C. Middleton, *Miscellaneous Works*, 2nd edn (1755); A. le Moine, *A Treatise of Miracles* (1747); S. Parvish, *An Inquiry into the Jewish and Christian Revelation* (1739); J. Rogers, *The Necessity of Divine Revelation*, 2nd edn (1729); T. Sherlock, *The Use and Intent of Prophecy*, 2nd corr. edn (1726); T. Stackhouse, *A Complete Body of Speculative and Practical Divinity*, 2nd corr. edn (1734); *idem*, *A New History of the Holy Bible* (1752); A. A. Sykes, *An Essay upon the Truth of the Christian Religion* (1725); W. Warburton, *The Divine Legation of Moses* (1738–41); D. Waterland, *Scripture Vindicated* (1730); F. Webber, *The Jewish Dispensation Consider'd and Vindicated*, 2nd edn (1751); W. Whiston, *The Accomplishment of Scripture Prophecies* (1708); T. Woolston, *Six Discourses on the Miracles of our Saviour* (1727–30).

very time when those sources formed the battleground of organized religion. And large sections of the librettos which now seem pointless or inexplicable fall into place within the context of the debate.

The recurrent and seemingly laboured references to and instances of prophecy (e.g. in *Deborah*) make sense as demonstrations of fulfilled prophecy – that is, as statements that biblical prophecy is valid. When we realize that the prophecies of Daniel were those most minutely and extensively analysed in the deist debate, his appearance in person in *Susanna*, proving his credentials at the outset of his career, ceases to seem a rather pointlessly inflated episode and becomes the point for using this part of the story. Similarly Daniel's role in *Belshazzar* gains in significance. Like the author of *Susanna* (who perhaps took the hint from him), Jennens does not associate Daniel with his hotly contested prophecies of Christ. But by showing him as the interpreter of earlier prophecies of a historically attested redeemer that can be, and are, fulfilled in the course of the drama, Jennens implies the validity of Daniel's prophecies of the Redeemer – a skilful piece of rhetoric. The special prominence and weight accorded to the prophetic Scriptures (in scene descriptions and marginal references to chapter and verse) is such that Cyrus' victory assumes the status of a miracle; and so impressed is Cyrus by scriptural ratification of his victory that one miracle begets another, namely his conversion and his pledge to fulfil the remainder of the prophecy. In this drama the Scriptures are elevated to the role of protagonist – and a more active one than is usual in the librettos. But all the Old Testament oratorios similarly underwrite prophecies and miracles, since they all report God's encouragement or promise of success in battle, and show its fulfilment as the climax. Yet just as in the contemporary polemical defences, a second cause is admitted: God personally intervenes, sending Cyrus an inspiring dream; but Cyrus conquers Babylon by intelligent strategy. While the deists rejected the concept of a personal God, the librettos made the alliance between God and Israel their main theme (in *Judas Maccabaeus*, for example, it is the topic of half the numbers) and trumped the opposition by presenting the Jews not as a savage, warmongering, faction-ridden, conceited and unstable tribe (as the deists showed them to be in the Bible), but as images of eighteenth-century Englishmen of refined moral and emotional sensibility, successfully united in defence of universal peace, liberty and virtue against an immoral aggressor.

The text that springs most startlingly into new life in the light of the debate is of course *Messiah*, which corresponds in such detail to contemporary writing that it demands full reconsideration against this background. Instead of skirting the real issue of revelation, as he cleverly does in *Belshazzar*, Jennens here sets forth precisely those essentials of Christianity that were being attacked: the Old Testament prophecies of Christ's birth, life and death, and his chief miracles, resurrection and redemption. And the texts that he uses are the bases of attack and defence in scores of contemporary publications about the nature and mission of Christ. Even his title is rooted in the debate, which revolves around and constantly asks in so many words, Was Jesus the Messiah? When we set it beside (for example) Entick's double-column arrangement of Old Testament ('prophesy'd') and New Testament ('accomplish'd') texts, twenty-nine of which recur in *Messiah*, Jennens's libretto seems less celebratory than polemical: his statement of faith is combative, pointed and coherent as well as latitudinarian. In its epigraph and text it boldly announces that the mysteries of Christianity *are* mysterious, just at the time when the orthodox defence was beginning to relax its rationalist position and make positive use of non-rationalist arguments. And by bringing Old Testament prophecies to a conclusion in a promise of general salvation it exonerates Christianity from the deist charges of partiality and restrictiveness. For its theology is latitudinarian, like that of the other librettos: God is bountiful and accessible; His service is enjoyable; and only those who deny His existence will be destroyed. (Indeed, it is tempting to see in the citation of Romans viii a rebuttal of the deists themselves.)

The religious sublime

Apart from *Samson Agonistes*, Hamilton's chief source was Milton's psalm translations. At this time the psalms and, indeed, Milton were loci classici of the religious sublime, and the fashion for versification and adaptation of those parts of the Bible which were thought to exemplify this style provides another illuminating background to the oratorios. The extensive literature recommending religion, especially the Bible, especially the Old Testament – style and content – as material for modern composition has been excellently surveyed by D. B. Morris,[17] who suggests a connection between this taste and Handelian oratorio but declines to pursue it; so various remarkable parallels remain to be investigated.[18]

On the question whether scriptural subjects could with propriety be used for plays, it had already been established in the seventeenth century that unstaged, closet religious drama was permissible, provided the holy narrative was not altered, the characters were simple, exalted and edifying, and the language respected the style of the original; and certain other aspects of the resulting dramas anticipate oratorio, such as the interspersing of the dramatic episodes with elaborate and lofty odes, often hymns of praise. Such hymns – poems on the attributes of God – acquired the status of a literary genre in the eighteenth century, and of course form a major constituent of the oratorios.

17. *The Religious Sublime* (Lexington, Kentucky 1972).
18. Especially relevant works include Addison, *Spectator* Nos. 160 (3 September 1711) and 405 (14 June 1712); R. Blackmore, *A Paraphrase on . . . the Songs of Moses, Deborah, David, on 6 Select Psalms, and the 3rd Chapter of Habakkuk*, 2nd rev. edn (1716); A Cowley, *Davideis* (1650); H. Felton, *A Dissertation upon Reading the Classics*, 5th edn (1753); Gildon, *Laws*; A. Hill, *Preface to Mr Pope concerning the Sublimity of the Ancient Hebrew Poetry* (1720); Hooker, ed., *Dennis*; Humphreys, *Sacred Books*; J. Husbands, *A Miscellany of Poems by Several Hands* (Oxford 1731); R. Lowth, *De Sacra Poesi Hebraeorum Praelectiones* (Oxford 1753); C. Rollin, *The Method of Teaching and Studying the Belles Lettres* (1753); W. Smith, *Dionysus Longinus on the Sublime*, 3rd corr. edn (1752); J. Spence, *An Essay on Pope's Odyssey* (1726); Trapp, *Lectures*; I. Watts, *Horae Lyricae*, 2nd much enlarged edn (1709); L. Welsted, *Treatise on the Sublime by Dionysus Longinus*, 3rd corr. edn (Dublin 1727).

There are striking recurrences in the librettos of the topics proposed by the advocates of religious drama. Cowley, whose *Davideis* Jennens used for *Saul*, suggests Samson (whom he compares, conventionally, with Hercules), Jephtha's daughter, the wars of David and of Joshua, and the passage of Moses and the Israelites into the Holy Land, as well as the friendship of David and Jonathan; he is followed by Blackmore and Watts. Husbands rebuts Shaftesbury's objections to the lack of refined feeling in potential biblical subjects by commending the tender sentiments and dramatically heightened emotion in David's lament, Jacob's love for his sons and the whole story of Joseph, which he recommends for dramatic (rather than only poetic) treatment; he also admires the Song of Solomon as 'a very regular dramatic poem', ignoring the traditional allegorical interpretation as completely as Handel's librettist did. Joseph was a much-discussed subject, because of his denigration by the deist Morgan; David was similarly denigrated and defended (see above, note 16).

Repeatedly the most admired scriptural passages recur in the librettos. The Songs of Moses, Miriam and Deborah, cited by Sidney as instances of the world's first poetry, became favourite eighteenth-century examples, as did much of Isaiah and the psalms (especially Milton's versions). The crossing of the Red Sea is referred to in *Jephtha* (where its mention makes sense once we recognize it as a stock figure for God's transcendant power), in the *Occasional Oratorio*, and by analogy in *Joshua* (paralleled in the crossing of the Jordan, to which Act I is devoted), and it forms the major part of *Israel in Egypt*. (The literary fashionableness of the Songs of Moses and Miriam sheds light on the fact that Handel set this part of the text first, and as a self-sufficient unit.) But there are many other such parallels. For instance Charles Rollin, besides devoting seventeen pages of appreciative analysis to the Song of Moses, particularly praises Isaiah ix.6, the prophecy of Cyrus the deliverer, the final scene of Racine's *Esther* (examplary as a psalm translation), and Joseph's reconciliation with his brothers (which he offers as a specimen of perfectly heightened emotion); and all these passages are drawn on in the oratorio librettos. Aaron Hill, who urged Handel to revitalize English opera, produced sample paraphrases of the Song of Moses, David's lament and the psalms.

Biblical paraphrase was a major branch of the religious sublime, and stylistic prescriptions for this respected kind of poetic creation (for so it was regarded), and the detailed praise accorded to the style of the originals, make interesting reading alongside the librettos. Many of the most keenly valued qualities are those which distress modern critics of the oratorios: repetition; the use of abstract terms for concrete; the attribution of sense and action to inanimate objects; adjectives followed by a noun in the genitive; and that 'lofty impenetrability' which at its best combines the ambiguity, density, obscurity and surprise which denote the true sublime and even at its worst imparts a sense of higher mysteries to the receptive reader. But simplicity and strength of diction in the Pentateuch were also admired; and Husbands's praise for the 'nervous' quality of Moses' writing gains interest for students of the oratorios when we remember that this was, after 'sublime', the word most frequently applied to Handel's style in his own century.[19] The terms of Hill's criticisms of other authors' paraphrases and his descriptions of the Scriptures as glowing with 'a kind of terrible simplicity' and 'a magnificent plainness' show how natural it was for contemporaries to turn to the Bible for material for the composer currently regarded as the master of the sublime style in the musical setting of religious texts. Addison's *Spectator* No. 405 has been pointed out as a singular and impressive anticipation of oratorio, but in fact (what is more impressive) he was original only in his arrangement of his material, the literary and musical commonplaces of his time.

The national epic

In the estimation of eighteenth-century writers the best vehicle of the religious sublime was the epic, established at least since Milton as the noblest literary form, and defined by Dryden as 'the greatest work that the soul of man is capable to perform';[20] honoured precedents included *Samson Agonistes* as well as *Paradise Lost*. Prescriptions for the modern epic provide a further context for the librettos and make their insistent religious nationalism appear conventional rather than peculiar.[21]

Writers of this period campaigned for an epic which bore as little resemblance to the Classical model as their adaptations of Greek tragedy. It was to have a Christian framework, partly for Christianity's sake and partly because the epic glorifies a nation and should therefore celebrate the national religion. It was to show a personal, moral God whose mystery was manifested in miracles and angelic appearances, the agents of His intervention in men's lives; yet there must also be free action by men, since blind destiny (a concept resisted as fervently here as in discussions of Greek tragedy) would make a mockery of the human virtue that the epic is intended to teach. All of which finds a realization in the oratorios. The hero should be virtuous (though a flawed hero can be sublime and is therefore admissible); and he should be passive as well as, or rather than, active. The liking for passive suffering again links this genre with the librettos and other contemporary writing. As in the drama, the Classical sense of continuing endurance and uncertainty is shunned, and a happy ending is required for the virtuous – a requirement fulfilled by the librettos, for example in the final choruses of *Saul* and *Samson*, which are not dramatically prepared for or appropriate to the tragic climax but which make a final resounding statement of God's care of His

19. E.g. by C. Avison, *Reply to . . . Remarks on His Essay* (1753); J. Mainwaring, 'Observations on the Works of George Frederic Handel' in *Memoirs of the Life of the Late George Frederic Handel* (1760).
20. 'A Discourse on Epick Poetry' in *Dryden's Prose Works*, ed. E. Malone (1800), vol. 3, pp. 425–6.
21. Besides works cited in note 18 above, see Addison, *Spectator* Nos. 297 (9 February 1712) and 369 (3 May 1712); J. Baillie, *An Essay on the Sublime* (1747); R. Blackmore, *Alfred, an Epick Poem* (1723); *idem*, *Creation, a Philosophical Poem* (1722); *idem*, *Essays* (1716); *idem*, *Prince Arthur, an Heroick Poem* (1695); H. Blair, *A Critical Dissertation on the Poems of Ossian* (1763); T. Blackwell, *An Enquiry into the Life and Writings of Homer* (1736); T. Trapp, *The Aeneis of Virgil* (1718).

people. Blackmore's suggestions (1723) for the contents of an epic provide sanction for the many passages in the librettos that, like these, seem to us irrelevant
and sometimes unrelated to the heightening of character or emotion: he advises
authors to include 'moral and political Discourses and Soliloquies, as well as
Devotions and Thanksgivings . . .' apt to produce great and exalted Idea's and
worthy Resolves', as Jennens did in *Belshazzar*. And Blair's praise of Ossian's
'agreeable diversity', the mixing of 'martial with tender scenes', gives us a context
of appreciation of librettos constructed to such a pattern, for example *Joshua*
(which is also notable among the epic librettos for its self-conscious embodiment
and commemoration of national history). The sublime affections, the virtues that
(according to Baillie) the personages should demonstrate, are also shown in the
librettos: heroism; desire for conquest; contempt of death, danger and rank;
aspirations to fame and immortality; patriotism; justice; universal benevolence;
and love of God.

In these discussions the nation is regarded as the epic's central concern, the
individual hero being primarily the barometer of national strength. Trapp (1718)
thought Virgil superior to Homer because 'the Moral of the Aeneis, properly so
called' is that a virtuous nation which obeys God has the reward of being
'flourishing and happy' – for notwithstanding the proposed Christian
framework, the epic was to be centred in this world. Morris states that, despite
critical interest, not only the religious epic but the whole genre was defunct in
eighteenth-century England; but this is to ignore Handelian oratorio, which
conforms to all the contemporary prescriptions. Finding analogies for current
events in Old Testament history by identifying the English with the Jews was a
commonplace in the seventeenth century, and there are signs of its continuance
in the eighteenth, outside the oratorio as well as within it, despite the seculariz-
ation of politics.[22] Loftis shows (though he does not himself make the point)[23] that
in Augustan England music drama was the favourite vehicle for the most overt
political allegory, and it may be possible (without oversimplifying them as Whig–
Protestant–Hanoverian or Tory–Catholic–Jacobite) to understand all the librettos
in which the Chorus represents the Israelites, and not just those with an avowed
political parallel, as comments on the condition of England.

Such an understanding demands a thorough knowledge of contemporary
politics, but even preliminary reading gives rise to far more complex and sympathetic interpretations of religious nationalism in the oratorios than the received
one of blinkered aggressive optimism (a view which awareness of the deist
controversy in any case qualifies). I would suggest that some librettos celebrate
the restoration of safety; others depict national triumphs as surrogates for the
victories that were lacking in reality; and others embody the ideas and programmes of the opposition to the government.

The analogy of the Old Testament Jews would have appealed in an un-

22. E.g. E. Gibson, *The Deliverances and Murmurings of the Israelites, and these Nations, Compar'd* (1716); T. Morell, *The Surest Grounds for Hopes of Success in War* (1740).
23. J. Loftis, *The Politics of Drama in Augustan England* (1963).

precedented fashion to Englishmen of this period – ruled by a foreigner who inspired no sense of national identity – in that their history attests to the direct co-operation of God with an entire nation. It is not necessary (though it is inviting) to see Saul as a figure for Walpole, or Samson as an amalgam of the thwarted admirals of the current war, for us to recognize in their dramas a reflection of the prevailing sense (given vehement expression even in Parliament) of lack of leadership and national disgrace. And the fabrication of and insistence on a sense of Israelite unity in the librettos, the elimination of all reference to faction (which demands a highly selective reading of the Old Testament), acquires meaning and even poignancy when we set it by the side of the impassioned contemporary pamphleteering (e.g. in *The Craftsman* and *The Champion*) on the threat of faction to national strength. In *Belshazzar* it is tempting to detect deliberate transcription of the opposition's manifesto, Bolingbroke's *Idea of a Patriot King*:[24] both the passages in which Nitocris and Daniel contemplate the decline of empires and the se- quences in which Cyrus pledges himself as the saviour monarch echo its theories. Such a connection would explain not only the material of the plot but also the very extended passages of political philosophy and the essentially undramatic charac- terization of Cyrus, which have puzzled modern critics.

In all the librettos that chiefly concern military operations there are central episodes of defeat, doubt or temporary peril for the Israelites, which are paral- leled in contemporary sermons and pamphlets warning against complacency and relaxation of effort. The lesson is the same in both contexts: God does not effect His people's salvation without their active co-operation. And the oratorio battles, more heroic and decisive than the muddled engagements of the contemporary English forces, and almost always more successful, make excellent sense as morale-raisers, as stimulants to patriotic fervour, especially when we take account of the anxiety and frustration aroused by the handling of national affairs. Such librettos as *Deborah* become intelligible as forms of self-encouragement; even *Judas Maccabaeus*, which does celebrate a real military success, is seen by this light to be as much concerned with the preservation of safety and independence; and praise of the vital principle of liberty, with all the weight of contemporary meaning, recurs throughout the librettos – often through unlikely agents (e.g. Iole in *Hercules*). The most obviously Whig libretto, *Solomon*, transcends the problem of current political failure by substituting the illusion of peaceful triumph for that of military success, side-stepping the humiliating terms of the Treaty of Aix by celebrating peace as the basis of trade. Here liberty is, as in *Alexander Balus*, 'the soul of property', but by making commercial success dependent on virtue the librettist both gives trade the sanction of religion and raises a credible edifice for the glorification of the monarch. (The text bears comparison with other Whig panegyrics such as Young's *Ocean* and Thomson's *Liberty*.) Like all the politically relevant librettos *Solomon* combines reality, possibility and wishful thinking. They

24. Written 1738 and privately printed by Pope 1740, and so well known before its official publication in 1749 that phrases from it were shouted as slogans in public demonstrations against Walpole.

all, except *Belshazzar*, have the dunce's political outlook of incurable optimism; but in as much as they dramatize the history of the nation at the expense of the drama of the individual they can lay claim to the Augustan principle of public relevance.

Handel's successor:
notes on John Christopher Smith
the younger

Alfred Mann

'He was an excellent composer in his own right', wrote Charles Cudworth in his notes for a record of Shakespeare songs by John Christopher Smith the younger; one of them, the setting of a song from *A Midsummer Night's Dream*, he described as 'an unforgettable musical picture'.[1] It seemed characteristic of both the charm and the learning of the Pendlebury Librarian that he used to speak of Handel's successor simply as 'John Christopher' – very few of Charles Cudworth's generation could claim an equal familiarity with the work and the artistic personality and spirit of this arresting figure in English eighteenth-century music.

The need for a monograph presenting biographical detail on John Christopher Smith has long been felt. This need has now been served with a fine essay by Percy Young in which the evaluation of Smith as a composer is formulated in less favourable terms than those quoted above. Both views are justified, and a brief discussion of this fact may help towards regaining a perspective for Smith's historical role, a perspective that has tended to prove elusive to the modern observer.

Young's biographical sketch forms part of a new edition of the *Anecdotes of George Frederick Handel and John Christopher Smith*, a little book of rare documentary value that was first published in 1799, four years after Smith's death.[2] Immediately one is aware again of the crucial legacy attached to Smith's name: it is impossible to separate this name from that of his great predecessor. The original text is almost evenly divided between Anecdotes of Handel and Anecdotes of Smith; the modern editor's introduction is, however, devoted entirely to John Christopher Smith. An appendix to the book consists of thirty-two pages containing several compositions by Smith which are recommended to the reader by the original

1. *Eighteenth Century Shakespearean Songs*, April Cantelo (soprano), English Chamber Orchestra, Raymond Leppard (conductor): L'Oiseau-Lyre OL 50205.
2. The facsimile reprint, with introduction by Percy Young, was issued by Da Capo Press (New York 1979).

compiler as 'never before published' – a recommendation that is not necessarily a strong one. In fact, when one compares the style of these decently written but rather conventional excerpts from opera and oratorio with the fresh lyrical invention of the Shakespeare songs mentioned earlier, one cannot help regretting that the memory of the composer was not better served in this volume. The *galant* spirit of his vocal phrases, unquestionably belonging to a new era, is at times imbued with Handelian touches in clarity of melodic design and refinement of orchestration, and the natural ease with which these different elements merge in his writing cannot be denied a certain originality – it was the fate of his creative mien that eclecticism and originality cannot be totally disentangled.

The *Anecdotes* were published anonymously, but the book was compiled by the Reverend William Coxe, Smith's stepson. Having been widowed early in life, Smith married in later years the widow of his close friend Dr William Coxe, a court physician. It is through William Coxe Jr that basic detail, not only of Smith's biography but also of Handel's biography, was documented, for in recording Smith recollections he confirmed the fact that the first Handel biography, John Mainwaring's *Memoirs of the Life of the late George Frederic Handel* (published within a year of Handel's death), was 'written under the inspection of Mr. Smith'.

While thus much of Mainwaring's work overlaps with the *Anecdotes*, there is a fundamental difference in the style of the publications. The scope of Mainwaring's writing goes notably beyond the anecdotal, as professed in the lines appended to his title – 'to which is added a Catalogue of his Works and *Observations* upon them'. For these *Observations* the author was indebted to Robert Price, a friend of Smith's and himself a composer of some skill; and in recognizing the need for a critical commitment, Mainwaring became the true pioneer of musical biography.[3] As biographer of J. C. Smith, Coxe proved unequal to such a task; and though the modern observer may hold that the need for a critical commentary was considerably less acute, he is faced with both the advantages and the disadvantages of exploring uncharted territory.

That Smith can be called 'an excellent composer in his own right' is perhaps most strongly argued by Handel's own attitude; and while Percy Young issues justified warning that Mainwaring's and Coxe's accounts have numerous inaccuracies in common, we are dealing here with facts that admit little doubt.

One of the circumstances that have obscured the figure of John Christopher Smith is that Smith stands not only in the shadow of Handel but also in that of his own father, John Christopher Smith the elder. And here it is not only the identity of names but the parallel and unusually close working associations with Handel that complicate a critical assessment. John Christopher Smith snr, a friend of Handel's from early days, followed Handel after the composer's brief return to Germany, probably in 1716, to England, 'where he regulated the expenses of his public performances, and filled the office of treasurer with great exactness and

---

3. See Peter Kivy, 'Mainwaring's *Handel*: Its Relation to English Aesthetics', *Journal of the American Musicological Society* xvii/2 (1964), pp. 170ff.

fidelity'.[4] In the municipal records of his native Ansbach, Smith senior was listed as 'tradesman', and he apparently conducted a successful business there. In London, he became both Handel's manager and his principal copyist, and this proved eventually the cause of particular confusion between the professional roles of father and son. Handel autographs are variously intermingled with copies by both Smith senior and Smith junior, which has given rise to the impression that the younger Smith may have served as a kind of junior manager and copyist in Handel's employ. It was Jens Peter Larsen who first clarified this picture and proved that the copies of the younger Smith identify him as Handel's successor rather than as his copyist.[5] With a few unimportant exceptions, he copied only material that he was called on to conduct, and some of his later conducting scores were in fact copied out for him by his father.

No one could have been more deliberately chosen and groomed for the role of successor than was John Christopher Smith. His birthdate marks a midway point between those of Wilhelm Friedemann and Carl Philipp Emanuel Bach, and Handel's share and – one might say – paternal interest in Smith's early training is not unlike that of J. S. Bach at the time when he was compiling different versions of an instructional clavier book for members of his family. When the boy's talent became evident, Handel had him taken out of school so that he could concentrate on his musical studies under the composer's personal guidance. The clavier book apparently used for these lessons was the priceless document lost in later years but described in detail in the *Anecdotes*: the collection Handel had compiled in the course of his own early studies – the first musical manuscript known to have come from Handel's hand. This book, dated 1698 and inscribed with the initials G.F.H., contained copies of works by some of the keyboard composers most highly esteemed at the time: Johan Jakob Froberger, Johann Krieger, Johann Caspar Kerll, Wolfgang Ebner, Delphin Strungk, and above all Friedrich Wilhelm Zachow, Handel's teacher.[6]

It is clear that this notebook, like the similar collections from Bach's hand, served not only for the purpose of keyboard instruction but also for instruction in the contrapuntal style. Coxe, who obviously had the manuscript before him when he referred to it in the *Anecdotes*, remarked that 'the composition is uncommonly scientific'. The book remained in the possession of the younger Smith, who eventually used it in teaching his own students, among them Martha Coxe, his stepdaughter, to whom it was bequeathed after Smith's death.

It was with keyboard compositions that John Christopher Smith first presented himself to the public as a composer. His Op. 1 (1732) was unmistakably fashioned after Handel's first publication of keyboard works as *Suites de Pièces pour le Clavecin* and subsequently issued by Handel's publisher John Walsh in a design duplicating that of Handel's own publication.

4. *Anecdotes*, p. 37.
5. Jens Peter Larsen, *Handel's 'Messiah'* (London 1957), pp. 206f, 261f.
6. See the discussion of the manuscript in Paul Henry Lang, *George Frideric Handel* (New York 1966), pp. 13ff.

We must not underestimate the difficulties encountered by a young man of Smith's generation in entering on a musical career. One of his early patrons, the theologian Dr Samuel Clarke, had admonished him: 'you follow a dangerous profession, which may lead you into late hours, and excesses of all kinds, that will injure your constitution'.[7] But Smith's efforts were rewarded with success from the outset. 'Under the tuition of Handel Smith made so considerable a proficiency in music, that in the eighteenth year of his age, he commenced teacher, and instantly obtained, through his master's recommendation, and his own merit, so much employment, as to enable him to maintain himself without assistance from his father.'[8] In the course of time, Smith had continued his studies with Handel's eminent colleagues John Christopher Pepusch and Thomas Roseingrave. The latter seems to have taken a particular interest in him, and for some period Smith lived in the same house as Roseingrave, where 'Roseingrave was a constant guest at his table'. As Coxe mentions, Smith remembered with gratitude that this 'was the only recompense he would ever receive'.[9]

In his twentieth year, Smith had presented his first opera, *Teraminta*, written on a text by Henry Carey, also a pupil of Roseingrave. It was followed a year later by his second English stage work, *Ulysses*, written on a text by one of Handel's librettists, Samuel Humphreys. Young points out that the production of these works – in 1732 and 1733 – coincided with Handel's own turn from Italian to English dramatic texts. The turbulent decade which saw the rise of Handelian oratorio affected Smith's career in various ways. Both he and his father were active in assisting Handel in the new venture that eventually proved to be a decisive beginning of modern concert life. In 1740, the year of Handel's last opera production, we encounter a work by Smith which, though apparently staged, may be considered his first contribution to the emerging genre: 'Rosalinda . . . perform'd at Mr. Hickford's Great Room, near Golden Square . . . Set to Music by Mr. J. C. Smith. To which is prefix'd, An Enquiry into the Rise and Progress of Operas and Oratorios, with some Reflections on Lyric Poetry and Music'.

But Smith's life was headed for a critical change. Having been married at the age of twenty-four, he lost his wife after a few years. 'She died of a decline', runs the laconic account given in the *Anecdotes*. We find the same vague terms applied earlier in the book to Smith's own illness: 'At the age of eighteen he had so greatly injured his health, by intense application, that he was declared by Dr. Mead to be in a decline.' Several children of the brief marriage had died in infancy. Smith accepted the offer of a wealthy friend to receive financial independence for accompanying him on an extended journey to Southern Europe, to be undertaken both for reasons of health and for the sake of meeting a distinguished literary circle.

From this sojourn Handel's call for help brought Smith back to London. His return has generally been associated with the onset of Handel's blindness, but the chronology given in the *Anecdotes*, as well as some facts relating to the oratorio performances, suggest an earlier date.

---

7. *Anecdotes*, p. 38.   8. *Ibid.*, p. 39.   9. *Ibid.*, p. 42.

The oratorio seasons, now well established, took on another dimension with the yearly presentations of *Messiah* beginning in 1749. During this season Handel established a new pattern in which *Messiah* performances at the Foundling Hospital were regularly added to the other oratorio concerts. *Messiah* had been written for the benefit of three Dublin charity organizations: Handel obviously wanted to transfer the original purpose of the work to the London scene and begin a tradition of benefit performances – an aim given final expression in his bequest of a special set of *Messiah* performing parts to the Foundling Hospital. The charity Handel had chosen – the Hospital for the Maintenance and Education of Exposed and Deserted Young Children – received special donations from the composer, elected as one of its Governors in 1750, through a benefit concert for which he composed the *Foundling Hospital Anthem*. The proceeds were to be applied to the completion of a hospital chapel, for which Handel presented an organ whose specifications he personally supervised.

Aside from the philanthropic purpose, there were apparently special artistic considerations that guided Handel in these actions. The confluence of cathedral and operatic performance principles that had arisen through the creation of Handelian oratorio presented issues never fully resolved by performing conditions in the various theatres and music halls which served for oratorio performances: Handel must have had an ideal setting in mind, a setting which depended in large measure upon the co-operation of conductor and organist (choirmaster). Smith was engaged as organist for the Founding Hospital performances and, upon Handel's recommendation, was eventually given a regular appointment as chapel organist.

Smith's appointment represented the final answer to a question with which Handel had been concerned from the earliest performances of *Messiah*. We know from the details given in Charles Burney's 'Sketch of the Life of Handel' (contained in his *An Account of the Musical Performances in Westminster Abbey and the Pantheon*) that Handel, detained on his Dublin journey by unfavourable weather in Chester, sought out the organist of Chester Cathedral to enlist his help in preparing for the première. Handel's first interest was in gathering singers for a reading session to check the choral parts. But before leaving Chester, he also engaged an organist who had been introduced to him there (a Mr Maclaine) to assist him at the Dublin performances. It seems that Handel had brought a small organ from London for this purpose.[10]

Max Seiffert, in the course of analysing a drawing preserved in the British Museum, was the first to call attention to the fact that the direction of oratorios was, in fact, divided among three conductors – concertmaster and organist served as assistant conductors to the composer as principal conductor, with specific responsibilities for orchestra, chorus, and soloists ensemble distributed in a manner that confirms the merging of opera and church practice.[11] Larsen has issued a word of caution in connection with the British Museum drawing to which

10. See Lang, *Handel*, p. 338.
11. *Sammelbände der Internationalen Musikgesellschaft* VIII (1907), pp. 601ff.

Seiffert referred – it is not an authenticated Handel portrait, but as documentary evidence for the oratorio performance situation it retains unquestionable value.[12]

The organist's role was that of *maestro di cappella* – the choirmaster who supervised the singers, supplying what discreet doubling of choral voices he considered necessary on the evidence of rehearsals. But Handel wished to have an organ available for the oratorio performances for another purpose as well. As the virtuosity of the solo voice was not the central attraction in oratorio that it had been in opera, its place was taken by the virtuosity of the orchestra in interpolated concerti grossi and by Handel's own legendary performance as organ virtuoso and improviser. Oratorio presentations were customarily announced to be given 'With a Concerto on the Organ, by Mr. Handel'. In this case, principal conductor and assistant conductor exchanged instruments, the latter assuming the direction at the harpsichord.

The manner in which the performance of both the oratorios and the organ concertos was executed underwent an inevitable change with Handel's increasing blindness. When Smith received his appointment as chapel organist, the minutes of the General Committee of the Foundling Hospital explicitly stated that, on account of his health, 'Mr. Handel . . . excused himself from giving any further Instructions relating to the Performances'.[13] This change is reflected in new performance material for the organ concertos, extant in Smith's hand, in which the organ part is omitted. And it is further documented in the *Anecdotes*: 'When Handel became blind, though he no longer presided over the Oratorios, he still introduced concertos on the organ between the acts. At first he relied on his memory, but the exertion becoming painful to him, he had recourse to the inexhaustible stores of his rich and fertile imagination. He gave to the band only such parts of his intended composition, as were to be filled up by their accompaniment; and relied on his own powers of invention to produce, at the impulse of the moment, those captivating passages, which arrested attention, and enchanted his auditors.'[14]

Smith must have found his way into the role of Handel's successor with great sensitivity. Handel continued to be present at the oratorio performances until the end of his life; the last of them was the *Messiah* performance on 6 April 1759, a week before Handel's death. On 7 April the following note appeared in London's *Public Advertiser*:

> Hospital,
> For the Maintenance and Education of Esposed and Deserted Young Children
> This is to give notice, That towards the Support of this Charity the sacred Oratorio MESSIAH Will be performed in the Chapel of this Hospital, under the Direction of George-Frederick Handel. Esq; on Thursday the Third of May next, at Twelve o'Clock at Noon precisely . . .[15]

12. Larsen, *Handel's 'Messiah'*, p. 191.
13. Otto Erich Deutsch, *Handel: A Documentary Biography* (London 1955), p. 753.
14. *Anecdotes*, p. 25; Burney gives a similar description – evidently also derived from Smith – in the biographical sketch contained in his *Account*, p. 30.
15. Deutsch, *Handel*, p. 813.

Apparently at the same time, the budget for the announced performance was prepared, a document which has been preserved at the Foundling Hospital and which gives a moving account of the events. Along with a list of the orchestra members, written in two columns, there is a list of the singers and stagehands (Plate 1). Under the names of the singers is added that of J. C. Smith, whereas the name and signature of his father appear in the opposite column. The note above the elder Smith's name indicates that the services of Thomas Bramwell, who led the blind composer on stage, were no longer required. As his fee, crossed out above in the same column, was subtracted from the total bill, the name of Samuel Howard was entered in the left column. Howard, a singer, composer, and organist, who had been active in Handel's oratorio performances from their very beginning, replaced J. C. Smith at the organ, and Smith's place as principal conductor at the harpsichord received its final confirmation.

Smith's historic mission, however, is more complex, for we must consider the fact that he succeeded Handel not only as conductor of the oratorio seasons but also as Royal Music Master. This aspect of the Handelian legacy, the pedagogical activity at court, is easily obscured because it seems so clearly a minor artistic chore.

In a recent volume of the new critical edition of Handel's works (a volume which originated in much spirited discussion with Charles Cudworth), I have had the opportunity of showing that the didactic work which arose through Handel's court appointment is inseparable from his creative career.[16] Handel's own words, recorded by the Groningen organist Jacob Wilhelm Lustig, a pupil of Johann Mattheson and G. P. Telemann who was born and trained in Hamburg, attest to the fact that Handel's initial lack of interest in the pedagogical task underwent a decisive change in London: 'After I left your home town anno 1706 in order to go to Italy and eventually enter service at the court of Hanover, no power on earth could have moved me to take up teaching duties again – except Anne, the flower of all princesses.'[17]

Princess Anne, eldest daughter of George II, proved a highly gifted musician, and her association with Handel turned into a lifelong friendship. We owe it to Smith that the exercises which Handel may have used in teaching the princess have been preserved, and some of them may have been originally designed for the instruction of Smith, which commenced some three years earlier. They remained in his possession after Handel's death and were put to fresh use when Smith received the court appointment in order to teach Princess Augusta, widow of Frederick, Prince of Wales. The *Anecdotes* report: 'The Princess was uncommonly gracious and condescending, and derived so much satisfaction and improvement from his instructions, that she was often heard to say, that in her

16. See Hallische Händel-Ausgabe, Supplement, vol. I: *Georg Friedrich Händel, Composition Lessons.*
17. *Inleidung tot de Musiekkunde* (Gröningen 1771), p. 172; see p. 11 of the edition cited in note 16, above.

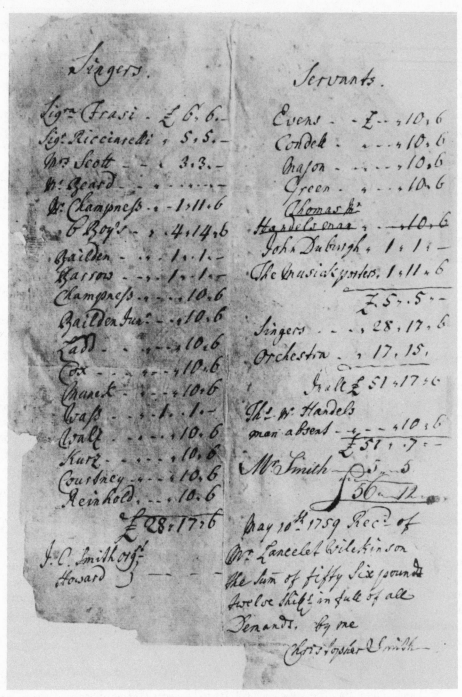

Plate 1. General Bill for the *Messiah* performance at the Foundling Hospital on 3 May 1759
Reproduced by permission of the Thomas Coram Foundation, London

advanced age, she had acquired a new taste for music, and had received notions of harmony, which she had never before experienced.[18]

'Harmony' is in this context still to be understood in the sense of polyphonic texture, and not in the meaning the term holds in present-day conventional instruction. In fact, as may be expected, Handel's teaching of composition was far removed from the methods that were to become conventional music theory. The point of departure was vocal and instrumental instruction. The technique of part-writing grew out of the study of thoroughbass, but the figures denoting the keyboard realization of a bass were so introduced, through chromaticism and dissonance resolution, that the fabric became immediately contrapuntal. Eventually the lessons included the task of designing four-part fugues and double fugues from a figured bass (see Plates 2 and 3).

Smith's continued use of these assignments must be seen in connection with his judicious preservation of the entire body of Handel autographs. He fell heir to this invaluable legacy partly by inheritance from his father, to whom Handel had bequeathed all his manuscripts, partly by a transfer of material from the master's library to his own, a transfer which originated in their working relationship.

Apparently at the time Smith became Royal Music Master, he made final disposition of the autographs. 'The Great Frederick, King of Prussia, offered Smith two thousand pounds for Handel's manuscripts; but he was unwilling to let such a treasure go out of England.'[19] As we know, Smith presented the Handel autographs to the royal family, and they went eventually from Buckingham Palace to the British Museum (and are now in the British Library). But quite logically, Smith's donation represented precisely the inheritance that had passed from his father to him. The autographs that formed part of his personal library remained in his possession and finally went to the manuscript collection of the Fitzwilliam Museum.

It seems likely that Smith himself had made the arrangements by which Lord Fitzwilliam became the owner of this special collection of Handel autographs; a biographical sketch, written by Charles Cudworth, gives a detailed description of the collecting activities of this remarkable connoisseur and devoted Handelian.[20] In the end, a single Handel autograph stayed in the possession of the Smith family, the notebook of 1698 by which Handel and Handel's pupils and later Smith's pupil were taught. It passed from Smith to Martha Coxe, who in 1768 married the Rev. Sir Peter Rivers. For her Smith also recopied those Handel autographs in the Fitzwilliam collection that seem to have formed the notebook of assignments Handel had written for the instruction of Smith and Princess Anne. The copy is contained in the 'Lady Rivers Manuscript' now in the possession of Gerald Coke, Esq., Bentley (Hants), and it represents the last extant document originating from the impact of Handel's teaching of composition.

A curious passage in the *Anecdotes* relates the story of a court invitation which

18. *Anecdotes*, p. 54.   19. *Ibid.*, p. 49.
20. Programme booklet, *Fitzwilliam Museum 150th Anniversary Concert*, Senate House, Cambridge, 14 July 1966.

Plate 2. A page from the Lady Rivers Manuscript showing Smith's copy of the beginning of Handel's
thoroughbass assignments
Reproduced by permission of Gerald Coke, Esq., Bentley, Hants

Handel's successor as Royal Music Master received whilst living in retirement in
the city of Bath. 'When the Commemoration of Handel was celebrated with such
wonderful effect in Westminster Abbey, under the direction of Joah Bates, Esq.
the King was desirous that Smith should be present at the performance, and sent
him a gracious and pressing invitation to come to London for that
purpose . . . Smith was fully sensible of this gracious mark of condescension; but
declined the honour with reluctance, apprehensive that from his advanced age,
so exquisitely powerful a performance of the works of his great master, would
excite such emotions as might too much affect his feeble frame.'[21] The famous
Handel Commemoration took place in 1784, when Smith was seventy-two. He
lived another eleven years and apparently remained active. The *Anecdotes* record
that even 'at the advanced age of eighty-one, he instructed a few young ladies
who had genius for music'; and one wonders, on the basis of its very formulation, if Smith's reply to the king might have been given for reasons of health
alone.

There was a basic difference between the manner in which Handel's pupil had

21. *Anecdotes*, p. 57.

Plate 3. A page from the Lady Rivers Manuscript showing a fugal thoroughbass assignment: the fugal entrances not written out in the different clefs are indicated by letter notation
Reproduced by permission of Gerald Coke, Esq., Bentley, Hants

guarded the Handel legacy and the 'powerful performance of the works of his great master' staged by Joah Bates. A crucial error was responsible for the dimensions of the great Commemoration, namely the assumption that the monumental setting of Handel's own performances at state occasions such as the coronation of George II might be applied to the lyrical style of *Messiah* – it was an error perpetuated well into the twentieth century. At its root, in the last analysis, was the fact that the musical director of the Commemoration represented a new type of professional conductor, a *maestro* no longer directly associated and familiar with the technique of composition from which the work had arisen. A modern dictionary entry for Joah Bates concludes with the brief sentence 'No compositions of his appear to be extant.'[22] The career of Handel's assistant and successor is characteristic of an era in which the functions of conductor and composer were still invariably linked – indeed, his own assistants were trained and experienced as composers (ironically, John Stanley, the blind organist and composer, became his assistant conductor). Did he realize that with him a great living tradition had reached its end?

22. *Baker's Biographical Dictionary of Musicians*, 6th edn (New York 1978).

The late additions to Handel's oratorios and the role of the younger Smith

Anthony Hicks

A famous and moving document forms parts of the autograph score of Handel's last oratorio, *Jephtha*. On the final page of the first section of the chorus 'How dark, O Lord, are thy decrees' the music peters out into the merest skeleton of notes. At the bottom of the page the composer explains, in German, that having reached that point on 13 February 1751 he could not continue because of the 'relaxation' of his left eye. It was an early indication of the blindness which within eighteen months became virtually total, tragically clouding the last six years of the composer's life. By 14 March, according to a letter of Sir Edward Turner,[1] Handel had lost the use of his left eye altogether, though his skill as an organist was apparently unimpaired. On 30 August *Jephtha* was completed. Handel directed the first performances at Covent Garden theatre on 26 February 1752 during one of his Lenten oratorio seasons, by then well established, concluding as usual with *Messiah* at the chapel of the Foundling Hospital on 9 April. If Handel had any special difficulties with this season as a result of his failing eyesight, no hint of them has come down to us. The real disaster struck in the summer. On 17 August the *General Advertiser* reported that Handel had succumbed to 'a Paralitick Disorder in his Head, which has deprived him of Sight'. Despite later rumours of recovery, there is little doubt that this notice signified the onset of effectively permanent blindness. Apart from shaky signatures on a letter and on the codicils to his will, no document of any kind written after 1752 survives in Handel's own hand.

Nevertheless, Handel somehow contrived to maintain his musical activities as before. Oratorio seasons were given under his supervision each Lent to within a week of his death on 14 April 1759. They were not without musical novelty. Many oratorios were revived with 'additions' and in 1757 there was even a 'new' oratorio, *The Triumph of Time and Truth*. The newness of the music which appeared

1. Unless another reference is given, all documents quoted are to be found in O. E. Deutsch, *Handel: A Documentary Biography* (London 1955) under the date mentioned.

in these years is open to question, as we shall see, but certainly some kind of compositional activity was going on in addition to the work of rehearsing and directing the oratorio concerts themselves. Obviously Handel was receiving help. His first biographer, John Mainwaring, remarks that when unable to manage the oratorio seasons alone Handel 'sent to Mr Smith to desire that he would play for him, and assist in conducting the oratorios'.[2] We are told that Handel continued composing, but nothing is said of the process by which the music was put down on paper. It was Burney who later wrote that the duet and chorus 'Sion now her head shall raise' were 'dictated to Mr Smith by Handel, after total privation of sight'.[3] This appears to be the earliest reference to the use of an amanuensis, and perhaps the only source for subsequent references to the matter. Mainwaring and Burney were of course referring to the younger John Christopher Smith (1712–95) rather than to his father (1683–1763) who bore the same name. The father figures more prominently in Handel literature because of his work as the composer's chief copyist from about 1720 onwards, but the son was better known to the contemporary London public as an organist and composer.[4]

Until recently Smith's role as amanuensis and the nature of his work for Handel has not been seriously discussed. Smith's handwriting was known to A. H. Mann in the 1890s, as is shown by his correct identification of it in his catalogue of the Handel manuscripts in the Fitzwilliam Museum,[5] but the hands of the two Smiths and other copyists associated with Handel became widely familiar only when facsimile examples were published in J. P. Larsen's study of *Messiah*.[6] Details of the late revivals of the oratorios were given by Winton Dean in his major study of the subject.[7] He included much information about the additional numbers and

2. [J. Mainwaring], *Memoirs of the Life of the Late George Frederic Handel* (London 1760, repr. Amsterdam 1964), p. 138.
3. Charles Burney, 'Sketch of the Life of Handel', printed with separate pagination as part of *An Account of the Musical Performances . . . in Commemoration of Handel* (London 1785, repr. Amsterdam 1964), p. 30.
4. In this essay 'Smith' is always a reference to the son. The foundation work for information on Smith is the variably reliable *Anecdotes of George Frederick Handel and John Christopher Smith* (London 1799, repr. New York 1979), issued anonymously but certainly compiled by Smith's stepson William Coxe. Unfortunately it has nothing to say about Smith's activity as Handel's amanuensis. The most helpful recent article on Smith's music is Andrew D. McCredie's 'John Christopher Smith as a Dramatic Composer', *Music & Letters* xLV (1964), pp. 22–38, which gives the sources of Smith's major works and other relevant information. Percy M. Young's introduction to the 1979 reprint of the *Anecdotes* seems to take no account of McCredie's study and barely fulfils its promise of making a 'critical assessment' of Smith's music; it is, however, extremely valuable for comprehensive background information on Smith's circle of acquaintances and the *Anecdotes* themselves. As both McCredie and Young fail to recognize the text of Smith's early cantata *The Mourning Muse of Alexis* (1729), it may perhaps be identified here as William Congreve's pastoral ode of 1694 'lamenting the Death of Queen Mary'.
5. J. A. Fuller-Maitland and A. H. Mann, *Catalogue of the Music in the Fitzwilliam Museum, Cambridge* (London 1893), pp. 157–227 ('Manuscripts and Sketches by G. F. Handel'); see in particular Mann's notes concerning pp. 83–108 of MS 265.
6. Larsen, *Handel's 'Messiah': Origins, Composition, Sources* (London 1957, 2nd edn New York 1972).
7. Dean, *Handel's Dramatic Oratorios and Masques* (London 1959).

noted Smith's connection with an air added to *Theodora*. Finally in 1972 Hans Dieter Clausen published as part of his description of Handel's working copies (or 'conducting scores') a more particular discussion of Handel's oratorio revisions in the time of his blindness.[8] He dismissed several proposed instances of Handel's handwriting after 1752 (in the form of corrections or annotations to musical scores), identifying some of them as being in the hand of Smith. He also printed a list of oratorio additions subsequent to 1752, distinguishing between 'parodies', or old music adapted to new texts without significant change, and items not known to be derived from earlier material. Clausen's most interesting remark occurs in connection with two airs extant in Smith's hand. These, he says, must have been written by Smith at Handel's dictation 'unless he was their composer or editor'; he does not however pursue this thought any further.

The purpose of this essay is to look more closely at the oratorio additions of 1753–9 and to suggest that Smith's involvement may well have been more than that of an amanuensis. In the absence of specific documentation it can do no more than suggest, as no description of Handel's method of composition at this period exists; only an eyewitness account could determine how creativity might have been shared between nominal composer and scribe. Two other preliminary points must be made. Handel's lifelong practice of re-using old material (by himself and others) in new contexts makes it unlikely that he would be strongly moved to create wholly original music in his declining years. Apparently 'new' music stemming from this period must therefore be treated with suspicion, especially if it possesses features untypical of the composer. Secondly, Smith was a competent and active composer in his own right, capable of working out hints from the older master without having to be instructed in every detail.

Whether or not the conclusions of this study prove acceptable, it is hoped that the examination of a body of music too little represented in modern editions of Handel's works will be of interest in itself. As the posing of a new question is sometimes as useful as finding an answer to an old one, it has been pleasing to find that the search for the origins of some of this music has led to an unexpected line of thought: to what extent do the late oratorio additions preserve earlier music that might otherwise be lost?

When considering additions to any of Handel's major works it is essential to distinguish between those cases where some musical creativity has taken place (whether or not old material is being used) and those where airs or choruses are simply transferred from one work to another, possibly with some alterations to the words alone. Transfers of the second kind are of little interest and are generally ignored here. Examples of the re-use of operatic or other Italian airs with new English texts are also comparatively unimportant and are mentioned only for the sake of completeness. It is noticeable that until 1753 cases of opera airs being

---

8. Clausen, *Händels Direktionspartituren* (Hamburg 1972), pp. 25–32 ('Excurs: Händels Revisionspraxis nach seiner Erblindung').

used in the oratorios are extremely rare. After that year, however, usage of operatic material becomes common.

The contrast between creative and non-creative additions is at once apparent in the two numbers added to the first revival of *Jephtha* in 1753, a year after its original production.[9] No other oratorio acquired 'new' material that season. The first addition was the bass air 'Freedom now once more possessing', a simple parody of 'La mia sorte fortunata' in the opera *Agrippina* (1709). As in other adaptations of this kind the new English text mimics the rhyme scheme and metre of the Italian original, with ungainly results. The effort of finding rhyming feminine endings produces a mélange of inversions and appositional phrases typical of many of the late oratorio additions:

Agrippina (1709)	*Jephtha* addition (1753)
La mia sorte fortunata	Freedom now once more possessing,
delle stelle oggi me scende	Peace shall spread with ev'ry blessing
se vien oggi da te;	Triumphant joy around.
che in te sol, bella adorata,	Sion now no more complaining
la mia stella mi resplende	Shall in blissful plenty reigning
per gloria di mia fè.	Thy glorious praise resound.

The second addition is the setting of 'All that is in Hamor mine' (originally an air for Iphis) as a quintet – an example of the more interesting kind of adaptation, where the musical material of the source is substantially reworked. The duet 'T'amo, si' from *Riccardo Primo* (1727) provides the basic themes of the quintet, but the treatment is quite different and the result is effectively a new composition. There are several surprising features. The quintet begins with what seems like the main section of a regular da capo duet, but the 'middle section' that follows turns out to be extremely brief – just 7 bars – and three additional voices suddenly join in. The duet resumes, then unexpectedly shifts to the tonic minor. Once again the three extra voices (echoed lugubriously by a pair of bassoons) appear, and the piece swiftly closes in the minor key.

Whether this close in the tonic minor should be hailed as a psychological subtlety is a moot point. Certainly a mood of unrestrained rejoicing at this point seems dramatically inept: Iphis, consigned to perpetual virginity, has had to relinquish all hope of marrying her lover Hamor and has no cause for joy. And it is true that Handel had occasionally made a point of contradicting inappropriate suggestions of happiness at the conclusions of dramatic works, notably in *Tamerlano*, *Alexander Balus* and *Theodora*. The replacement of a bright major-key air with a quintet turning to the minor could be a natural sequel to these precedents. If so,

9. Unless otherwise stated, all musical items mentioned will be found in *The Works of George Frederic Handel*, ed. F. Chrysander (Leipzig 1858–1902, repr. Farnborough 1965–6 and New York n.d.) – usually referred to as the Händel-Gesellschaft or HG edition. It should be noted that Chrysander often omits the late additions from his oratorio volumes, and when he does include them, he does not always place them in their proper contexts or distinguish them from the original content of the oratorio. At the time of writing (1980) the new Hallische Händel-Ausgabe has not covered any of the oratorios which acquired additions in the period 1753–9.

one questions whether it achieves the same effect. The close of the quintet is immediately swamped by a determinedly bright concluding chorus, in D major with trumpets, and it is hard to accept the quintet itself as a satisfactory whole. If Handel had intended to create tension between words and music it would surely have been better to re-use one of the poignant minor-key duets which occur in a number of the Italian operas. What is impressive about the finales of the three works mentioned earlier is that the minor key is sustained throughout, whereas the shift in the *Jephtha* quintet (it can hardly be called a modulation) sounds gratuitous, a desperate measure to relieve the fairly static harmonic scheme.

Judging purely by the music itself, the *Jephtha* quintet could easily be the work of a competent follower of Handel with limited powers of invention. The identification of Smith as the follower concerned is suggested by documentary evidence. Clausen[10] points out that certain corrections to the copy of the quintet in the *Jephtha* conducting score attributed by Schoelcher[11] to Handel are more probably Smith's; and it was Smith who wrote the notes of the altered recitative introducing 'Freedom now', the other 1753 addition to *Jephtha*.

In the 1754 season there appears to have been no creative enhancement of the oratorios performed. The only works receiving additions were *Alexander Balus* and *Joshua*. In *Alexander Balus* the new numbers were items from the abandoned *Alceste* music of 1750 which had not found a place in *The Choice of Hercules*, while all but one of the *Joshua* additions are readily identifiable as items from the *Occasional Oratorio* of 1746. The exception is an air with chorus in Act I, 'Now before our ravish'd eyes', but it is almost certain that this too is from the *Occasional Oratorio*, as the text can be easily fitted to 'Then will I Jehovah's praise' and its pendant chorus 'All his mercies shall endure.'

In 1755 it was the revival of *Theodora* that received additional music, the only oratorio so favoured that season. It is not immediately obvious what the additions were. The Händel-Gesellschaft score shows only the music of the original 1749 version, regrettably defaced by the silent incorporation of several cuts made at later dates. Arnold's score of 1787 more helpfully prints five additional numbers found in the conducting score.[12] Three of these are parodies of operatic airs, resetting texts already in the oratorio; the musical alterations are trivial, though slightly in excess of what was strictly necessary. Dating these additions is problematic because no *Theodora* wordbook dated 1755 is known; in any case wordbooks cannot help to decide when new versions of airs are introduced without any changes being made to the words. However, in 1759 a wordbook was printed in anticipation of a performance that never took place, and it contains the two additions printed by Arnold which have new texts. Winton Dean[13] suggests that both these and the three operatic parodies date from 1755. Clausen, on the basis of his paper studies, accepts this date for the two items on new texts but con-

10. *Händels Direktionspartituren*, p. 28.
11. V. Schoelcher, *The Life of Handel* (London 1857), pp. 324–5.
12. The inserts are those designated E6, E10, E5, E8 and E9 by Clausen, pp. 239–40.
13. *Handel's Dramatic Oratorios and Masques*, p. 575.

vincingly puts the three operatic parodies into the post-1760 period when the conducting scores unfortunately continued to be used and altered.

Thus for 1755 we have just two additions in *Theodora* to consider. The first is the solo and chorus 'Blessed be the power', which replaced Theodora's air 'When sunk in anguish and despair'. It is quite Handelian in style but oddly short: a 6-bar solo for Irene (here a soprano instead of the original mezzo) concluded by a mere 3-bar coda for full chorus and orchestra. Despite Dean's reasonable comment that the music was 'almost certainly' not new, there seems to be no direct model, though one notices a fleeting reminiscence of the gavotte finale of the Concerto Op. 3 No. 2. Clearly this piece could be a brief exercise in the Handelian manner by anyone familiar with the basic characteristics of the style. With the second addition, the air 'Lost in anguish, quite despairing', there is direct evidence of Smith's involvement. The air, for Theodora, was inserted in Act III before the chorus 'How strange their ends'. Though the copy inserted into the conducting score is, as usual, in the elder Smith's hand, a second manuscript in his son's hand exists.[14] It bears a number of corrections, sometimes said to be Handel's, but they would appear to be Smith's own adjustments.[15] Despite the Italianate structure and metre of the text, the music does not appear to have come from an earlier Handel work. Possibly the *Flavio* air 'Quanto dolci' inspired the opening idea (Ex. 1 shows the two incipits) but no more, as the airs are in contrasting modes and the continuations are quite different. The *Theodora* air is again short (41 bars, through-composed) and does not stray far from the home key. A startling interrupted cadence on the word 'die', like the minor-key shift in the *Jephtha* quintet, sounds more contrived than inspired.

The revivals of *Athalia* and *Deborah* in 1756 received three additions between them, but all were parodies. Two airs from *Il Parnasso in Festa* (1734), 'Torni pure' and 'Da sorgente', became respectively 'Happy Judah' and 'Lovely youth' in *Athalia*.[16] The *Deborah* addition, printed in skeleton form in the appendix to Arnold's edition, was 'Hateful man', musically identical to 'Piangi pur' in *Tolomeo*.

In the season of 1757 the amount of newly adapted material added to the oratorios increased dramatically. Major additions were made to *Esther*, and a new English oratorio, *The Triumph of Time and Truth*, was given its first performance. The latter was not, in fact, particularly well favoured with fresh material; it was basically an English version of the Italian oratorio *Il Trionfo del Tempo e della Verità* of 1737, itself an extensively recomposed version of *Il Trionfo del Tempo e del Disinganno*, written in Rome in the spring of 1707. The new English recitatives were not adapted from the earlier ones, and there is no way of determining who

14. In the Library of Congress, Washington, D.C., MS ML96.H156 (Case). A facsimile of the first page is given in E. Winternitz, *Musical Autographs from Monteverdi to Hindemith* (Princeton 1955, 2nd edn New York 1965), vol. 2, plate 39. Apart from one ambiguous sentence, the description of this plate (vol. 1, p. 63) misleadingly treats the manuscript as if it were a Handel autograph.

15. Clausen, *Händels Direktionspartituren*, p. 28 n. 2.

16. *Ibid.*, p. 29, refers 'Lovely youth' to 'Io vorrei' in the 1707 *Il Trionfo del Tempo*. This indeed supplied the basic musical material, but 'Da sorgente' is the actual air parodied.

Example 1
(a) *Flavio* (1723): 'Quanto dolci'
(b) *Theodora* (1755): 'Lost in anguish, quite despairing'

(a)

(b)

composed them. Otherwise the amount of material not taken directly from earlier works was small. Out of twenty-nine numbers (excluding the recitatives) twenty came from the 1707 or 1737 Italian versions, while most of the rest were parodies of items in *Lotario* (1729), the expanded *Acis and Galatea* of 1732, *Athalia* (1733), *Il Parnasso in Festa* (1734), *Susanna* (1749) and three anthems. Only three vocal sections, none a complete piece in itself, required some creative involvement. These were:

(i) the soprano solo section of 'Happy, if still they reign in pleasure' – a simple extension of the main section, which is a parody of the *coro* 'Viva e regni fortunato' in *Lotario*;

(ii) the opening 8 bars of the chorus 'Strengthen us, oh Time' – a straightforward harmonic progression from F to G, preparing for C minor;

(iii) the main sections of 'Like clouds stormy winds them compelling' – freely adapted from 'Come nembo che fugge col vento' in the 1707 *Trionfo*; the brief concluding reprise, turning to the tonic minor, brings the formal scheme close to that of the *Jephtha* quintet.

None of these required any great powers of musical invention. More intriguing is the overture, the last item one would expect to be new, yet the slow opening and closing sections, quite Handelian in manner, do not appear to have been taken from an earlier work. The Allegro incorporates portions of the corresponding movement of the overture to *Il Pastor Fido* (1712) sandwiched between some very dull material largely made up of repeated chords. In short, none of the really 'new' music in *The Triumph of Time and Truth* is sufficiently original or remarkable to rule out the possibility that the compilation of the oratorio was entirely the work of a collaborator.

The *Esther* additions of 1757 present a very different picture, at least one of them having strong claims to be considered Handel's unadulterated work. They may well be a reflection of the improvement in the composer's health noted by his friends at this time. On 8 February the Earl of Shaftesbury, one of Handel's keenest supporters, wrote to James Harris:

> Mr Handel is better than he has been for some years and finds he can compose Chorus's as well as other music to his own (and consequently to the hearers) satisfaction. His memory is strengthened of late to an astonishing degree.[17]

Actually just one choral item appeared in 1757, and it remained the only substantial piece for chorus among the late oratorio additions. It was the well-known duet and chorus 'Sion now her head shall raise', written for *Esther* and first performed in that oratorio but shortly afterwards transferred to *Judas Maccabaeus*.[18] Based on a motive from a Bononcini cantata,[19] 'Sion now' is thoroughly Handelian in its magisterially sustained development of simple material. Of all the late oratorio additions, it alone is plainly in the main stream of Handel's mature work. Burney's particular reference to this piece as having actually been dictated to Smith by Handel significantly confirms its authenticity.

Three airs were also added to *Esther* in 1757. One ('May thy beauty') was simply an English version of 'Tua bellezza', an Italian air included in Handel's 1737 revival of *Esther* and also used with a different text ('La speranza, la costanza') in *Israel in Egypt* in 1739.[20] The other airs – incipits are shown as Exx. 2 and 3 – are more puzzling, as they have no known sources yet the music hardly suggests late Handel. Both are lightweight pieces scored for violins and continuo only, such as one might come across in the operas of the 1720s or early 1730s; the airs of Boyce's *Solomon* (1743) are also called to mind. Possibly they are the 'other music' mentioned by Shaftesbury that Handel found he was capable of composing, but if so the reversion to an airy, not to say trite, style is surprising, and one would have expected Walsh to have published them as he did all the other additional airs in the late oratorio revivals that were not direct parodies. There is no documentary evidence to connect them with Smith, and they present a contrast with the more turgid style of the other late oratorio additions with which he does seem to have been involved.

There were further substantial additions to the oratorios in both 1758 and 1759,

17. B. Matthews, 'Handel – More Unpublished Letters', *Music & Letters* XLII (1961), pp. 127–31.
18. Chrysander included it only in *Judas Maccabaeus* (HG vol. 22); his edition of the London versions of *Esther* (HG vol. 41) does not include any of the 1757 additions.
19. The bass of the air 'Se al morir' in the cantata 'Peno, e l'alma fedel'.
20. Both Dean (*op. cit.*, p. 213) and Clausen (*op. cit.*, p. 29) erroneously describe 'May thy beauty' as a parody of 'So much beauty', one of the 1732 *Esther* additions. 'Tua bellezza' is not in any HG volume and remains unpublished in its original form. Walsh included a treble-and-bass version of it in his *Sonatas, or Chamber Aires, for a German Flute, Violin or Harpsicord*, a collection of instrumental arrangements of opera and oratorio airs which appeared in instalments between about 1726 and 1760.

Example 2. *Esther* (1757): 'How sweet the rose'

amounting to fourteen airs over the two seasons, only one being a direct parody. A further letter of Shaftesbury's, dated 31 December 1757, explains the inspiration behind several of the 1758 additions:

> I saw Mr Handel the other day, who is pretty well and has just finished the composing of several new songs for Federica his new singer, from whom he has great expectations. She is the girl who was celebrated a few years since for playing on the Harpsichord at eight years old.[21]

'Federica' is Cassandra Frederick, who had played a Handel concerto on the harpsichord at the New Theatre, Haymarket, on 10 April 1749. She received no less than five new airs in the revival of *The Triumph of Time and Truth*, and two more in *Judas Maccabaeus*. The other additions of 1758, two airs for Giulia Frasi, appeared in *Belshazzar*. One of them was (like 'Sion now') quickly transferred to *Judas Maccabaeus* and found a permanent home there.[22]

21. Matthews, 'Handel – More Unpublished Letters', p. 130.
22. Full scores of the nine 1758 additions were published by Walsh in August of the same year as *A Grand Collection of Celebrated English Songs introduced in the Late Oratorios*. The HG edition prints only the five airs added to *The Triumph of Time and Truth* (without distinguishing them from the rest of the score) and 'Wise men flatt'ring', which appears only in *Judas Maccabaeus*.

Example 3. *Esther* (1757): 'This glorious deed defending'

Shaftesbury's reference to Handel's 'composing' notwithstanding, the additional airs of 1758 draw heavily on earlier material and display the structural awkwardness and harmonic quirks already noted in the 1753 *Jephtha* quintet and the 1755 *Theodora* additions. There is likewise evidence of Smith's involvement. A new feature is the extensive use of material from the operas and cantatas of Handel's Italian period. It will be simplest to give a brief description of each air in turn, omitting for the moment 'Charming beauty', one of the additions to *The Triumph of Time and Truth*.

Additions in *The Triumph of Time and Truth* (1758)

'Sorrow darkens ev'ry feature'
> A vocal line closely based on 'Già superbo' from the cantata *Lucretia* ('O numi eterni') is ingeniously married to an accompaniment derived from 'Perchè viva il caro sposo' in *Rodrigo* (1707). The *Lucretia* aria also supplies the metrical scheme of the text.

'Happy beauty'
> The model is 'Ogni vento' in *Agrippina* (1709) – itself based on 'Fiamma bella' in the cantata *Arresta il passo* – but the infectious waltz-like episodes which are such an attractive feature of the model are consistently replaced with passages based on a dull three-note figure. Development of the material of the first section, which is extremely leisurely, continues in the middle section. Words from the first section then begin to return haphazardly, the tonic is regained almost by accident and the end comes very quickly. There is nothing here of Handel's sense of formal balance. The orchestral sound is dominated by a wind group of oboes, horns and bassoons.

'No more complaining'
> The vocal sections are taken without musical change from *Rodrigo* ('Allor che sorge'), but for no obvious reason a new ritornello is added to close the first section and the final ritornello is significantly expanded.

'Pleasure's gentle zephyrs playing'
> The first section is musically identical to the corresponding portion of 'Volo pronto' in *Agrippina*. Here Smith's involvement is apparent because it was he who added the new English text to the aria in the *Agrippina* autograph.[23] The middle section appears to have been newly composed. The air retains its original pure da capo form.

23. A facsimile of the relevant page is given in A. Hyatt King, *Handel and His Autographs* (London 1967), plate x. The handwriting of the added text is incorrectly stated to be Handel's, and the adaptation is dated 1757 instead of 1758.

Additions in *Belshazzar* (1758)

'Wise men flatt'ring'

The model is 'Se vuoi pace' in *Agrippina*, from which the vocal line comes more or less directly, with 'modernized' cadences.[24] The middle section is rewritten and the whole air expanded by much use of the attractive figure shown in Ex. 4. (The figure has several Handelian antecedents, notably in 'Crede l'uom' from the 1707 *Trionfo del Tempo* and the later versions of that oratorio.) The wind group noticed earlier is prominent

Example 4. *Belshazzar* (1758): 'Wise men flatt'ring'

again, now augmented by recorders. Although the wind are used skilfully there is a general thickening of the orchestration as compared to the three-part string writing of the model. A tendency to use the middle register of the horns for harmonic filling-in is of course more typical of Smith's generation than of Handel's. There is a noticeable similarity between the use of the orchestra in this air and that in the air 'Bid her learn the gentler arts' from Smith's unfinished opera *Medea* (1760–1),[25] the opening of which is shown in Ex. 5.

'Fain would I know, if virtue confessing'

This is an expanded and fully orchestrated version of a keyboard 'sarabande' (or rather minuet) in E, well attested to have been written while Handel was paying a visit to the Earl of Shaftesbury at St Giles's House, his seat in Dorset.[26] Each half of the original is separately extended with new material of no great interest. The four-part string writing again lacks Handelian clarity.

24. Dean (*Handel's Dramatic Oratorios and Masques*, pp. 469–70) shows in detail the development of the vocal line from the earlier models.
25. Quoted in the appendix to the *Anecdotes* (see note 4, above).
26. Matthews, 'Handel – More Unpublished Letters', prints a facsimile of the autograph in the Earl of Malmesbury's family collection; it bears a note (not in Handel's hand) stating that Handel improvised the piece while on a visit to St Giles's House, the seat of the Earl of Shaftesbury. A copy added at the end of a manuscript volume of organ concertos presently at St Giles's bears a similar note. The piece (not in HG) is printed as no. 16 in G. F. Händel, *Pieces for Harpsichord*, ed. W. Barclay Squire and J. A. Fuller-Maitland (London [1928]).

Example 5. J. C. Smith, *Medea* (1760–1): 'Bid her learn the gentler arts'

Ex. 5 (contd)

Additions in *Judas Maccabaeus* (1758)

'Far brighter than the morning'

        A joint derivation from 'Il dolce foco mio' in *Rodrigo* (1707) and 'È un incendio fra due venti' in *Rinaldo*, which is a recomposition of the same material. The accompaniment is closer to the *Rinaldo* model, but the shape of the vocal line and the metre of the text derive from *Rodrigo*. Unlike the models, both regular da capo airs, 'Far brighter' is in effect through-composed. Once more the wind group is prominent, and there is a good deal of unnecessary doubling and harmonic padding from the horns (Ex. 6).

'Great in wisdom, great in glory'

        The accompaniment is apparently based on 'Tacerò' in *Agrippina* (1709), which in turn derives from the air 'Gaude tellus' in the Pentecost motet 'O qualis de coelo sonus' of June 1707.[27] Neither of these supplies the vocal line, however. The expected da capo is replaced by a shortened reprise. A remarkable feature of the instrumentation is that the busy figures in the continuo line of the models are transferred to unison bassoons, a conventional continuo line being extracted for the string basses: this is without Handelian parallel. Smith's intimate connection with the production of this air is displayed by a manuscript in his hand covering bars 36–108 of its 128 bars.[28] It contains many amendments and corrections suggestive of a composition autograph.

After this survey we can return to the one addition in *The Triumph of Time and Truth* which was passed over: 'Charming beauty'. The style of this da capo air gives the impression that, like most of the other additions reviewed, it is based on an air from Handel's Italian period. No such model can now be found, but newly

27. Not in HG. Edited by R. Ewerhart (Cologne 1957).
28. Fitzwilliam MS Mus.265, pp. 105–8.

discovered information about the opera *Rodrigo* allows the speculation that one did exist in Handel's time. Thanks to the researches of Reinhard Strohm,[29] the printed wordbook of the original performances of *Rodrigo* has been located. It shows that the opera was produced in Florence in the autumn of 1707 under the

Example 6. *Judas Maccabaeus* (1758): 'Far brighter than the morning'

29. R. Strohm, 'Händel in Italia: Nuovi Contributi', *Rivista Italiana di Musicologia* IX (1974), pp. 152–74. See also R. L. Weaver and N. W. Weaver, *A Chronology of Music in the Florentine Theater (1590–1750)* (Detroit 1978), p. 210.

Ex. 6 (contd)

title *Vincer se stesso è la maggior vittoria* and supplies the full verbal text of the sections missing in the autograph and all known manuscript copies. The text of the first air in the opera, part of the lost section of Act I, turns out to have a strong affinity with that of 'Charming beauty':

Rodrigo (1707)	*The Triumph of Time and Truth* addition (1758)
Occhi neri,	Charming beauty,
voi non siete a pianger soli	Stop the starting tear from flowing
dopo il punto del goder;	All adown the rosy cheek.
resta, o bella, e ti consoli	Pleasure still new charms bestowing,
la memoria del piacer.	Ever cheerful Pleasure seek.

Not only is the metrical scheme of the Italian paralleled exactly, but 'tear' relates to 'pianger' in line 2 and 'pleasure' to 'piacer' in line 5. There is also some similarity of general sense. Unfortunately, it is not possible to produce a convincing 'reconstruction' of the *Rodrigo* air simply by grafting the Italian text on to the music of 'Charming beauty', even though the fit is perfect. As in the case of the other 1758 *Triumph* additions, it is clear that the music has been recomposed, acquiring un-Handelian features in the process. The middle section is most suspect: in *Rodrigo* Handel would have followed his normal procedure of ending in the mediant minor, but the *Triumph* air, after reaching this key at the fourth bar of the mid-section, goes on to establish the subdominant as the preparation for the da capo, an exceedingly rare proceedure.[30] Nevertheless, 'Charming beauty' offers an excellent starting point for anyone wishing to fill up the gaps in the *Rodrigo* score to provide a performing text.

With this hint, the question arises whether any other music belonging to the lost sections of *Rodrigo* may lie hidden in the late oratorio additions. Generally speaking the material is adequately accounted for in extant compositions, as we have seen, but the *Judas Maccabaeus* addition 'Great in wisdom' is worth reconsidering, since the shape of the vocal line cannot be related to the models which provide the material for the accompaniment. It happens that the *Rodrigo* libretto does contain a text with virtually the same rhyme scheme and metre as 'Great in wisdom', and whose sense would be appropriately expressed by vigorous and angry figures in the bass line:

Rodrigo (1707)	*Judas Maccabaeus* addition (1758)
Vibri pure iniqua sorte	Great in wisdom, great in glory
Dardi, piaghe e crudeltà;	Thee all nations shall proclaim;
sarò grande, sarò forte,	Future times record thy story
l'alma mia temer non sà.[31]	And with wonder sing thy name.

The Italian requires an elision in the first line ('Vibri pur'iniqua sorte'), but Handel may well have set the first two words on their own to start the air. If this licence is allowed, the *Rodrigo* text may be fitted to the *Judas Maccabaeus* music (Ex. 7). The result is less convincing than is the case with 'Charming beauty', but still plausible; again one would assume some recomposition of the music.

All the oratorio additions of the 1759 season, the last under Handel's nominal direction, appeared in a drastically revised version of *Solomon*.[32] As Winton

30. The only other examples known to me occur in 'All'orror delle procelle' (*Riccardo Primo*, 1728) and 'Father of Heav'n' (*Judas Maccabaeus*, 1746).
31. This air, for Evanco in Act I scene 6, appears in the wordbook in place of 'Heroica fortezza'. Comparison between the wordbook and the surviving portion of the autograph shows that significant changes were made to *Rodrigo* before the first performances, presumably in a lost conducting score.
32. Full scores of all the *Solomon* additions plus 'The Lord is a man of war' from *Israel in Egypt* were published by Walsh in March 1763 as *A Second Grand Collection of Celebrated English Songs introduced in the Late Oratorios*; the pagination continues that of the first volume (see note 22 above). In the form of keyboard transcriptions with separate instrumental parts they had appeared earlier as nos. 381–5 in Walsh's general collection *Handel's Songs Selected from his Oratorios*, Vol. V (November 1759). The only *Solomon* addition to appear in HG is 'Wise, great and good', which is included in the appendix to *Saul*.

Dean's detailed account of the revisions[33] includes a descriptive list of the additions, only a summary review, with a little fresh information, is necessary here. There is no doubt that Smith played a major part in creating the 1759 version of

Example 7. *Judas Maccabaeus* (1758): 'Great in wisdom, great in glory'

33. Dean, *Handel's Dramatic Oratorios and Masques*, pp. 527–8.

Ex. 7 (contd)

Solomon. It was he who annotated the original conducting score of 1749 so that it could be recopied in its new form by his father for the 1759 performances.[34] He was also concerned in adapting the texts of two airs which were straight parodies of airs in earlier works. 'Wise, great and good' was originally 'Wise, valiant, good', an air written for *Saul* in 1738 but discarded before first performance; Smith entered the new *Solomon* text in the *Saul* autograph.[35] 'When the sun gives brightest day', apparently intended in 1759 as a replacement of 'When the sun o'er yonder hills', is also a parody, based on 'Clouds o'ertake the brightest day' in *Susanna*.[36] Once again it was Smith who fitted the new words to the music, this

34. Clausen, *Händels Direktionspartituren*, p. 231. The 1749 and 1759 conducting scores of *Solomon* are respectively the MSS M c/268 and M c/268a in the Staats- und Universitäts-bibliothek, Hamburg.
35. In the appendix to the HG score of *Saul*, Chrysander follows the old English editions of *Saul* in printing the air in its *Solomon* form, but adds the original *Saul* words above the stave. In the Kritischer Bericht to the edition of *Saul* in the Hallische Händel-Ausgabe (Ser I, vol. 13), pp. 137–41, the music of the air is shown in its original *Saul* form but inexplicably with the *Solomon* words, the correct words being relegated to the commentary on p. 88. The editor notes the presence of both texts in the autograph but does not point out that one of them is not in Handel's hand.
36. As 'When the sun gives brightest day' does not appear in the 1759 *Solomon* wordbook but only in later undated editions, Dean (*op. cit.*, p. 527 n. 2) assigns it to a post-1760 revival. Clausen (*op. cit.*, p. 232 n. 4) asserts, however, that it was copied as an integral part of the 1759 conducting score, so its omission from the wordbook is probably a mistake.

time in the *Susanna* conducting score, adding the direction 'to be plac'd into Solomon'.[37]

The remaining *Solomon* additions follow the pattern of using Handelian material in un-Handelian ways, but derive from a wider range of sources than do the 1758 additions; there is only one borrowing from Handel's Italian period. In many ways the oddest addition is the new setting of 'How green our fertile pastures look', which seems not to use any earlier material but is rather a feeble paraphrase of the original setting. Dean relates the music of the air and chorus 'Love from such a parent sprung' to a subsidiary theme in another *Solomon* air ('Indulge thy faith and wedded truth', sung in 1759 as 'To view the wonders of thy throne'), but the resemblance is slight and some other unrecognized model may have been called upon; as in the case of the 1757 *Esther* airs there is a suggestion of Handel's lighter operatic style.[38] 'Sad, solemn sounds' is based on a *siciliana* theme used by Handel in three discarded airs[39] before ending up in the Concerto Grosso Op. 6 No. 8; none of these treatments, however, includes the peculiar shift to the mediant minor, in a minor key, that occurs in the *Solomon* version (Ex. 8). This air and 'Thy music is divine, O King' mark a return to the harmonic quirkiness noticed in earlier additional airs. The opening of 'Thy music' has a remarkable joint parentage from an early cantata and an air in *Radamisto*, as shown by the comparison in Ex. 9.[40] In *Radamisto* the twist to the minor is properly developed within the air, whereas in the *Solomon* air it has no function beyond the initial effect of surprise. The second section of the air, an arioso Largo in Eb, should be regarded as a separate number, since it is designed to lead directly into the following air ('Pious King') in C minor. The material is unrelated to the first part of the air and seems to be original, though not very striking.

Although all the vocal additions to Handel's late revivals of his oratorios have now been discussed, this essay would not be complete without some consideration of that species of instrumental music which played an important part in the oratorio concerts from 1735 onwards: the organ concerto. Burney says that even after Handel's sight had failed, 'he continued to play concertos and voluntaries between the parts of his Oratorios to the last, with the same vigour of thought and touch, for which he was ever so justly renowned'.[41] At first, Burney continues,

37. A facsimile of the first page of this air in the *Susanna* conducting score, showing Smith's annotations, is printed in Larsen, *Handel's 'Messiah'*, p. 312.
38. Three airs in *Tolomeo* (1728) – 'Respira almen', 'Il mio core' and 'Senza il suo bene' – are based on similar thematic material, though none is a direct model for the *Solomon* air.
39. 'Love from such a parent sprung' and the first setting of 'Capricious man', composed for *Saul*, and 'Se d'amore amanti siete', composed for *Imeneo*. The *Imeneo* air (autograph in Fitzwilliam MS Mus.258, pp. 29–32) is unpublished. 'Love from such a parent sprung' is not in HG but is printed as an appendix to the old English editions of *Saul*, and in the Kritischer Bericht of the HHA edition (pp. 158–61). The C minor setting of 'Capricious man' is printed only in the HHA Kritischer Bericht (pp. 149–53), regrettably in an erroneous form: it is a *dal segno* air, with the reprise beginning at the first entry of the voice, not a full da capo air as shown in HHA.
40. The *Radamisto* fragment is transposed down a tone for the purposes of the comparison.
41. 'Sketch of the Life of Handel', pp. 29–30.

Example 8. *Solomon* (1759): 'Sad, solemn sounds'

he played several of his *old* organ concertos, which must have been previously impressed on his memory by practice. At last, however, he rather chose to trust to his inventive powers, than those or reminiscence: for giving the band only the skeleton, or ritornels of each movement, he played all the solo parts extempore, while the other instruments left him, *ad libitum*; waiting for the signal of a shake, before they played such fragments of symphony as they found in their books.

An arrangement of one of the organ concertos conforming exactly to Burney's description survives – in the hand of Smith.[42] The first movement is made up of four tutti sections from the first movement of the Concerto Op. 7 No. 3 in B flat, linked by 'ad libitum' directions. Then comes the instruction 'Adagio ad libitum', signifying an improvised second movement, and finally the 'Spiritoso' movement of Op. 7 No. 3, again reduced to four tutti sections with intervening gaps for improvisation.

Another way of getting over Handel's handicap would have been to use purely orchestral movements in the organ concertos, and there is a hint of this in the posthumously published Op. 7 set. As published, the fifth concerto, in G minor,

42. Fitzwilliam MS Mus.265, pp. 83–9.

Example 9
   (a) *Solomon* (1759): 'Thy music is divine, O King'
   (b) Cantata, *Tu fedel? tu costante* (1707): 'Se non ti piace'
   (c) *Radamisto* (1720): 'Ferite, uccidete'

ends with a gavotte without a concertante organ part, though this movement is not in the autograph and Handel clearly intended the previous movement, a minuet, to be the last. The only known manuscript source for the gavotte[43] is in Smith's hand and, as with certain of the vocal items mentioned earlier, it contains

43. Fitzwilliam MS Mus.265, pp. 97–102, headed 'This after the Menuet'.

amendments suggestive of a composition autograph. It is of course modelled on the gavotte finale of the earlier G minor Organ Concerto, Op. 4 No. 3, but differs considerably from it. Use of the wind group alone for the opening statement of the theme is untypical of the organ concertos, though one may feel it to be in conformity with the prominent wind writing of some of the additional oratorio airs.

What emerges from this survey of the music added to Handel's oratorio concerts from 1753 onwards is that when the additions are not simply copied from other works they often display un-Handelian features conforming to a fairly consistent pattern. Da capo or *dal segno* forms tend to be avoided in favour of through-composed structures, sometimes awkwardly balanced with a shortened, not to say perfunctory, reprise. Material from the early Italian works is prominently used, but with the original freshness dulled by thickened orchestration and conventional melodic shaping. On the other hand, material harmonically unadventurous at its first appearance may be agitated by surprising tonal shifts; where these occur, they produce little of the *frisson* of the harmonic daring in Handel's earlier and unquestionably authentic work. Wind instruments feature in a manner more typical of the Rococo than the Baroque; the horns, in particular, tend to 'fill in' instead of ringing out heroically in the way Handel usually favoured. There are exceptions to these generalizations – notably the *Esther* additions of 1757 – but in broad terms they are not unfair.

The affinities between the un-Handelian features found in the late oratorio additions suggest they are the product of a single musical mind, that of a composer a generation younger than Handel. The evidence of the manuscripts is consistent with this hypothesis and identifies the composer as Smith. With the exception of the fair copies by the elder Smith inserted into the conducting scores, manuscript scores of the additions or annotations connected with them are always in the younger Smith's hand. To conclude that Smith 'composed' many of the late additions would obviously stretch the evidence too far: we do not know how closely Smith worked with Handel, or how much was genuinely 'dictated' either verbally or by illustration at the harpsichord. But there is enough to indicate that Smith's role was likely to have been more creative than has hitherto been recognized.

Finally one must note the genuine musical fascination of the late additions, quite apart from the question of their authorship or the possibility that they may preserve some early Handel movements otherwise lost. Many clearly represent attempts to mould out-of-date music according to the manners of a new era, epitomizing a key moment of transition in musical history. As such, they deserve the full representation in editions of Handel's works that has so far been denied them; they will repay further study; and they should be allowed a hearing from time to time, both independently and in the contexts for which they were designed.

Handel's harpsichord music: a checklist

Terence Best

Introduction

Most of Handel's important compositions for the harpsichord were printed in his lifetime by the London publishers Cluer and Walsh, but a significant number remained unpublished and have survived only in manuscript. A few of these found their way into the editions of Arnold (*c.* 1793) and Chrysander (1859 and 1894), which reprinted the text of the early editions with little attempt at correcting their mistakes and omissions, and which despite their additional material were far from complete. Two twentieth-century editions printed some of the unpublished works – the two volumes of *Aylesford Pieces*, so called from the name of the manuscript collection in which they were found,[1] and a volume of three early suites in manuscripts in Berlin,[2] but still the list was incomplete, and there was no comprehensive survey of the corpus.

The research undertaken for the preparation of the new edition of the keyboard works, now published in four volumes of the Hallische Händel-Ausgabe, has brought to light much new information and a few compositions previously unknown. We can for the first time put into perspective Handel's activity as a composer for the harpsichord, make some attempt at dating the music, and in most cases establish a correct text. The chronology, in particular, has never been properly examined, so that early and later works have been jumbled together, and performers have never known whether they were playing an immature piece from Handel's boyhood or a work of his maturity.

The boy Handel received his early training from the organist Zachow in Halle, so he must have studied the keyboard music of seventeenth-century German composers such as Froberger, Buxtehude, Pachelbel and Kuhnau, and their influence is detectable in several works which must be among his earliest surviv-

---

1. Schott (London [1928]), ed. W. Barclay Squire and J. Fuller-Maitland.
2. Bärenreiter (Kassel 1930), ed. Walther Danckert.

ing compositions. We have no autographs from this youthful period – the earliest surviving autograph of a Handel keyboard piece dates from his Italian years – but some of these early compositions exist in copies made by contemporary scribes, whose attributions seem accurate, since certain clearly defined stylistic features are already present. We have no means of dating these works, and 'early eighteenth-century' is the nearest we can get at present to dating the manuscripts that contain them, so we have to rely almost entirely on stylistic criteria; the only historical evidence we have is a remark which Handel is reported to have made to one J. W. Lustig, who knew him in London in the 1730s, that four pieces published by Witvogel in 1732 were 'written in his early youth'.[3]

We know that Handel went to Hamburg in 1703, and remained there until about 1706, and that while he was there he earned his living partly by giving harpsichord lessons. It is very likely that he wrote music for his pupils, as was the custom, and stylistic evidence suggests that an important part of his extant keyboard music was written at this time. The music survives of only one work which we can certainly date to the Hamburg period, the opera *Almira*, which was first performed in January 1705. In this opera there is extensive use of a distinctive cadence figure which is rare in later works. It occurs in both duple and triple time (the 3/4 version is Ex. 1): the cadence, which I call '*Almira* 1', occurs fifty-three times in this opera, while in the next group of dateable works, those of the Italian period beginning in 1707, it appears hardly at all: in *Dixit Dominus* (1707) two occurrences; in *Rodrigo* (1707) eleven occurrences; in *Agrippina* (1709) none; and it is very rare in later works. It is clearly typical of the *Almira* period, and we find it widely used in some of the keyboard works, in particular several suites which were later published in the *Second Set* of 1733.

Example 1

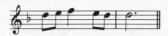

A second cadence figure characteristic of *Almira* ('*Almira* 2') takes two forms: full close (Ex. 2), and half close (Ex. 3). This is less certain as a guide to dating, since it occurs only eighteen times in this opera, compared with two in *Agrippina* and five in *Rinaldo* (1711); but it disappears by 1718, and its appearance still suggests a comparatively early date.

Example 2   Example 3

---

3. In F. W. Marpurg, *Kritische Briefe über die Tonkunst* (Berlin 1763), vol. 2, p. 467.

A third feature of the Hamburg period appears to be what has often been thought of as the typical Handel sarabande, in 3/2 time, with a rhythm of

Everyone will think of the famous 'Lascia ch'io pianga' in *Rinaldo*: yet this most perfect example of the type is in fact the last in Handel's work, and 'Lascia ch'io pianga' is in any case a revision of 'Lascia la spina' in *Il Trionfo del Tempo* of 1707, which is itself a reworking of an instrumental sarabande in *Almira*; and there is another very similar one in the same opera. There are in all only eight such sarabandes in Handel, if we count 'Lascia ch'io pianga' and its earlier versions as one piece: two are in *Almira*, and one is in some instrumental music now shown to belong to the lost Hamburg opera *Florindo*;[4] while five are in keyboard works. Of these, one is in a Partita in G which has every sign of belonging to a very early period, while the remaining four are in suites which have examples of the cadences '*Almira* 1' and '*Almira* 2'. The Suite in G minor which was printed in the 1733 collection is a good example of the characteristics which seem to me to indicate the Hamburg period – the Allemande is followed by a Courante which is largely based on the same musical material, in the manner of some seventeenth-century Germany composers, but with the bizarre peculiarity that the second halves of the two movements match more exactly than the first halves; the Courante has several '*Almira* 1' cadences. Then comes a 3/2 Sarabande (omitted from the 1733 edition because it had been borrowed meanwhile for the seventh suite of the 1720 set), and finally a Gigue of enormous length, which exists in manuscript in two shorter and presumably earlier versions. He we find a particularly significant clue: in the two early versions the opening idea is Ex. 4, but in the

Example 4

final version Handel improved it by reducing the quaver movement as in Ex. 5. In

Example 5

Almira, Act I scene 4, is an aria, 'Du irrst dich, mein Licht', which begins as in Ex. 6. The conclusion is obvious: the two early versions of the Gigue were probably written before *Almira*.

Example 6

4. I am grateful to Dr Bernd Baselt of Halle for information on this point.

It is on these criteria that my dating of works to the Hamburg period is based; the few works which I believe to be even earlier, from his years in Halle, are reckoned so because their style seems less mature, but it is difficult to separate the two groups, and they are all listed simply 'before 1706'. In the whole group of pieces which I have assigned to the period before 1706 there are many similarities of theme and figuration, too numerous to be listed here, which corroborate the idea that they belong to the same period. Anyone who studies them carefully will easily detect these features.

We do not know if Handel composed much keyboard music in the next stage of his life, the Italian period from 1706–7 to 1710. One piece certainly belongs to this time, the Allemande in A, the earliest surviving autograph; the dating is given by the paper and the writing. Another piece is probably contemporary, the Sonata in G for a two-manual harpsichord, which derives from the Organ Sonata in *Il Trionfo del Tempo* and has some figuration very typical of the early part of the Italian period; it later provided material for the aria 'Vo' far guerra' in *Rinaldo*. There is no evidence of any other keyboard composition at this time, and it is probably to the period 1710–20, the years of his brief stay in Hanover and his first years in England, that almost all the rest of the keyboard music belongs. We have many autographs from this period, and dating is possible within certain limits by a study of Handel's handwriting and the characteristics of the paper – the watermarks and the dimensions of the rastra used to rule the staves. The first dated evidence now appears, a manuscript anthology of a large proportion of his keyboard music, which is written partly by John Christopher Smith the elder, who became his copyist about 1716–17. The manuscript (cited below as MS B), which was originally owned by Elizabeth Legh of Adlington Hall in Cheshire, now forms part of the collection of the Earl of Malmesbury. The title-page reads:

Pieces for the HARPSICORD
compos'd by
Sign^r G. F. HANDEL
1718

and Elizabeth Legh has written on the flyleaf 'Elizabeth Legh her book 1717'. Another manuscript (cited below as MS A), written wholly by Smith, which we can date a little earlier on the evidence of his musical handwriting,[5] is in the Ripin Collection of the Boston Museum of Fine Arts. It is clear from these manuscripts that the bulk of Handel's harpsichord music was composed by 1717–18; a third manuscript, whose contents are closely related in text and disposition to those of the Legh Manuscript, was written by Smith about 1721 (New York Public Library), MS Mus. Res. Drexel 5856 – cited below as MS C). These manuscripts must have been prepared for patrons who were friends of the composer, for as yet none of the works had been published. In 1719 Handel went abroad, to recruit singers for the newly founded Royal Academy of Music, and it was possibly during his

5. See Hans Dieter Clausen, *Händels Direktionspartituren* (Hamburg 1972).

absence that a pirated edition of a selection of the keyboard works was issued. The culprit was unquestionably John Walsh, whose engraving style is unmistakable; the edition, of sixty-eight pages, has a title-page as follows:

PIECES à un & Deux Clavecins COMPOSEES par Mr HENDEL
A AMSTERDAM Chez Jeanne Roger   No. 490

The English origin of the edition is confirmed by the titles of some of the pieces: 'Corrant', 'Jigg', 'Sonata for a Harpsicord with Double Keys'; Walsh must have had some business arrangement with the Amsterdam firm founded by Estienne Roger in 1696. Most of the pieces occur in the three manuscripts already mentioned, in very similar texts and groupings, so that they and the 'Roger' edition taken together give a clear picture of Handel's harpsichord music as it was about the year 1719.

On his return to London at the end of the year, Handel must have been annoyed to find that his music had been pirated, and he took out a Royal Privilege to protect himself: this was issued in June 1720, and he then set about producing an authoritative edition of his own. He took sixteen of the pieces which had been published in the 'Roger' (significantly revising some of them), composed a few new ones, and added some other pieces already written, including four fugues. The edition was published by J. Cluer on 14 November 1720, with the following dedication, which may contain a reference to the 'Roger' edition:

> I have been obliged to publish some of the following lessons because surrepticious and incorrect copies of them had got abroad. I have added several new ones to make the Work more usefull which if it meets with a favourable reception: I will still proceed to publish more reckoning it my duty with my small talent to serve a Nation from which I have receiv'd so Generous a protection.
>
> G. F. Handel[6]

This *First Set* of suites contains Handel's finest and maturest work for the instrument, and after its publication he virtually abandoned keyboard composition. However, he did compose an important new Suite in D minor some time before 1726 (the approximate date of its earliest copy, in MS E – the autograph is lost), three small pieces in 1726–33, and two charming little suites for George II's daughter Princess Louisa about 1739 – but that is all, except for what is possibly a keyboard arrangement of a sonata for a musical clock, written about 1750.

The promised second volume of suites appeared in 1733, by which time Walsh was Handel's sole publisher. An earlier issue of the same pieces, arranged in a different order, had appeared about 1727; this was probably another piracy by Walsh, since the imprint is blocked out in surviving copies, and it is unlikely to have had Handel's authority. Some copies of this issue were printed in about 1730, with a few corrections to the music text, and with the Walsh imprint no longer blocked out (copy in the Rowe Library, King's College, Cambridge).

6. F. Lesure, in *Bibliographie des Éditions musicales publiées par Etienne Roger et Michel Charles le Cène* (Paris 1969), gives 1721 for a Roger plate no. of 490. If this is correct, the 'Roger' postdates the Cluer, but Handel may have known of its impending publication.

Whether these changes indicate some authorization by the composer is difficult to say; certainly the 1733 edition was printed from the same plates, without further alteration to the text. The major rearrangement in the order of the pieces in 1733 may have been decided by Handel himself, but no attempt was made to correct the music in detail, and the edition therefore has little textual authority compared with the manuscript sources. Apart from the new D minor Suite, an early Chaconne with sixty-two variations, and an early Suite in G, the whole contents of this volume are pieces from the 'Roger' edition which Handel had not reprinted in 1720 – that is, mostly the earlier ones, some dating from the Hamburg period. The only 'Roger' pieces left out in 1733 are two short preludes and the Sonata for two-manual harpsichord. So it is clear that much of the *Second Set* of 1733 consists of music written as much as thirty years earlier, and this explains why a lot of it is less mature than the *First Set* of 1720.

It was at about this time that two other sets of Handel keyboard pieces were published: in 1732 Witvogel of Amsterdam, who had issued the Chaconne with sixty-two variations the previous year, printed four more pieces (the music referred to by Lustig as 'written in his early youth'), and these were reprinted by Walsh in 1734 in *The Lady's Banquet*, Fifth Book; and in 1735 Walsh issued *Six Fugues or Voluntarys for the Organ or Harpsichord*, which had been written around 1717. Apart from French and Dutch reprints of the existing volumes, no more genuine harpsichord music by Handel was published in his lifetime; nor was there ever any 'Third Collection', as Chrysander misleadingly implies in the preface to his edition.

The checklist gives the keyboard works in the following sequence:
1 *Suites de Pièces pour le Clavecin* (*First Set*) published 'for the Author' by J. Cluer, 1720.
2 *Suites de Pièces pour le Clavecin*, Second Volume (*Second Set*) published by J. Walsh, 1733. There are a few copies extant of the withdrawn issue, c. 1727.[7]
3 *Six Fugues or Voluntarys for the Organ or Harpsicord*, published by J. Walsh, 1735.
4 The remainder, arranged as far as is possible in chronological order.

Manuscripts:

1 Autographs: the location of autographs is shown thus:
   i A shelf-mark of the type '20g14' indicates a manuscript volume in the Royal Music collection in the British Library, e.g. (in full) R.M. 20.g.14.
   ii The type '263' indicates a volume in the Fitzwilliam Museum, Cambridge, e.g. MS Mus. 263 (formerly known by the shelf-mark '30.H.13').
2 Copies: contemporary manuscript copies are given sigla, as follows:
   A Boston Museum of Fine Arts, Edwin M. Ripin Collection of Musical Instruments and Library (no shelf-mark). Copied by Smith, c. 1717. Second part after 1730.

7. To those listed in W. C. Smith and Charles Humphries, *Handel: A Descriptive Catalogue of the Early Editions*, 2nd edn (London 1970) add a copy in the Rowe Music Library, King's College, Cambridge, and one in the British Library, e.438.o.

B MS in the collection of the Earl of Malmesbury, originally owned by Elizabeth Legh. Copied partly by Smith, dated 1717–18.

C MS in the New York Public Library, Drexel Mus. Res. 5856. Copied by Smith, *c.* 1721.

D MS in the collection of Mr Gerald Coke, formerly owned by Charles Wesley. Copied by Smith, *c.* 1721.

E MS volume mostly of overtures, Malmesbury collection. Copied by Smith and others, *c.* 1722–7.

F MSS originally in the Aylesford Collection, owned by Charles Jennens, Handel's friend and librettist.

   F1 R.M. 18.b.4. Various copyists, *c.* 1732.

   F2 R.M. 18.b.8. Various copyists, *c.* 1718–32. (For the Handel copyists, see J. P. Larsen, *Handel's 'Messiah', Origins – Composition – Sources* (1957), ch. 4.)

   F3 R.M. 19.a.3. Copied by S2, *c.* 1732.

   F4 R.M. 19.a.4. Copied by S2, *c.* 1732.

   F5 Manchester Public Library, 130 Hd4, vol. 268. Copied by S1 and S2, *c.* 1740.

G British Library, Add. 31577. Copyist unknown, *c.* 1723.

H Coke Collection. MS mostly in the hand of J. C. Smith junior, *c.* 1727. Belonged to Lady Rivers, stepdaughter of Smith junior.

J 'IIX Fuge's For an Organ or Harpsichord Compos'd by George Fred^k Handel Esqr', Malmesbury collection. Copied by Smith junior, *c.* 1727.

K MSS in the Staatsbibliothek, Berlin (West), Preussischer Kulturbesitz. All early 18th century unless otherwise indicated.

K1 9161 (H.2).		K8 9181. 19th century.
K2 9162/3.		K9 9163.
K3 9164/1.		K10 9164/4.
K4 9164/3.		K11 9164/6.
K5 9168.		
K6 9182. 19th century.		
K7 9171. *c.* 1717.		

L Four Italian MSS, copies of Capriccio in G.

   L1 Fitzwilliam MS Mus. 265.

   L2 British Library, Add. 14248. Copied 1732.

   L3 Genova, Conservatorio A.7b.63. Cass.

   L4 Napoli, Conservatorio MS 71.

M Darmstadt, Hessische Landes- und Hochschulbibliothek, MS 1231. After 1719.

N Fitzwilliam MS Mus. 161.

O Royal College of Music, MS 2097. Copied by J. Stafford Smith, *c.* 1780.

P Coke Collection, MS formerly owned by W. Walond of Chichester. Dated 1778, but some of it is by Smith, *c.* 1720–30.

Q Zürich, Zentralbibliothek, Car xv 249. Copied by Hermann Nägeli, early 19th century.

R British Library, Add. 31573. Copied by M. Rophino Lacy, *c.* 1858. Includes a
   copy of part of the Lennard MS; see Chrysander vol. 48.
S Vienna, Minoritenkonvent, MS xiv, 743.
T British Library, R.M. 19.d.11. Copied by S13, *c.* 1750–60.
U Oxford, Bodleian Library, Tenbury MS 1131, *c.* 1725.

Two early printed editions other than the Cluer and Walsh editions already
listed:

V *A General Collection of MINUETS made for the BALLS at COURT, etc.* Walsh,
   1729.
W Five separate issues by G. F. Witvogel, Amsterdam.
   W1 The Chaconne with sixty-two variations, with a Prelude, *Opera Primo,*
      c. 1731.
   W2, 3, 4, 5   Sonata, Capriccio, Preludio et Allegro, Fantaisie, *Opera Seconda,*
      Terza, Quarta, Quinta, c. 1732.

The principal later editions

About 1793, Arnold reprinted for his 'complete' edition the two sets of suites and
the six fugues, together with what he called *A Third Set of Lessons for the Harpsichord,*
a miscellaneous collection of pieces which he acquired from manuscript sources
and the Witvogel and other prints (one by Goodison, 1787).

   In 1859 Chrysander published in volume 2 of his Händel-Gesellschaft edition
(known as HG) four collections of keyboard music: (1) the 1720 set, (2) the 1733
set, (3) Arnold's 'Third Set' with some additions, (4) the six fugues. In volume 48
(1894), he added some early works from manuscript and printed sources, including an important early German manuscript, once in the Barrett Lennard Collection but now lost, which Chrysander dated *c.* 1710, and whose contents included
nos. IV, VI and VII from the 1733 set, thus confirming their early date. Manuscript
R contains a copy of part of the Lennard Manuscript.

   The Hallische Händel- Ausgabe published the keyboard music in four volumes,
Ser. iv, vols. 1, 5, 6 and 17 – cited below as 'I' to 'IV' respectively.[8]

Symbols: Pieces in the 1720 and 1733 collections which had previously appeared in
the edition of *Pièces à un & Deux Clavecins*, issued *c.* 1719 with the Roger imprint,
are marked *. Those which appeared in the Roger print and were revised by
Handel for the 1720 edition are marked †. It is to be understood that the manuscript copies of the latter group of pieces always show the original form, as printed
in Roger.

'fr' indicates a fragmentary autograph.

Dates: The attribution of some works to the early period is made on stylistic
criteria; these are all given as 'pre 1706'. Those whose style suggests a later date,
and which appear in MS B, are given as 'pre 1718'. More precise indications, such
as '1713–17' or '*c.* 1717', are arrived at by a study of the watermarks, rastralogical
characteristics and handwriting in the autographs, or on historical evidence.

8. References in the form 'IV:2' etc. mean HHA Ser. iv, vol. 17, the second item.

1. First Set of Suites, 1720. HG 2, HHA I[9]

No.	Key	Movts	Autog.	MS copies	Date of comp.	Comments
I	A	Prelude	—	A B	pre 1718	
		Allemande	—	A B	pre 1718	
		Courante	—	A B	pre 1718	
		Gigue	—	A B	pre 1718	
II	F	Adagio†	—	A B	pre 1718	
		Allegro*	20g14	A B	c. 1717	
		Adagio*	—	A B	pre 1718	
		Allegro (Fugue)*	263	A B J	c. 1717	Autog. has only last 9 bars, and an extra Allegro which is in Roger and MSS; see 1733 IX, below.
III	d	Prelude	—	A F2 (sketch)	1720	Rev. of preludes in HHA IV:12 and Roger. Copy in A c. 1730.
		Allegro (Fugue)	20g14	F2 J	c. 1717	
		Allemande	263	—	1720	
		Courante	20g13	—	1720	
		Air & 5 var.	—	A B C F5 G P	pre 1718	Rev. of movt in HHA IV:12. MS version lacks vars. 2 & 3.
		Presto	—	A (early v.) H	c. 1720	Rev. of an earlier piece, which has versions in Ov. *Pastor Fido*, Conc. Grosso Op. 3 No. 6, Organ Conc. Op. 7 No. 4.
IV	e	Allegro (Fugue)	20g13 (fr)	F2 J K7	c. 1717	K7 has 'Fuga di Sr Hendel 1717'.
		Allemande†	263	A B C	pre 1718	Autog. of Allemande and last 8 bars of Sarabande have rev. text of 1720.
		Courante*	—	A B C	pre 1718	
		Sarabande†	263 (fr)	A B C	pre 1718	
		Gigue†	—	A B C	pre 1718	
V	E	Prelude	—	—	1720	See HHA IV:28 for early version.
		Allemande	—	A B (early v.) C E	pre 1718 rev. c. 1720	
		Courante	—	A B (early v.) C E	pre 1718 rev. c. 1720	
		Air & 5 var.	—	B (early v.)	pre 1718 rev. c. 1720	Two early versions in G in MSS A B C F5 G P.
VI	f♯	Prelude	—	—	1720	See HHA III:15 for early version.
		Largo	20g14	A B C G	c. 1717	
		Allegro (Fugue)	—	A B C G J	pre 1718	
		Gigue	20g14	A B C G	c. 1717	Autog. is of early version. All MS copies have later text.
VII	g	Ouverture†	—	C E G	pre 1706?	A version of ov. to cantata 'Cor Fedele', 1797. Hamburg period?
		Andante*	20g14	A B C G H	c. 1717	In A minor in Roger, preceded by prelude; see HHA III:21. Prelude also in MSS.
		Allegro*	—	A B C G H	pre 1718	

9. As noted above, in HHA references 'I' to 'IV' are HHA Ser. IV, vols. 1, 5, 6 and 17 respectively. Thus 'IV:12' is the twelfth item in 'IV', etc.

No.	Key	Movts	Autog.	MS copies	Date of comp.	Comments
		Sarabande†	—	B C K5 K9 K10	pre 1706	Originally part of suite pub. as 1733 VI (Roger and MSS).
		Gigue	—	C E G H	pre 1706	C E G have early version. Rev. for 1720?
		Passacaille†	—	B C F5 G H	pre 1706?	Similar to early chaconnes. Suite compiled from several sources: (a) Overture, two minuets and Gigue; (b) the 3-movt suite in Roger; (c) Sarabande and Passacaille.
VIII	f	Prelude	20g14	—	1720	
		Allegro (Fugue)	20g14	F2 J	c. 1717	
		Allemande†	—	B C G	pre 1718	
		Courante*	—	B C G	pre 1718	
		Gigue*	—	B C G	pre 1718	

2. Second Set of Suites, 1733. HG 2, HHA II

No.	Key	Movts	Autog.	MS copies	Date of comp.	Comments
I	Bb	Prelude*	Coke coll. (early v.)	A B C F5 G	1713–17	
		Sonata*	Coke coll. (fr)	A B C F3 G	1713–17	Based on orch. Sinfonia, c. 1707.
		Air & 5 var.*	—	A B C F3 G P	pre 1718	A B C P have early version. B C G P associate these 3 movts with the suite no. VII.
—	g	Minuet*	—	C E F2 F3 G P		Usually included with the above, but no obvious connection (items are unnumbered in 1733). Appears in C and E as part of a suite consisting of Overture 1720 VII, two minuets, and Gigue 1720 VII.
II	G	Chaconne*	—	K1	pre 1706	1st version.
			—	H	pre 1706	2nd version.
			—	—	?	3rd version, in Roger edition.
			—	—	?	4th version, in 1733 edition.
			—	A B C F3 G P	pre 1718	5th version; 1733 text is probably corrupt version and is inferior to 5th version. Complete edn, ed. Best, O.U.P. 1979.
III	d	Allemande	18c1	A E F3	1721–6	Autog. is early version in b (HHA II:Anhang); final version based on this and HHA IV:12. Copy in A is c. 1730. E is earliest copy, c. 1726.
		Allegro	—	A E F3	1721–6	
		Air	—	A E F3	1721–6	Based on movts in HHA IV:12.
		Gigue	—	A E F3	1721–6	
		Minuet & 3 var.	—	A E F3	1721–6	
IV	d	Allemande*	—	B C F5 G K10 P	pre 1706	MSS and Roger have a Prelude which was rev. and used for 1720 III. B C F5 G have at end a Sonatina, HHA IV:13.
		Courante*	—	B C F5 G K10 P	pre 1706	

No.	Key	Movts	Autog.	MS copies	Date of comp.	Comments
		Sarabande & 2 var.*	—	B C F5 G K10 P	pre 1706	
		Gigue*	—	B C F5 G K10 P	pre 1706	
V	e	Allemande*	—	A B C F3 P	pre 1718	
		Sarabande*	—	A B C F3 P	pre 1718	
		Gigue*	—	A B C F3 P	pre 1718	A B C have variant (HHA II:Anhang); F3 has both versions.
VI	g	Allemande*	—	B C F3 K5 K9 K10	pre 1706	B C K5 K9 K10 Roger have a Sarabande which was rev. and included in 1720 VII. F3 follows Courante with the Minuet in 1733 I and puts Gigue separately.
		Courante*	—	B C F3 K5 K9 K10	pre 1706	
		Gigue	—	D E F3 (early v. 1)	pre 1706	Early version 1 associated with Ov. *Agrippina* in D E. Early versions in HHA II:Anhang, not in 1733.
		Gigue	—	F1 (early v. 2)	pre 1706	
		Gigue*	—	B C F3 K5 K9 K10 (last v.)	pre 1706	
VII	Bb	Allemande	—	F4 G K5 HG48 (1st v.)	pre 1706	Early version in HHA II:Anhang, not in 1733.
		Allemande*	—	A B C F5 H P (2nd v.)	pre 1718	
		Courante*	—	F4 G K5	pre 1706	
		Sarabande	—	F4 G K5 HG48 (1st v.)	pre 1706	Early version in HHA II:Anhang, not in 1733.
		Sarabande*	—	A B C F5 P (2nd v.)	pre 1718	
		Gigue*	—	A F4 G P	pre 1706	B C G P associate this suite with 1733 I: B C P in the order Prelude/Allemande/Sarabande/Sonata/Air. G has Prelude/Sonata/Air+Suite in first version.
VIII	G	Allemande	—	C	pre 1706	
		Allegro	—	—	pre 1706	
		Courante	—	—	pre 1706	
		Aria	—	—	pre 1706	
		Minuet	—	—	pre 1706	
		Gavotte & Double	—	—	pre 1706	
		Gigue	—	—	pre 1706	
IX	G	Preludio*	20g14 (1st v. in F)	—	c. 1717	1st version printed in HG 2, 3rd coll., as 'Courante'. 2nd version originally finale of 1720 II.
			263 (2nd	A B F5	c. 1717	

| Chaconne | — | | B C F5 P | pre 1706 | W1, *c.* 1731, has a prelude consisting of 20 bars of Babell's fantasia on 'Vo' far guerra' in *Rinaldo*. W text from *c.* 1727 Walsh edn. |

The earlier issue of *c.* 1727 has the pieces in the order IX i, VIII, III, IV, V, II, VI, VII, I, IX ii.

3. Six Fugues or Voluntaries for Organ or Harpsichord, 1735. HG 2, HHA III:1.

No.	Key	Autog.	MS copies	Date of comp.	Comments
1	g	20g14	F2 F3 J	*c.* 1717	Autog. of 1, 3–6 are composition autographs; 2 is fair copy, *c.* 1717, ?composed earlier. Subject of 1 rev. for 'He smote the first born of Egypt' in *Israel in Egypt*.
2	G	20g14	F2 F3 J	pre 1717?	Scored for orch. in Conc. Grosso Op. 3 No. 3.
3	Bb	20g14	F2 F3 J	*c.* 1717	Rev. of Sinfonia in *Brockes Passion*.
4	b	20g14	F2 F3 J	*c.* 1717	
5	a	20g14	F2 F3 J	*c.* 1717	Adapted for 'They loathed to drink of the river' in *Israel in Egypt*.
6	c	20g14	F2 F3 J	*c.* 1717	

4. The remainder

I. Before 1706

Style suggests that the first five items are earlier than the rest, possibly dating from the Halle years, before 1703. There are no autographs for the period before 1706.

Title	Key	MS copies	HG	HHA	Comments
Suite	C		—	IV:1	
Praeludium		K2 M			Fugue subject also used in Italian Trio II 'Quel fior', and in the chorus 'Let old Timotheus yield the prize' in *Alexander's Feast*.
Allemande		K2			
Courante		K2			
Sarabande		K2 M			
Double		K2			
Gigue		K2 M			Rev. for HHA III:6.
Chaconne (1st v.)		K2 M			With 26 var. in K2, 27 var. in M.
Chaconne (2nd v.)		B C F3 K6 P			With 49 var. as independent piece.
Partita	G	K3	—	IV:2	Title 'Partie' in source.
Praeludio					
Allemande					
Courante					
Sarabande					
Gigue					
Minuet					
Prelude	d	B D F5	—	IV:3	
Allemande & Courante	g	S	—	Suppl.	Material re-used in HHA IV:11 and IV:12.
Prelude & Capriccio	G	K1 R A B C F3 K1 L R	48	IV:4	'Allegro' in K1 R HG; 'Toccata' in L.

Title	Key	MS copies	HG	HHA	Comments
Overture	g	F4	—	IV:5⎫	?orchestral origin, from *Nero*, *Daphne* or
Entrée	g	F4	—	IV:6⎬	*Florindo*? Opening of IV:5 re-used
Chaconne	g	F4	—	IV:7⎭	*Agrippina*, 1709.
Preludio	d	F4	—	IV:8	
Allegro	C	F4	—	IV:9	
Chaconne	F	B D F3	—	IV:10	For two-manual hpchd.
Suite	d		48	IV:11	
Overture		R			Opening re-used in Ov. *Pastor Fido*.
Allemande		K5 R			
Courante		K5 R			
Sarabande I		K5 R			
Sarabande II		R			
Chaconne		R			
Suite	d	K1 R	48	IV:12	
Prelude					Rev. for 1720 III.
Allemande					The source for several later Allemandes.
Courante					
Sarabande					
Air & 7 var.					Rev. for 1720 III.
Gigue					⎫ Rev. for 1733 III. In HG R, Gigue
Minuet					⎭ follows Minuet.
Sonatina	d	B C F5 G	48	IV:13	As finale of 1733 IV in B C F5 G R HG.
		K5 P R			
Sonata	C	K8 Q	2	III:2	Printed 1732, W2; K8 Q are early versions.
Capriccio	F	—	2	III:3	Printed 1732, W3.
Preludio &	g	—	2	III:4	Allegro called 'Sonata' and 'Sonatina' in
Allegro		F2 H			MSS. Coke coll. has additional MS on a
					single leaf. Printed 1732, W4.
Fantaisie	C	—	2	III:5	Printed 1732, W5.
Allemande	a	F2	—	IV:14	
Fugue	F	F2 J	—	IV:15	MS of first 19 bars, Durham Cathedral,
					Mus. MS E.24.
Chaconne	g	F2	—	IV:16	
Partita	c	K4	—	IV:17a	Title 'Partie' in source.
Prelude					
Allemande					
Courante					
Gavotte					
Minuet					
Suite	c	F2	—	IV:17b	
Prelude					
Allemande					Allemande is rev. of the one in 17a.
Courante					Courante is a version of Sarabande in the
					suite following.
Suite	c	B C D F5 G R	48	Suppl.	For two hpchds. Sources have part for one
Allemande					hpchd only. Ed. Dart, O.U.P. 1951, with
Courante					reconstruction of second hpchd part.
Sarabande					
Chaconne					
Prelude & Allegro	a	A (Allegro)	—	IV:18	Theme of Allegro used (in g) in Oboe Conc.
		F1			in g, Trio Sonata Op. 2 No. 5, Organ
					Conc. Op. 4 No. 3. Copy in A is c. 1730.
Partita	A	—	48	III:20	No 18-century source. Pub. Senff, Leipzig
Allemande					1864, ed. Mortier de Fontaine, and
Courante					lithograph by Fontaine, 1863. Based on
Sarabande					early MS now lost.
Gigue					

II. 1706–10

Title	Key	Autog.	MS copies	HG	HHA	Comments
Allemande	A	260	—	—	III:9	Italian paper; title 'Allemanda'.
Sonata	G	—	F1 Q	—	III:22	Printed in Roger as 'Sonata for a Harpsicord with Double Keys'. . . Used in 'Vo' far guerra' in *Rinaldo*.
Sonata	g	—	F2	—	IV:22	?violin original; theme used in Sonata *a5*, 1707; Chandos Anthem 'I will magnify thee' and derivatives (Trio Sonata Op. 5 No. 1, Oboe Conc. in Bb, pub. 1740).

III. *c.* 1710–20

Title	Key	Autog.	MS copies	HG	HHA	Comments
Sonatina	G	263	F2	—	III:13	No title in autog. F2 'Fuga'. *c.* 1720.
Sonatina	Bb	263	H	—	III:14	This and preceding possibly teaching pieces; see HHA Suppl. 'Handel's Kompositionslehre' *c.* 1720.
Air	g	—	F2	—	IV:19	Rev. for HHA III:17.
Toccata	g	—	F2	—	IV:20	
Sonatina	g	—	F2	—	IV:21	No title in source, only 'A tempo giusto'. Motif used in 'They are brought down and fall'n' in Chandos Anthem 'The Lord is my light', and Conc. Grosso Op. 6 No. 6.
Concerto	G	—		—	IV:23	Copy in A is *c.* 1730. ?orchestral. 1st movt has passages similar to 'Ritorna adesso Amor' in *Il Pastor Fido*; rev. for *Scipione* III/5. 2nd movt based on 'Disserratevi o porte d'averno' in *La Resurrezione*; rev. for Conc. Grosso Op. 3 No. 4.
Allegro			A F2 H N O			
Andante			A F2			
Air	Bb	—	F2 H	—	IV:24	Printed in V, 1729, in key of G.
Preludium	F	—	F2	—	IV:25	
Preludium	f	—	F2 G	—	IV:26	G has it as prelude to 1720 VIII; probably the original prelude.
Prelude	g	—	F1	—	IV:27	Source has it before early version 2 of the Gigue 1733 VI.
Prelude	E	—	C E	—	IV:28	Precedes Allemande and Courante of 1720 V; probably original prelude.
Air	g	—	A F2	—	IV:29	F2 'air for 2 rowed Harpsicord'. Copy in A *c.* 1730. ?upper part originally for violin.
Air	Bb	—	A F2	—	IV:30	F2 title as preceding. Copy in A after 1734. ?originally oboe duet. See Ov. *Teseo*, 2nd Allegro.
Impertinence	g	—	F2	—	IV:31	Could be earlier, ?Hamburg.
Air & 2 Doubles	F	—	F2 H	—	IV:32	?orchestral.
Allegro	d	—	A F2 H	—	IV:33	Copy in A is *c.* 1730.
Lesson	a	—	U	2	III:19	U has two copies, one in g. Printed Arnold, Third Set.
Prelude	g	—	A B C F5 G	—	III:21	Prelude to suite consisting of Andante and Allegro in 1720 VII. Printed Roger, all three pieces in a. Pre 1717.

Title	Key	Autog.	MS copies	HG	HHA	Comments
Prelude	d	263	B C F5	—	III:12.	1712–17. Autog. lacks last 2 bars.
Prelude	f♯	20g14	B C G	—	III:15	c. 1717. B C G have it as a prelude to 1720 VI. Must be original prelude.
Prelude	a	20g14	—	2	III:18	c. 1717. HG joins it with HHA III:19.
Capriccio	g	263	—	2	III:8	c. 1720. No title in autog. Pub. by Goodison, 1787, as 'Capriccio'. Repr. Arnold. Re-used in 'Alza il ciel' in *Lotario*, and 'Now strike the golden lyre again' in *Alexander's Feast*.

To this period belongs a Fugue in E which exists in a MS copy in the Royal College of Organists, pub. Novello 1974, ed. H. D. Johnstone. The subject is similar to that of the Allegro in the *Water Music* Overture, and the piece is probably genuine until the closing bars, which are obviously spurious. ?original incomplete. (To be pub. in HHA Ser. IV vol. 19, Suppl. to the instrumental music.)

IV. After 1720

Title	Key	Autog.	MS copies	HG	HHA	Comments
Allemande	b	18c2	E	—	II:Anhang	Pre 1722. Rev. for 1733 III.
Courante	b	—	E	—	IV:34	Pre 1722.
Air	A	20e5	—	—	III:16	c. 1733. Related to 'Chi ben ama' in *Aci, Galatea e Polifemo*; 'Diasi lode' in *La Resurrezione*; Cantata 'Ah crudel'; 'L'alma mia' in *Agrippina*; 'Molto voglio' in *Rinaldo*; 'Heroes, when with glory burning' in *Joshua*.
Gigue	F	263	—	—	III:11	c. 1726.
Allemande	F	263	—	—	III:10	c. 1733. Rev. for Sinfonia in *Serse* Act III.
Suite Allemande Courante Sarabande Gigue	d	261	265 (two copies) F5 T	2	III:6	c. 1739. F5 has in Jennens's hand for this and the following: 'Two Sets of Lessons for the Princess Louisa'. T has similar information. Louisa was born 1724. First printed in Arnold.
Suite Allemande Courante Sarabande Gigue	g	263 261	F5 T	2	III:7	c. 1739. See preceding. Autog. in 263 is draft, 261 fair copy. First printed by Thompson, c. 1770, then Arnold. Allemande related to Conc. Grosso No. 8, 1st movt.
Sonata	C	261 20g13	—	2	III:17	c. 1750. Probably originally for musical clock. 261 is 1st version, 20g13 fair copy with changes, ?arrangement for hpchd.
Allegro						Based on 'Hallelujah, Amen' in F for sopr., b. c., c. 1744.
Trio – Larghetto						Rev. of HHA IV:19.
Gavotte – Non troppo presto						From *Alexander's Feast* Conc.

The Minuets

The contemporary sources contain a large number of minuets; some are arrangements of well-known orchestral pieces, such as those in the *Water Music*, and others are based on popular opera arias. Of the original ones, most are in two parts – treble and bass – and cannot be considered true keyboard music; consequently they are all to be published together in the section 'Works of unspecified instrumentation' in the Supplement-Band of HHA Ser. IV (vol. 19).

One in G minor, clearly written in keyboard style, was published in the 1733 set, no. I; four others are fully harmonized, appear in several of the manuscripts of keyboard music (B, C, E, P), and could be included among the keyboard works: three are in B♭ (nos. 88–90 in the list of contents of R.M. 18.b.8 in W. Barclay Squire's *Catalogue of the Handel MSS in the King's Music Library*), and one in G minor (no. 73). The latter is found in MSS C and E as part of a suite with the one in the same key already mentioned (see note on 1733 I).

Doubtful and spurious works

There are many eighteenth- and nineteenth-century manuscripts which contain keyboard pieces attributed to Handel, but which could not possibly be by him because of their style. In some cases we can establish the composer, and these are listed as spurious works; the others are given as doubtful.

The many pieces which have remained in manuscript are not listed here in detail: this will be done in the Kritische Berichte for the HHA volumes. The Staatsbibliothek in Berlin has most of them, including 'Fünf Capriccios von G. F. Händel' (by Froberger). Others are in the Fitzwilliam Museum, the Santini collection in Munster, and MS P, the 'Walond' MS in the Coke Collection.

The doubtful and spurious works which have appeared in print are as follows:

1. Possibly authentic:
(i) Air in c, from a manuscript copied by John Barker, *c*. 1735, British Library, Add. 31467. At the end is 'Mr Handell'. HHA IV:Anhang, no. 1

(ii) Sonatina in a, copies in MSS A and F2. In F2 it is in the hand of Smith junior, who calls it 'Sonatina del Sg^r Hendel'. HHA IV:Anhang, no. 2.

(iii) Aria in c, in MS F4. No composer's name, but all other keyboard works in the volume are by Handel. HHA IV:Anhang, no. 3.

2. Unlikely to be authentic:

(i) TWELVE Voluntaries and Fugues for the ORGAN or HARPSICHORD with Rules for Tuning by the celebrated MR. HANDEL. Book IV . . . LONDON Printed by LONGMAN and BRODERIP no. 26 Cheapside . . . [*c*. 1780]
From these works, some of which are marked with organ registrations, six

movements in fugue form have been extracted and published many times as 'Fughettas' or 'Fugues Faciles' by Handel. They are not separate compositions, as each is preceded by a voluntary, and they are not indicated as being by Handel – it is the 'Rules of Tuning' which are attributed to him, as the first inside page makes clear – 'RULES for Tuning the HARPSICHORD &c. by the celebrated Mr. HANDEL'. Contemporary manuscript copies attribute several movements in the voluntaries to John Robinson, Pepusch and Greene, and they seem to be of composite authorship.

(ii) *12 Fantasien und Vier Stücke von G. F. Händel*, ed. G. Walter, (Hug), Zürich 1942. This edition is based on a nineteenth-century manuscript, MS Q in the present checklist. The first Fantasia is the Sonata in C by Handel (HHA III:2), but the rest cannot be by him. The second of the 'Vier Stücke' is the first movement of a Sonata in A by Fortunato Kelleri (1690–1757), published in London in 1762.

(iii) Sonatina in d and Allemande in g, published in *Deutsche Klaviermusik aus dem Beginn des 18. Jahrhunderts*, ed. T. E. Werner, Hanover 1927.

(iv) Fugue in f, ed. K. Anton, Halle 1940.

(v) *G. F. Handel – Pieces for Harpsichord*, ed. Ferenc Brodsky (Editio Musica), Budapest 1964.
These are said by the editor to come from a manuscript compiled by an eighteenth-century Hungarian musician. The pieces are clearly Italian of the early and mid eighteenth century, and cannot be by Handel.

3. Spurious:

(i) Minuet in a, published in a pirated edition consisting mostly of arrangements of overtures, concertos and arias:
    Pièces Pour le CLAVECIN Composées par G. F. HANDEL Vᵉ OUVRAGE . . .
    LONDON. John What, Musical instrument Maker and Musick Printer at the
    Golden Viol et hautboy in St. Pauls church yard. A PARIS . . . Mᵈ Boivin . . . A
    LYON . . . Chez Mʳ de Brotonne . . . [*c.* 1739]
The minuet occurs in British Library Add. 31577, where it is attributed to Loeillet; comparison with Loeillet's pieces shows that this attribution is almost certainly correct.

(ii) Two preludes and fugues in C for 4 hands, published as *Zwei Fugen*, ed. H. Schüngeler, Magdeburg and Leipzig 1944. By J. Marsh, *c.* 1783.

New light on the libretto of *The Creation*

Nicholas Temperley

The English text of Haydn's *Creation* has been held up to ridicule from the early nineteenth century until quite recent times. Various attempts have been made to improve it, and it is now rarely to be heard in its original form, though the Peters vocal score still prints it essentially unaltered.

Of course, *The Creation* is far from being the only musical masterpiece with an inferior literary text. We do not, nowadays, think it right to tamper with the text of a great composer's music. Even if it is infelicitous or illogical, or changes the poet's words, its use by the composer confers an authenticity that is beyond argument.

Much of the rough treatment accorded to the English text of *The Creation* has been justified by the assumption that it was a translation or retranslation of a German original, and thus fair game for critical attack. This belief was firmly held, for example, by Donald Tovey, who based his opinion on statements by A. H. Fox Strangways.[1] He might have moderated his satire if he had thought that Haydn himself had regarded the English text as an integral part of the music. German critics have consistently treated the German text as the original one. Though acknowledging that Gottfried van Swieten based his text on an English libretto, written by one 'Lidley' according to Griesinger,[2] they have assumed that he altered it so much as to make what was virtually a new text. For example Martin Stern, in an elaborate and in many ways profound study of the *Creation* text, pointed out that joyful homage to the creation of man is characteristic of the Enlightenment, and was by 1800 out of step with prevailing Romantic pessimism;[3] but he explained this by positing the influence of earlier German

---

1. D. F. Tovey, *Essays in Musical Analysis*, vol. 4 (London 1937), p. 120.
2. G. A. Griesinger, *Biographische Notizen über Joseph Haydn*, ed. F. Grasberger (Vienna 1954), p. 37.
3. Stern, 'Haydn's "Schöpfung": Geist und Herkunft des van Swietenschen Librettos', *Haydn-Studien* i (1966), pp. 121–98, esp. pp. 143, 192.

writers,[4] ignoring the established fact that the libretto originated in England some fifty years before it was used by Haydn, and hence came by its Enlightenment philosophy quite naturally.

This misunderstanding was corrected by Edward Olleson, who, after reviewing the documentary evidence, showed by a penetrating textual analysis that the English text originally published with the score was not a mere translation, but must have incorporated much of the lost English libretto on which van Swieten had based his German version. Olleson arrived at this conclusion by showing that in many cases the English text is closer to its model in the Bible or in Milton's *Paradise Lost* than is van Swieten's German translation. His summing-up is worth quoting at length:

> The English text to the *Creation*, as we know it from the printed score, was to a considerable extent simply compiled by van Swieten from his model. It seems safe to assume that those parts of the 'Lidley' libretto which were used in Haydn's oratorio have by and large survived – not dimly visible through a translation and a re-translation, but in their original form. Van Swieten's general method of working was to leave the English of his model as it stood, and to write his German text around it. His own metaphor describes the process exactly: he 'resolved to clothe the English poem in German garb' . . . The German libretto was written in such a way that Haydn's music would fit the original English too.[5]

Additional evidence on the point can be found in a source which has been neglected by German and English scholars alike: the printed English librettos associated with the first English performances of *The Creation*, given under the direction of John Ashley and Johann Peter Salomon in the spring of 1800. This evidence, which I will now examine, shows that the English text is even closer to the original than anyone has suspected.

Salomon's part in the plan for Haydn's *Creation* is attested by two sources close to the composer himself. According to Albert Christoph Dies, 'the first suggestion for this work was made by Salomon in London . . . Salomon resolved to have Haydn write a large-scale oratorio, and for this purpose handed over to him an already old libretto in English. Haydn had doubts about his familiarity with the English; he would not undertake anything, and finally left London on 15 August 1795.'[6] Griesinger gave a very similar version of the same story. He said that Haydn was at first supposed to set the 'Lidley' text for Salomon ('Haydn sollte Lidleys Text für Salomon komponieren') but changed his mind because of his uncertain command of English, and also because the text was too long. 'In the meantime Haydn took the text with him back to Germany; he showed it to Baron van Swieten, . . . and the latter put it into its present shape. Salomon wanted to

---

4. *Ibid.*, pp. 170–5.
5. Olleson, 'The Origin and Libretto of Haydn's *Creation*', *Haydn Yearbook* No. 4 (1968), pp. 148–66, esp. p. 160.
6. A. C. Dies, *Biographische Nachrichten von Joseph Haydn*, ed. H. Seeger (Berlin [1959]), pp. 158–9; trans. Olleson, p. 151.

take Haydn to law for this . . .'[7] Van Swieten's own account, though it does not mention Salomon by name, confirms the story.[8]

After the first performance of *The Creation* at Vienna on 29 April 1798, Salomon must have been anxious to have the honour of introducing it to London audiences. But the score was not generally available until it had been published by the composer himself. Haydn solicited subscriptions in 1799, and Salomon subscribed for no fewer than twelve copies of the full score.[9] Publication was delayed until 28 February 1800;[10] Salomon did not receive his copies until 23 March.[11] He then immediately set about arranging for a performance in his oratorio series at the King's Theatre. We can imagine his feelings when, the very next day, he read in the *Morning Chronicle* that John Ashley, manager of the rival oratorio concerts at Covent Garden, was proposing to give the first London performance later that week, on Friday, 28 March. The advertisement simply said that Ashley had received the score from Vienna.[12] According to a later authentic account, it had reached him 'on Saturday, 22 March, . . . at nine o'clock in the evening, by a King's messenger from Vienna; was copied into parts by Mr. Thomas Goodwin for 120 performers; rehearsed, and performed at Covent Garden on the Friday following'.[13] As a reward for this feverish activity, Ashley secured the honour of giving the first performance of *The Creation* in Great Britain, on Friday, 28 March 1800, at Covent Garden, with Mary Second, Charles Incledon, Charles Dignum, and John Sale in the principal parts.

Meanwhile Salomon inserted a paragraph in the main newspapers as follows:

> HAYDN's Celebrated ORATORIO, the CREATION of the WORLD.
> MR. SALOMON having received from Dr. Haydn a correct Copy of his New Oratorio, called The CREATION of the WORLD, and having been favoured by him, exclusively, with particular Directions on the Style and Manner in which it must be executed, in order to produce the Effects required by the Author, begs to acquaint the Nobility and Gentry, that he intends to perform it on Monday, the 21st of April next, at the King's Theatre, Haymarket.[14]

7. Griesinger, *Biographische Notizen*, p. 37; trans. Olleson, p. 150.
8. *Allgemeine Musikalische Zeitung* I (1798–9), pp. 254–5; quoted and trans. Olleson, pp. 149–50.
9. Joseph Haydn, *Die Schoepfung, Ein Oratorium . . . The Creation, An Oratorio* (Vienna 1800), list of subscribers. See also H. C. Robbins Landon, *Haydn: The Years of 'The Creation' 1796–1800* (London 1977), p. 630.
10. Landon, p. 542. I am grateful to D. W. Krummel for comparing several issues of the first edition at the Bayerische Staatsbibliothek, Munich.
11. *The Times*, 4 April 1800; quoted Landon, p. 575.
12. *Morning Chronicle*, 24 March 1800; quoted Landon, p. 573.
13. 'For the information contained in this paragraph, I am indebted to Mr. William Goodwin, of Charles Street, Covent Garden, and son of the above.' *The Creation . . . newly arranged for the Pianoforte by John Bishop* (London [1842]), preface, signed 'John Bishop, Cheltenham, Nov. 1842'. A slightly inaccurate version of this account is given in Anthony van Hoboken, *Haydn Verzeichnis*, vol. 2 (Mainz 1971), p. 48. C. F. Pohl, *Haydn in London* (Vienna 1867, repr. New York 1970), pp. 315–16, states that Salomon had to pay £30 16s postage on his copy while Ashley paid only £2 12s 6d, and Landon, p. 572, draws attention to the difference as showing that Salomon was 'even unluckier' than his rival. But, after all, Salomon had ordered twelve copies, while Ashley, as far as we know, received only one.
14. *The Times*, 27 March 1800; quoted Landon, p. 573.

Ashley, sure of his triumph, replied by assuring the public that he possessed an equally 'correct' copy of the work, which had been published by subscription, and that his performance had shown that 'no other directions are necessary to "produce the effect required by the Author"'.[15] Salomon answered that

> he did not assert to be alone in possession of a correct score of this excellent Work, but said, what he can prove by Dr. HAYDN's Letters, that he had been favoured, exclusively, by Dr. HAYDN with particular directions on the stile and manner in which it ought to be executed, to produce the effects required by the Author.[16]

There the public exchange ended; and at last, after three performances at Covent Garden, Salomon put on the work at the King's Theatre on 21 April, with Gertrude Mara, Sophia Dussek, James Bartleman, and other well-known singers.[17] A Mr Denman sang in both Ashley's and Salomon's performances, but otherwise separate casts were used.

In accordance with custom, both managers brought out librettos for sale at the theatres. Ashley's, published by himself,[18] was deposited at Stationers' Hall on 27 March, the day before his first performance; Salomon's,[19] on 16 April.[20] At about the same period, separate editions in full score of three of the most popular numbers from the work were hurriedly brought out, and judging by the names of the singers they were associated with Ashley's rather than Salomon's performance: indeed, they were deposited five days before Salomon had performed the work.[21] The piano/vocal score of the whole work, prepared by Muzio Clementi, appeared several months later.[22] It may be useful to summarize the timing of these events in tabular form (see Table 1).

Evidently both Ashley and Salomon had to wait for the arrival of the printed full score before they could either mount a performance or prepare a libretto, and Ashley was able to carry out both tasks with the greater despatch. The librettos, as

15. *The Times*, 1 April; quoted Landon, p. 575.
16. *The Times*, 4 April; quoted Landon, p. 575.   17. Landon, p. 576.
18. *The Creation. A Sacred Oratorio, Composed by Joseph Haydn, Doctor of Music . . . As performed at the Theatre Royal, Covent-Garden, 1800. Under the Direction of Mr. Ashley, Sen.* London: Printed by E. Macleish, No. 2, Bow-Street, Covent-Garden. For John Ashley. M,DCCC. Price Sixpence. (Copies: British Library, 641.h.13(5); University of Michigan, Ann Arbor, PR3991.A1c9.)
19. *The Creation: A Sacred Oratorio, Composed by Dr. Haydn, as performed at The Concert Room, King's Theatre, Hay-market, under the direction of Mr. Salomon.* London: Printed by Henry Raynell, No. 21, Piccadilly, near the Hay-market. 1800. Price One shilling. [Entered at Stationers' Hall]. (Copy: British Library, 644.k.21(20).)
20. Hoboken, *Haydn Verzeichnis*, vol. 2, pp. 40, 48.
21. 'Outrageous storms' (nos. 3, 4; Hob. xxi/2/3^b), 'With verdure clad' (nos. 7, 8; Hob. xxi/2/6^{a,b}), and 'Graceful consort' (no. 32; Hob. xxi/2/16^b), all published at London by Corri, Dussek & Co. for G. H. M[aurell], deposited at Stationers' Hall on 16 April 1800, and advertised in the *Morning Herald* on 13 May. (Copies: Cambridge University Library.)
22. In a letter to Artaria & Co., dated 22 August 1800, which survives only in a copy by Pohl, Haydn reports receiving a letter from Clementi dated London, 16 July, in which he reads with surprise that 'the copies of my Creation had not arrived there . . . They were dispatched more than 3 months ago. Because of this delay, I am in danger of losing two thousand Gulden, because Herr Clementi has already published the work himself' (Landon, p. 556). But Clementi's vocal score was not deposited at Stationers' Hall until 6 January 1801. Haydn in this letter refers not to the full score, but to the piano/vocal score made by his pupil Sigismund Neukomm and advertised on 8 March 1800 by Artaria (Landon, p. 542).

Table 1. *Chronology of the introduction of* The Creation *to London*

1795	15 August	Haydn leaves London, taking the original libretto with him
1797	autumn	Haydn completes primary composition of *The Creation*
1798	29 April	First performance at the Palais Schwarzenberg, Vienna
1799	15 June	Haydn announces the proposed publication of the full score by subscription in 'three or four months'
1800	28 February	Full score on sale in Vienna shops; advertised by Artaria on 1 March
	8 March	Neukomm's piano/vocal score advertised by Artaria
	22 March	Ashley receives his copy of the full score
	23 March	Salomon receives his copies of the full score
	24 March	Ashley advertises performance for 28 March
	27 March	Salomon advertises performance for 21 April
	27 March	Ashley's libretto deposited at Stationers' Hall
	28 March	Ashley's first performance at Covent Garden
	16 April	English editions of three songs deposited at Stationers' Hall
	16 April	Salomon's libretto deposited at Stationers' Hall
	21 April	Salomon's first performance at the King's Theatre
1801	6 January	Clementi's piano/vocal score deposited at Stationers' Hall

one might expect, substantially follow the English text printed in Haydn's score. They have their share of misprints, no doubt owing to the great haste with which they were prepared. One misprint in Ashley's text is compounded in Salomon's, suggesting that Salomon had Ashley's libretto in front of him when he prepared the copy for his own.[23] Both impresarios corrected some misspellings and similar imperfections in Haydn's printed English text.

But the London librettos also contain a number of passages which differ from the text in Haydn's score in ways that cannot be explained as either new errors or the correction of old ones, on the part of Ashley and Salomon or their printers. These are listed in Table 3, on pp. 202–3 below. Several of them correspond closely to variants found in earlier versions of the German text. The most striking of these is variant 2, where the words 'mark out their way' correspond to 'bahnet seinen Weg' in both van Swieten's autograph[24] and the German libretto printed at Vienna for the first performance.[25] In the published full score, and also in Neukomm's piano reduction, these words had disappeared from both the

23. Haydn: 'Here vent their fumes the fragrant herbs'; Ashley: 'Here went their fames the fragrant herbs'; Salomon: 'Here what their fames the fragrant herbs' (no. 8). Both librettos have 'streams' instead of the clearly correct 'steams' in 'Now from the floods in steams ascend' (no. 3). (I cite the movements as they are numbered in the Peters vocal score, no. 7619, the Eulenburg miniature score, no. 955, and Landon, pp. 388–90. Most British and American editions, unfortunately, have different numbering.)

24. Budapest, National Library, Ha.I.12, described and annotated in Horst Walter, 'Gottfried van Swietens handschriftliche Textbücher zu "Schöpfung" und "Jahreszeiten",' *Haydn-Studien* I/4 (1967), pp. 241–77. Walter collates the German text in the early sources but pays little attention to the English text.

25. *Die Schöpfung. In Musik gesetzt von Herrn Joseph Haydn Doktor der Tonkunst und Kappelmeister in wirklichen Diensten Sr.Durchl.des Hrn. Fürsten von Esterhazy*. Vienna: gedruckt bei Matthias Andreas Schmidt, k.k.Hoffbuchdruker.1798. (Copy: Vienna, Gesellschaft der Musik-freunde.) It was reprinted, with trivial corrections, in *Allgemeine Musikalische Zeitung* I (1798–9), Beilage VII (after p. 288), pp. xxi–xxiv (30 January 1799). See Walter, pp. 249–50.

German and the English texts. The fact that they occur in both London librettos shows that Ashley and Salomon must have had access to a source of the text earlier than the printed score.

In other cases, the variant wordings in the London librettos can be found in the copy of Haydn's lost autograph made by Johann Elssler and an assistant, which contains what is probably the earliest surviving text of the original English libretto. This important document, preserved in the Stiftung Preussischer Kultur-besitz (formerly the Prussian State Library), Berlin,[26] has a number of holograph corrections by the composer, and has the English text added by van Swieten above the vocal staves.[27] It is evidently the actual document in which the English text was first fitted to the music. There are some corrections in the English text, and in several such cases, the first version is the same as that in the London librettos, while the corrected wording agrees with the published full score (see Plates 1 and 2). Again, this points to an earlier source available to Ashley and Salomon.

What was this source? We can at once discount the possibility that they used the Vienna libretto. There was no motive for retranslating into English a German text that differed from that in Haydn's score; and, in any case, many of the variants cannot be explained as retranslations. An explanation more plausible at first sight is that Salomon was favoured by Haydn with manuscript versions at some earlier stage, before the final revisions had been made in the English text. But it hardly seems likely that Haydn would have sent Salomon the text alone; why should he? A manuscript copy of the score would have been more to the point: Elssler did indeed prepare several of these in 1798–9.[28] Had Salomon been in possession of such a prize, he would surely have used it to scoop the first English performance. The last thing he would have done is to show it to his rival. And his own advertisement reveals that he had to await the printed score, 'Dr. HAYDN's wish having been that this Composition should be performed first in this country, under the direction of Mr. SALOMON, for which purpose he forwarded the first Printed Copy to him from Vienna'.[29] His claim to have been 'favoured, exclusive-ly, by Dr. HAYDN with particular directions on the stile and manner in which it ought to be executed' would hardly cover the provision of rejected versions of the text. Indeed this claim sounds remarkably like those commercial puffs often found for patent medicines in this period, which warn the public to beware of imitations that do not bear the signed certificate of Dr So-and-So.

It seems clear, then, that the *original* English libretto was still available in London and was used as a source for the London librettos. Ashley must have had access to it: the timetable shows that he could not have copied from Salomon. Salomon must have had access to it: some significant variants occur in his libretto only, not in Ashley's. It is much easier to see how Salomon could have had a copy

26. Mus. ms. 9851. I am most grateful to the librarians of the Stiftung for providing me with a microfilm of this MS.
27. Landon, *Haydn: The Years of 'The Creation'*, p. 392.
28. *Ibid.*   29. *The Times*, 4 April 1800; quoted Landon, p. 575.

Plate 1. Berlin, Stiftung Preussischer Kulturbesitz, Mus.ms.9851: corrections by van Swieten in the added English text (no. 30, bars 82–5)
Reproduced by permission of the Stiftung Preussischer Kulturbesitz, Berlin (West)

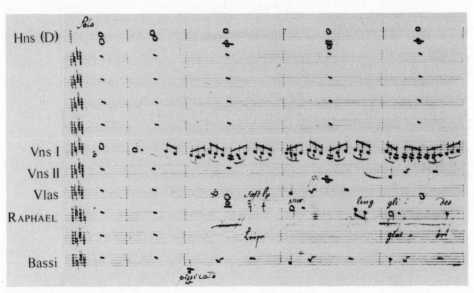

Plate 2. Berlin MS 9851: corrections by Haydn (no. 6, bars 75–7)
Reproduced by permission of the Stiftung Preussischer Kulturbesitz

than Ashley. No doubt, when he handed Haydn the libretto in 1795, he prudently kept a copy for possible future use. Ashley may have found a copy at Covent Garden theatre. Thomas Linley, who is not a very likely candidate for authorship of the text but who may well have supplied it to Salomon,[30] may have left a copy at Drury Lane theatre, where he directed the oratorio concerts for some years, and it would have come into Ashley's hands after Linley's death in 1795. Unless one of these copies should come to light,[31] the exact circumstances are likely to remain conjectural.

Clementi in preparing his vocal score evidently made use of Salomon's libretto, for he restored the original English in several cases where the text published by Haydn was erroneous (see Table 3, variants marked 'C'). He also made a laudable effort to correct faults in syllabification and word-setting. But his score has no independent authority.

How much can we deduce about the original libretto from the variants in Table 3? It is clear that neither Ashley nor Salomon used it as the only source. For instance the names of the angels, not found in van Swieten's autograph, are in the London librettos, and must have been taken from the printed score. Common sense tells us that Ashley and Salomon would have compared their text with the score, and corrected it wherever they noticed deviations. Thus in all major respects they would have brought their librettos into conformity with the score. The variants that remain would be minor differences that escaped their notice.

Before we examine these minor differences in detail we may ask how much evidence there is of changes in structure. Van Swieten's own account tells us that he 'followed the plan of the original faithfully as a whole', but 'diverged from it in details . . . I often judged it necessary that much should be shortened or even omitted . . . and . . . that much should be made more prominent or brought into greater relief, and much placed more in the shade.'[32] Griesinger and Dies both confirm that van Swieten abridged the text.

In the first two parts of the oratorio, one can see a consistent plan for the six Days of Creation, and there are signs that the plan may have been still more consistent in the original libretto (see Table 2). Each act of creation is first stated in the words of the English Bible (the first chapter of Genesis, with one verse from the second account, Genesis ii:7) and then provided with a free paraphrase and commentary. In the case of the Third, Fifth, and Sixth Days, this procedure is followed twice. At the end of most days there follows a passage in biblical style

30. Olleson, 'The Origin and Libretto of Haydn's *Creation*', pp. 162–3.
31. I know nothing of what might have happened to Ashley's papers after his death in 1805. Salomon bequeathed his printed and manuscript music to William Ayrton (see A. Tyson, 'Salomon's Will,' *Studien der Musikgeschichte des Rheinlandes*, III, ed. U. Eckart Bäcker (Cologne 1965), p. 43; I have found no reference to Salomon's performance of *The Creation* in Ayrton's writings or the journals he edited, and there is nothing relevant in the catalogue of the auction of his library on 3 July 1858 (see A. Hyatt King, *Some British Collectors of Music c. 1600–1960* (Cambridge 1963), p. 137; I am grateful to Dr King and to Ms Lenore Coral for looking into this matter for me).
32. *Allgemeine Musikalische Zeitung*, I (1798–9), p. 255; trans. Olleson, p. 150.

Table 2. *Plan of Parts I and II of* The Creation
Note: The movement numbers (bold type) correspond with those in the Peters vocal score (no. 7619) and the Eulenburg miniature score (no. 955).

Day of Creation	biblical narrative (features of creation)	paraphrase and commentary (features of creation)	words introducing heavenly host*	praise by heavenly host
First	**1** *Accomp. Recit. &* *Chorus* (heaven, earth, light)	**2** *Aria & Chorus* (light, fallen angels)	[cut?]	[cut?]
Second	**3**, bars 1–6 *Recit.* (division of waters)	**3**, 7–43 *Accomp. Recit.* (storms, floods)	**4** *Solo & Chorus* [?intended Recit.]	[cut?]
Third	**5** *Recit.* (seas, earth) **7** *Recit.* (grass, trees)	**6** *Aria* (seas, rivers, streams) **8** *Aria* (grass, plants, trees)	**9** *Recit.*	**10** *Chorus*
Fourth	**11** *Recit.* (sun, moon, stars)	**12**, bars 1–42 *Accomp. Recit.* (sun, moon, stars)	**12**, bars 43–50 *Accomp. Recit.*	**13** *Chorus with Soli*
Fifth	**14** *Accomp. Recit.* (birds) **16** *Recit.; Accomp. Recit.* (whales; command to multiply)	**15** *Aria* (birds) **18**, bars 1–99 *Trio* (hills, birds, fish)	**17** *Recit.*	[**18**, bars 98–110;] **19** *Trio with Chorus*
Sixth	**20** *Recit.* (beasts) **23** *Recit.* (man, woman) **25**, bars 1–4 *Recit.* (survey of creation)	**21** *Accomp. Recit.;* **22** *Aria* (beasts; creation incomplete) **24** *Aria* (man, woman)	**25**, bars 4–9 *Recit.*	**26** *Chorus;* **27** *Trio;* **28** *Chorus*

*4 The marv'lous work beholds amaz'd the glorious hierarchy of heav'n, and to th'ethereal vaults proclaim the praise of God, and of the second day.
  9 And the heavenly host proclaimed the third day, praising God and saying:
  12 And the sons of God announced the fourth day in song divine, proclaiming thus his power:
  17 And the angels struck their immortal harps, and the wonders of the fifth day sung.
  25 And the heavenly choir in song divine thus closed the sixth day.

but not directly from the Bible, introducing a song of general praise by the heavenly host.

Haydn, following van Swieten's suggestions, set the biblical and pseudo-biblical passages in recitative, accompanied or otherwise, with one clear exception: the famous passage describing the creation of light, assigned to chorus (the chorus also takes part in Uriel's aria (no. 2), describing the fate of 'hell's spirits'). Perhaps for this reason, there is no chorus of angels at the end of the First Day. This change may well have been an example of van Swieten's bringing some things 'into greater relief' and casting others 'more in the shade'.

The pseudo-biblical recitatives closing the Third to Sixth Days, shown at the foot of Table 2, are all similar in character, as are the choruses of praise they introduce. Each uses a different phrase to describe the heavenly host. At the end of the Second Day we can find a very similar passage in the text of no. 4, set by Haydn as a solo with chorus. Here, yet another phrase describes the heavenly host: 'the glorious hierarchy of heaven'. These words are not like the verses of paraphrase and commentary, and sound very much as if they originally introduced a chorus of praise. They would sound even more like that if the word 'resound' was replaced by 'proclaim' – and that is just what we find in the Salomon libretto (see Table 3, variant 1). The word is echoed in nos. 9 and 12, the corresponding passages closing the Third and Fourth Days. Here, then, is evidence directly pointing to a probable cut by van Swieten.

At the end of the Fifth Day, it looks very much as if van Swieten reordered the materials he found in the original libretto, for reasons that are obscure. No. 18 is a typical 'paraphrase and commentary' section, except for its last two lines, which seem to belong with no. 19: 'How many are thy works, O God! Who may their numbers tell? The Lord is great, his glory lasts For ever and for evermore.' The four lines are printed thus together in the London librettos (and also, by the way, in the Vienna libretto). Van Swieten seems to have taken the first two lines and tagged them on to the end of the trio; Haydn further added the words 'Who? O God!'. The preceding recitative, no. 17, must surely have introduced no. 19 originally (see foot of Table 2): it makes little sense in the position in which van Swieten has placed it.

There is no way of guessing what changes van Swieten may have made in Part III, which ceases to follow any biblical account. The possibility that he made more extensive changes or additions here is more or less ruled out by his own statement that he 'followed the plan of the original faithfully as a whole'. But it is suggestive that the great song of praise sung by Adam and Eve (no. 30) is called 'Hymn' in the London librettos and is in a stricter verse metre than the rest of the libretto. Some signs of a regular structure of verse and chorus can be discerned here: each verse of four lines (8686 iambic) for Adam, Eve, or both may originally have been followed by two lines (88 iambic) for chorus, and some of these choruses may have been deleted by van Swieten. But this is pure speculation.

A suggestive point concerns the title of the work. Salomon's first printed advertisement (quoted above) called it *The Creation of the World*; later on, he adopted the familiar shorter form. He must surely have taken this longer title from the original libretto. On the other hand he called the introduction simply 'Chaos' (Ashley called it 'Caius'!); the longer title 'Representation of Chaos', found in all the German sources, was no doubt van Swieten's idea.

Let us now review the process by which the double text of *The Creation* was evolved through various stages leading eventually to the historic published full score, the first known example of a major work printed with bilingual underlay for performance in either language (see Plate 3). Van Swieten was responsible for

Plate 3. *The Creation*, first edition of 1800 (no. 33)

the German translation and made some changes, including cuts, in the words. He then prepared for Haydn his version of the German text alone, with certain suggestions for setting it to music which, in the main, were followed by the composer. Nevertheless he must have intended from the first that the music should fit the text in both languages so far as possible. This is shown most conclusively by the biblical passages, in which, instead of adopting one of the German translations in common use, van Swieten made his own translation that fitted closely, in sense, order, and rhythm, the words that were part of the English libretto,[33] even when these words departed slightly from the scriptural text.[34]

Haydn's surviving sketches[35] (the autograph is lost) show that he worked with the German text: I shall consider below whether there is any evidence that he had the English text also in mind during the process of composition. The first performance probably took place before any attempt had been made to fit the English text to the music in detail. This 'fitting' process can be seen primarily in the Berlin manuscript full score already referred to. Here we find the English text added in van Swieten's hand[36] to a score already completed by Elssler and his assistants. The text is intermediate between the original (as far as we can infer its details from the London librettos) and the printed score. In this manuscript also, especially in the recitatives, alternative notes were often provided to go with the English words, and these appear again in small type in the printed score; thus they were ultimately approved by Haydn. It is difficult to be sure that these notes are also in van Swieten's handwriting in the absence of authentic examples of his musical hand for comparison, but it seems overwhelmingly probable. The word-setting

33. This was pointed out by Olleson, 'The Origin and Libretto of Haydn's *Creation*', pp. 156–7.
34. For instance, no. 11 changes the order of phrases from Genesis i:14–15; and in no. 16 'Be fruitful' is changed to 'Be fruitful all'.
35. A useful list and description of the sketches is in Landon, *Haydn: The Years of 'The Creation'*, pp. 354–88.
36. Landon stated that the text was added 'apparently by van Swieten himself' (Landon, p. 392); I have confirmed this supposition by comparison with other non-German texts in the Baron's hand.

(15)

DUET.

Adam. Graceful confort! At thy fide
Softly fly the golden hours.
Ev'ry moment brings new rapture,
Ev'ry care is put to reft.

Eve. Spoufe adored! At thy fide
Pureft joys o'erflow the heart.
Life and all I am is thine;
My reward thy love fhall be.

Adam. The dew-dropping morn,
O how fhe quickens all!
Eve. The coolnefs of ev'n
O how fhe all reftores!

Adam. How grateful is
Of fruits the favour fweet!
Eve. How pleafing is
Of fragrant bloom the fmell!

Both. But without thee, what is it to me,
Adam. The morning dew,
Eve. The breath of ev'n,
Adam. The fav'ry fruit,
Eve. The fragrant bloom!

Both. With thee is ev'ry hour enhanced;
With thee delight is ever new.
With thee is life inceffant blifs,
To thee be vow'd it whole.

RECITATIVE.

URIEL.

O happy pair, and ever happy ftill,
If not, by falfe conceit mifled,
Ye ftrive at more than granted is,
And more to know, than know you fhould.

Plate 4. *The Creation*, Salomon's libretto (end of no. 32; no. 33)

contains many blunders, for example treating 'eagle' as one syllable and 'stately' as three.

A few further changes appear in the printed full score. So there were three phases at which revisions were made, and they can be differentiated with the help of the concordances listed in Table 3. I will call the phases *A*, *B*, and *C*.

(*A*) Van Swieten made any major structural alterations before he made his fair copy of the German translation for Haydn. At the same time, he made some smaller textual changes, chiefly to bring the English and German closer together.

These are listed below, by reference to the numbered variants (numbers in italic) in Table 3. They are assigned to this first phase because they can be explained without reference to the problems of fitting the English text to the music.

8, 9, 12, 30. These probably resulted from copying errors on van Swieten's part. The original version is clearly preferable in all respects.

20. I suspect that he intended to emend to 'Great is his name, and great his might', which accords well with the German, but accidentally omitted the word 'is'.

3, 4, 5, 13, 17, 19, 21, 24, 32. These can best be explained as efforts to make the English come closer to the German in rhythm, word order, or meaning; van Swieten had presumably taken a liking to his German text, or had found it impossible to provide a German translation close enough to the original English wording. (Some of them could equally have been made during phase *B*: see below.)

28, 29. These are clear cases of adaptation of the English to an already completed German translation.[37] The word 'als' could stand either for 'than', the original and clearly the correct reading, or for the meaningless 'as' of the authentic English text.

1. Van Swieten chose to translate 'to th'ethereal vaults' as 'aus ihren Kehlen' and then had to change 'to' to 'from' in the English text. But for some reason the original 'to' survived in the first two places (bars 10, 16), while 'from' replaced it in the rest of the movement. The change from 'proclaim' to 'resound' was possibly due to the omission of a following chorus of angels, as already suggested. (Either reading is ungrammatical: the subject, 'hierarchy', has already taken a singular verb, 'beholds', and is now provided with a plural one, suggesting some clumsy cutting and pasting on van Swieten's part.)

26, 31. No explanation for these changes suggests itself, though *31* gives an improved word order.

There is no evidence of further text revisions by van Swieten in advance of Haydn's musical setting of the German text. Of course, there is always the possibility that he made many other changes which have left no trace. Careful statistical reasoning, however, proves that this is not likely. I have already shown that Ashley and Salomon revised their copies of the original libretto in the light of Haydn's score, and that the surviving variants were the ones that escaped their notice. Suppose, for the sake of argument, that van Swieten made ten times as many verbal changes as these, and that nine-tenths of the total were noticed by Ashley and Salomon and incorporated in their librettos. We would then have to explain the fact that the ten per cent that escaped Ashley's notice were almost the same variants as the ten per cent that escaped Salomon's notice (see Table 3). This is clearly unlikely: Salomon and Ashley, as rival aspirants to the first English performance, would hardly have collaborated in this task. The inference is that van Swieten did not make many alterations in the original English libretto beyond those already discussed.

37. Olleson made the same inference without the help of the London librettos ('The Origin and Libretto of Haydn's *Creation*', p. 161).

Table 3. *Significant textual variants in the London librettos of* The Creation

Note: Movement numbers are in bold type: see note to Table 2. Text lines in roman type are from the authentic version published by Haydn in 1800; corresponding lines in italic type are from one or both of the English librettos published in London in 1800, edited respectively by Ashley (*A*) and Salomon (*S*). Variants clearly due to error are not included. Abbreviations in the last column, 'concordances', have the following meanings: G: variant corresponds to an earlier version of the German text (see Walter, pp. 249–57); H: variant corresponds more closely than authentic English text to the authentic German text in Haydn's score; B: variant found uncorrected in Berlin MS 9851; [B]: variant found in Berlin MS 9851, corrected so as to correspond with authentic English text; C: variant found in Clementi's piano/vocal score of 1801.

variant no.	movt no.	text line	bars	text	variant source(s)	concordances	notes
1	**4**	3	26–8 etc.	And from th'ethereal vaults resound *And to th'ethereal vaults resound* *And to th'ethereal vaults proclaim*	 A S		cf. bars 9–10, 16–17
2	**6**	7–8	75–119	Softly purling glides on Thro' silent vales the limpid brook. *In silent vales soft gliding brooks* *By gentle noise mark out their way.*	A S	G [B]	see Pl. 2
3	**8**	3–4	9–16 etc.	By flowers sweet and gay Enhanced is the pleasing sight. *Enhanced is the pleasing sight* *By flowers sweet and gay.*	A S	H	
4	**8**	9	45–50	The mountain brow is crown'd with closed wood, *With closed wood is crown'd the* *the mountain's brow.*	A S		
5	**16**	7	12–13	Multiply ye finny tribes, *Be multiplied ye finny tribes,*	A S		
6	**18**	—	111–14, 121–3	Who? O God! *[lacking]*	A S	G	
7	**19**	1	1–3, 13–15, 21–3	The Lord is great, and great his might. *The Lord is great, his glory lasts*	A S	G H [B]	cf. bars 4, 7 etc.
8	**21**	13	52–4	The fleecy, meek and bleating flock. *The fleecy, meek and bleating flocks.*	A S	C	
9	**21**	15	55–7	In whirl arose the host of insects. *In whirls arose the host of insects.*	A S	C	
10	**22**	1	11–14	Now heav'n in fullest glory shone; *Now heav'n in all her glory shone;*	A S	B	
11	**22**	2	17–20	Earth smiles in all her rich attire. *Earth smiles in her rich attire.*	A S	G H [B]	
12	**23**	3	5–6	Male and female created he him. *Male and female created he them.*	S	G H C	
13	**24**	5	19–23	The Lord and King of nature all. *The Lord of earth, and nature's king.*	A S		
14	**24**	8	32–5, 43–6	And in his eyes with brightness shines *And in his eyes with brightness shone*	A S	G H B	
15	**28**	4	10–11 etc.	He sole on high exalted reigns. *On high exalted reigns the Lord.*	A S		
16	**30**	2	8–11	The heav'n and earth are stor'd. *The heav'n and earth are fill'd.*	A S	G H [B]	
17	**30**	3	11–14	This world, so great, so wonderful, *This world, so wondrous and so great,*	A S		
18	**30**	11	82–5 etc.	Proclaim in your extended course *In your extended course proclaim*	A S	[B]	see Pl. 1
19	**30**	12	85–8 etc.	Th'almighty pow'r and praise of God! *The glorious power of the Lord!*	A S		
20	**30**	23	153–61	Great his name, and great his might. *His name is great, and great his might.*	A S		
21	**30**	31	207–10	And ye, that swim the stream, *Ye, that thro' waters glide*	A S		
22	**30**	33	218–26	Him celebrate, him magnify! *Your voices join, his pow'r proclaim.*	A S		
23	**30**	40	276–90	Thy pow'r adore the heav'n and earth. *Thy pow'r adore the earth and heav'n.*	A S	G H [B]	
24	**32**	18	117–21 etc.	With thee is ev'ry joy enhanced, *With thee is ev'ry hour enhanced,*	A S		see Pl. 4
25	**32**	21	158–74 etc.	Thine it whole shall be. *To thee be vow'd it whole.*	A S	G H [B]	see Pl. 4
26	**33**	1	1–2	O happy pair, and always happy yet, *O happy pair, and ever happy still,*	S		see Pls. 3, 4
27	**33**	2	3–4	If not, misled by false conceit, *If not, by false conceit misled,*	A S		see Pls. 3, 4

Table 3.—*cont.*

variant no.	movt no.	text line	bars	text	variant source(s)	concordances	notes
28	33	3	4–5	Ye strive at more, as granted is,			see Pls. 3, 4
				Ye strive at more than granted is,	*S*	C	
29	33	4	6–7	And more to know, as know ye should.			see Pls. 3, 4
				And more to know, than know you should.	*S*	C	
30	34	2	3–4	Utter thanks ye all his works.			
				Utter thanks, all ye his works.	*S*		
31	34	4	7–9	Let his name resound on high!			
				Let on high resound his name!	*A*		
32	34	5	10–12 etc.	The Lord is great, his praise shall last for aye.			
				The Lord is great, his praise shall last for ever.	*S*		
33	12	7, 9	26, 36	Piu Adagio . . . Allegro			
				In tempo . . . Ad libitum	*A S*	G	
34	16	3	6	Poco Adagio			
				In tempo	*A S*	G	
35	30	title		Duett und Chor			
				Hymn	*A S*	G	['Lobgesang']

(B) Van Swieten later made further revisions in the English text, especially for the purpose of fitting it to the music. In this category fall those variants in Table 3 that seem to be due to musical considerations, and those in which the original English text appears deleted in the Berlin manuscript.

7, 15, 18, 22, 25, 27. In these instances the English text would not fit the music because of the way Haydn had divided or repeated the German phrase; van Swieten accordingly altered the English text. In variant *18* we can see this process at work (Plate 1, on p. 195 above): van Swieten at first tried to fit the original text, but was defeated by Haydn's repetition of 'Macht kund' in the tenor, and so changed the English text to begin with the word 'Proclaim'. In variant *22* he at first entered 'Him magnify, him celebrate', then reversed the order for no apparent reason. In variant *7* the English was changed to 'and great his might' only in those places where the original line would not stand Haydn's repetition of it. (Other changes which could have been made for this reason are variants *3, 13, 17, 19, 21,* and *32.*)

2, 6. Here Haydn himself made changes in the German text which had to be accommodated in the English. In variant *2* the Berlin manuscript shows corrections, in Haydn's own hand, changing van Swieten's 'Sanft rauschend fliesst und windet sich' (his second attempt) to 'Leise rauschend gleitet fort' (see Plate 2), with corresponding changes in the musical rhythm. Van Swieten had to fit a new English version of this first line, 'Softly purling glides on', to these new rhythms, with 'softly' to correspond with 'leise'; and the changes in the second line were necessary to complete the sense. In variant *6*, Haydn had added a coda[38] which included an extra phrase of text, 'Wer? O Gott!'; this had to be translated into English.

38. See the composer's sketch of this passage, Vienna, Österreichische Nationalbibliothek, Codex 16835, fols. 16v, 17r. I am grateful to A. Peter Brown for letting me see the photocopies of these sketches provided to him by the Nationalbibliothek.

11, 16, 23. Van Swieten's alteration has no clear musical motivation, and appears to be due to literary considerations; but it was made after Haydn composed the music, for the correction can be seen in the Berlin manuscript. In variant *11* he at first treated 'smiles' as two syllables: perhaps someone pointed out his error, and the word 'all' had to be added to provide the extra syllable. (Similarly in no. 2, bar 21, he at first treated 'shades' as two syllables, but in this case no added word was necessary when the correction was made.) In variant *16* the correction of 'fill'd' to 'stor'd' might have been made to provide a rhyme for 'Lord', though rhyme is not a significant feature of this libretto in either language. Variant *23* replaces 'earth and heav'n' by the more idiomatic 'heav'n and earth'. (In these last two cases the motivation for the change seems very weak.)

(C) Further changes were made before the publication of the score: the original text of these passages is still found uncorrected in the Berlin manuscript. There are only two instances. They suggest the influence of someone who knew English better than van Swieten.

10. The change was probably made because the revised text accords better with the German translation.

14. The revision clearly improves the sequence of tenses, and must have been made by someone who knew enough English to recognize this fact.

It is clear enough from these details that the London librettos are substantially the same as the original English libretto, except for the possible omission of several sections. It is also clear that, generally speaking, Haydn himself worked with the German text. The fitting of the music to the English, which was always part of the plan, was accomplished (imperfectly enough) by van Swieten, in two principal stages. Before composition, he tried to make the two texts as closely parallel as he could, principally by tailoring his German to the original English, but here and there by altering a word or two of the English to fit his German. After composition, he made whatever further adjustments were necessary in the English text and in the musical rhythms. Though Haydn may not have played a direct part in either process, it seems certain that he must have looked over and approved the results.

But that is not quite the end of the matter. There are a few places in the oratorio where the music seems, in one way or another, better suited to the English text than to the German. It is difficult to resist the conclusion that Haydn had the English text in mind at these points, either in the original process of composition or during revision; and in one or two cases there is some objective evidence to support this position.

In the solo and chorus 'The marv'llous work beholds amazed' (no. 4), the third phrase of the vocal melody is introduced as the echo of an orchestral phrase, and the echo is more precise with the English text than with the German (Ex. 1). When this phrase of the text returns in a Handelian passage (Ex. 2), the English and German are fitted to the music in quite different ways. The German requires the repetition of one phrase in the chorus, and entails a discrepancy between chorus

Example 1. *The Creation* no. 4, bars 8–11

and soloist in bar 28. But the English text, with the first two chords of the chorus part omitted, fits the music exactly and effectively, with imitation in bars 26–7 that paints the English text only. It is tempting to think that this was Haydn's first conception of the passage. The two bracketed chords were then added to suit the German text, and van Swieten clumsily fitted 'and from' to them (similarly at bars 43–7). No sketch survives to prove or disprove the hypothesis. There are several other passages in which the musical phrase seems to fit the English masculine ending better than the German feminine ending. In no. 10, 'Awake the harp', this subjective view again receives some confirmation from the orchestral accompaniment (Ex. 3); the entry of the chorus after the beat in bar 3 also seems to fit the accompaniment better.

But the most striking superiority of the English text is in the wonderful passage 'Be fruitful all and multiply' (no. 16), where the potency of the Creator is expressed in a wide-ranging bass recitative in tempo, richly accompanied by divided lower strings (Ex. 4). The vocal line is superbly suited to the English biblical text, and one of its most impressive moments is at the word 'deep' on a low A, contrasting with a high C on 'tree' at the end of an earlier phrase. In the version with German text, not only do the feminine endings negate this word-painting effect: they also weaken the impact of the octave leaps in bars 10 and 12 by requiring further, and fortuitous, octave leaps in bars 11 and 14. To my mind it is too much to believe that the marvellous felicity of the English text setting here came about by chance, as the result of routine adaptations made by the not very skilful van Swieten. I can only attribute it to Haydn himself, despite the fact that the surviving sketch[39] shows only the melodic line that later accompanied the German text. The composer may have originally conceived this passage with the English text, and then sketched it out with the German; or he may, in this case,

39. Vienna, Österreichische Nationalbibliothek, Codex 16835, fol. 15r, partly reproduced in Landon, *Haydn: The Years of 'The Creation'*, p. 379.

Example 2. *The Creation* no. 4, bars 26–30

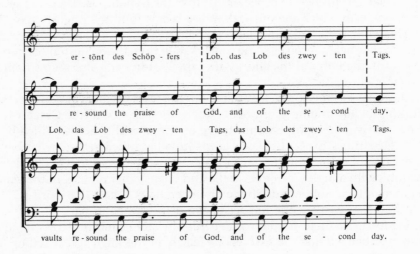

Example 3. *The Creation* no. 10, bars 1–4

Example 4. *The Creation* no. 16, bars 6–17

Ex. 4 (contd)

have taken in hand personally the adaptation to English. Certainly he worked on this passage after making the extant sketch, for the sketch shows only a bare continuo accompaniment which, as Landon puts it, 'pales beside Haydn's later version'.[40]

It is true that, in contrast to these places, there are many more at which the music fits the German better than the English – in some cases enormously better. But these do not really affect my argument. No one doubts that Haydn had the German in mind; it was, certainly, his main text. I am merely suggesting that he also had, at least in the back of his mind, the original English. After all, he wanted his work to be appreciated by English audiences as much as by German-speaking ones.

The remaining evidence for this is more nebulous in character. While in London, Haydn was approached by the Reverend William Tattersall with a request for some tunes for a book of church music he was about to publish by

40. Landon, p. 380.

subscription. The book appeared in 1794 as *Improved Psalmody*, with six original tunes by Haydn. One of them, a setting of James Merrick's version of Psalm 50 verses 1–6, is strikingly similar in both text and music to the famous chorus in *The Creation*, 'The heavens are telling': its repeated last line is especially prophetic (Ex. 5).[41] The impression made on Haydn by English religious choral music is well

Example 5. Haydn's tune for Psalm 50, from Tattersall's *Improved Psalmody* (1794)

41. See Nicholas Temperley, *The Music of the English Parish Church*, 2 vols. (Cambridge 1979) vol. 1, pp. 228–9; vol. 2, p. 130, Ex. 50. Facsimile in Landon, *Haydn in England 1791–1795* (London 1976), p. 368. Cf. *The Creation*, no. 13: bars 1–3, 54–62, 67–71, 95–9, 147–53.

Ex. 5 (contd)

known, and it was not confined to Handel's oratorios: he was deeply moved by the sound of the charity children singing hymns and chants at St Paul's.[42] It seems likely that the feeling of such music was strongly in his mind when he came to write 'The heavens are telling', which, like Psalm 50, surveys God's creation of the world; and he must surely have been aware of the English text when he was composing the music. That he succeeded in capturing the enthusiasm of the English public in this regard is shown by the enormous popularity of this chorus in England from 1800 to the present. From as early as 1802 it became a usual custom in England to perform Part I of the work only,[43] giving 'The heavens are telling' pride of place as the final, culminating statement. In the early nineteenth

42. Landon, *Haydn in England*, pp. 173–4.
43. See performances at Covent Garden on 7 April 1802; 9 March 1803; 14 March 1804; 13 and 27 March 1805; 28 February, 12 and 21 March 1806; etc., as advertised in the daily newspapers. Also at the Salisbury Festivals of 1810 and 1824 (Douglas J. Reid, 'Some Festival Programmes of the Eighteenth and Nineteenth Centuries,' *Royal Musical Association Research Chronicle* No. 5 (1965), pp. 51–79; No. 6 (1966), pp. 2–22: esp. No. 5, pp. 64, 66), the Cambridge Festival of 1811 (Reid, No. 6, p. 9), the Edinburgh Festival of 1815 (G. F. Graham, *An Account of the First Edinburgh Musical Festival* (Edinburgh 1816)), the Derby Festival of 1831 (*Harmonicon*, 1831, p. 272), and so on.

century it was more than once adapted as a hymn tune, sung, in the most popular version, to Addison's Psalm 18, 'The spacious firmament on high'[44] – another hymn of unqualified joy in creation, which has much in common with the mood of Haydn's oratorio, shaped as it was by the Augustan confidence of Handel's England.

Whatever the shortcomings of the English text of *The Creation*, we can see now that there are compelling reasons for preferring it to any other, German or English, for performances in the English-speaking world. The composer made clear by his actions that he wanted this text to have equal authority with the German; and in many ways it must be closer to his own thoughts than any 'improved' English version can be. To sing the English text as published by Haydn in 1800, it is necessary to modify the underlay in certain places. It is high time we had a scholarly English edition in which this task had been carefully and modestly carried out. Then, perhaps, we whose mother tongue is English could hear *The Creation* as Haydn meant us to hear it.[45]

44. By Bishop Simms, organist of St Philip, Birmingham; published about 1810. See Temperley, vol. 1, p. 232; vol. 2, pp. 138–45, Ex. 54.
45. Some of the ideas in this paper were worked out in a seminar on Haydn's *Creation* which I gave at the University of Illinois in the spring of 1978. I should like to acknowledge the help and suggestions of the students in that seminar: Aaron Appelstein, Christopher McGahan, Steven Schaufele, and Paulette Morgan Zalesiak.

The English symphony:
some additions and annotations
to Charles Cudworth's
published studies

Jan LaRue

Sound scholarship obviously must keep its feet well balanced in the past, but it should also keep an eye to the future. The pioneering work of Charles Cudworth on the English symphony nicely illustrates these requirements in a small but significant detail. When, owing to sudden illness, he was unable to transmit a last half-dozen incipits for his Thematic Index[1] of English symphonies, he provided blank staff-lines to allow later insertions – evidence of his long experience and practical approach to bibliography. More important, to various friends some months later he sent small sheets of music paper on which he had laboriously copied out the missing incipits. As a small response to this characteristically thoughtful and encouraging gesture, the following discussion attempts to carry on Cudworth's explorations from a continental perspective; a revised version of the Thematic Index, emended in the light of new information revealed by my union thematic catalogue of eighteenth-century symphonies,[2] may be found on pp. 219–43 below.

Cudworth's study provides the first comprehensive evidence of strength, continuity and diversity in the early English symphony, which has been totally ignored in surveys such as that of William Henry Hadow in the Oxford History of Music. Summing up the trends in his material, Cudworth remarks that 'after the middle of the eighteenth century there were two influences, that of the older Handelian baroque style on the one hand and the more modern, Galant, Mannheim style on the other'.[3] Certainly one feels the persistence of the Handelian influence, not only in English versions of the French overture, but also in the

1. Charles L. Cudworth, *Thematic Index of English Eighteenth-Century Overtures and Symphonies* (London 1953, repr. Liechtenstein 1969), published by the Royal Musical Association as an appendix to his paper 'The English Symphonists of the Eighteenth Century', *PRMA* LXXVIII (1953), pp. 31–51.
2. LaRue, 'A Union Thematic Catalogue of 18th-Century Symphonies', *Fontes Artis Musicae* VI (1959), pp. 18–20.
3. Cudworth, 'The English Symphonists', p. 50.

'grand concertos' of composers like Avison. As for the 'more modern' symphonists, however, any genetic tracing must be extended far beyond Mannheim:
England welcomed musicians from all parts of Europe, most notably the two
other great North Germans, Carl Friedrich Abel and Johann Christian Bach, who
together exercised an influence at least as strong as all of Mannheim.

British internationalism showed in other ways as well. In the New Oxford
History of Music[4] I have drawn attention to the wide representation of Continental music brought out by British publishers in the second half of the eighteenth
century. Robert Bremner, for example, in his long series of periodical overtures
includes more symphonies from Austria and Italy than from Mannheim. Possibly
the broadly international character of British musical taste – first seen at least as far
back as the Restoration – may have contributed to the relative decline of native
English music after Purcell. Whatever our evaluations of this background may be,
by 1760 the British musical public undeniably had become as catholic and
sophisticated in its taste as any audience in Europe.

One important aspect of the English symphonies, amply illustrated but never
specifically emphasized by Cudworth, concerns the split in the social purposes of
these works. A clarification of what kinds of performers and listeners were
involved helps us to understand the different currents in symphonic development more fundamentally than does an appreciation of the divergence between
Handelian and *galant* influence. Stated in the most general way, the English
symphony divided into two types consistently related to social strata: the concert-
hall/drawing-room symphony and the music-hall/ theatre symphony or overture.
Already at mid-century the concert symphony belonged mainly to the aristocracy. For example, Thomas Erskine (the Earl of Kelly, a Scottish peer) studied
about 1750 with Johann Stamitz and brought the symphonic mannerisms of
Mannheim back to England with considerable success, playing largely to an
aristocratic concert-hall audience. A decade later the concert symphony received
strong impetus from the arrival of Bach and Abel, who, following Handel's
precedent, entered English society at the top: Bach became music master to
Queen Charlotte, while Abel served as chamber musician in her household. The
symphonies played in the modish Bach–Abel concerts reflected the advanced
musical tastes of the Georgian aristocracy, differing comparatively little in size or
stylistic fundamentals from the three-movement concert symphonies familiar in
Germany, France and Italy about 1765 (the Viennese symphonists had already
begun to turn toward the four-movement plan).

The native English symphony emerged from an entirely different social stratum
and musical tradition. Few native composers at mid-century wrote concert symphonies, not only because the aristocratic posts in music were already occupied
by foreign artists (a circumstance deplored by English commentators[5]), but also
because the native symphony belonged to a less formal milieu. Whereas on the

4. *The Age of Enlightenment (1745–1790)*, The New Oxford History of Music, vol. 7, ed.
    E. Wellesz and F. Sternfeld (London 1973), chapter VI, esp. pp. 426–9.
5. See Cudworth's discussion, 'The English Symphonists', p. 39.

continent the counterpart of the concert symphony was the opera overture, in England the lack of any strong tradition of grand opera obviously reduced the need for grand symphony-overtures. Instead we find an extremely active, varied and flexible situation, with every imaginable combination of theatre and music, from plays with interspersed songs and dances to ballad operas and finally to full-scale comic operas, such as those of William Shield. Yet even these larger works, which expanded the dimensions of individual numbers and also maintained a general musical unity rather than a chain of incidental songs, never required elaborate symphonies or overtures.

It was just a short step from the theatre to music halls and pleasure gardens such as Vauxhall and Ranelagh, which also exercised a strong influence on the native symphony: the short attention span of strollers and beer-drinkers called for brief and lively instrumental introductions.[6] Elsewhere the informal character of preludes, interludes, and postludes can be imagined from the myriad of publications with titles such as 'The favourite Songs from the opera call'd X compos'd by Mr. Y . . ., together with their symphonys'. Turning the process around, many composers adapted currently popular songs into slow movements, while echoes of reels or strathspeys found their way into numerous symphonic finales.

With entertainment as a chief requirement, therefore, it is not surprising to find a concentration on brevity and sprightliness in the native English symphony. That a symphony is short and witty, however, in no way implies a lack of talent in its composer. The small size of many English symphonies somehow has directed attention away from their accomplishments in other respects. Though popular circumstances dictated the general tone of the native symphony much of the time, by several criteria that I have found applicable to continental symphonies, English masters were not altogether in the rearguard. As one example, with respect to thematic contrast and differentiation, an essential aspect of mature sonata forms, composers such as Collett, Fisher and Smethergell not only confirm the dominant modulation with suitably contrasting material but also connect primary and secondary areas with convincing transitions. In a number of works one can even find parallels to the highly active closing techniques perfected by Haydn to carry the momentum over the double bar into the development – one of the significant refinements of the original binary plan.

A more detailed test concerns melodic fluency and control, the power to project a line with logic as well as some element of special invention or surprise. The second slow movement from John Collett's *Six Simphonies or Overtures in 8 & 10 parts with a thorough bass for the Harpsichord . . . Opera Seconda* (London: Bremner, *c*. 1765) can stand as an equal beside J. C. Bach's best *cantabile* movements, freshly attractive for its touch of rhythmic intrigue when the second-beat dotted figure of the opening bars shifts to the first beat in bars 7–8; then, with a compelling upward sweep of semiquavers the melody travels two and a half octaves to reach an impressive peak of c'': Ex. 1.

6. For an appropriate illustration, see *Grove's Dictionary*, 5th edn (London 1954), vol. 5, plate 41 (opp. p. 374).

Example 1. Collett, Op. 2 No. 2; second movement (Andante), bars 1–12

A third argument that many English symphonies were progressive, or at least up to date, can be found in the key-relationships of their slow movements. For some years around the middle of the century continental symphonists most frequently chose tonic minor or dominant as keys for slow movements. These choices imposed rather narrow harmonic boundaries. By about 1770, however, the commoner choices were relative minor and subdominant, a perceptible expansion and refreshment of tonality. These later preferences characterize the English symphony taken as a whole, even including the mid-century works.

Near the end of his paper Cudworth attempted to assemble a few specifically English traits. Here he referred to 'a distinctive English style of melody, brief, but often of haunting charm, usually displayed in the small-scale slow movements'.[7] It is a bit difficult to interpret these words in any more specific way, particularly since one's natural association with English melody might be 'open-air' rather than 'haunting'. No doubt some day a computer will explain it all. Among traits more concretely identifiable as English, however, is the use of popular songs (as opposed to traditional or folk melodies) as thematic material. If we look at the eighteenth-century symphony as a whole, uses of borrowed melody are rather infrequent, and quotations of currently popular songs are even more rare, except in England.

The most numerically impressive difference of the English symphony appears in an unexpected area: preliminary statistics assembled from my union thematic catalogue make possible a full-scale comparison of the key and time-signature preferences of English symphonists with the choices of their Continental colleagues. For reasons presently obscure, the English wrote higher percentages of works in B♭, E♭ and D minor, but significantly lower percentages in C and A, as well as proportionately fewer works in minor keys.[8] The full details can be seen in

7. Cudworth, 'The English Symphonists', p. 47.
8. Except for Thomas Arne, who in keeping with his continuing interest in Baroque style wrote symphony–overtures not only in D minor but also in E minor and G minor – the only English symphonies in these two keys presently known.

Composers' symphonic preferences (percentages)

	Key									Time signature			
	C	D	Eb	E	F	G	A	Bb	D minor	4/4 2/2	3/4	2/4	other
England	8.1	29.4	14	3.7	11.8	4.4	11.8	11.8	3.7	75	18.4	1.5	5
Continent	13.5	28.9	9.5	3.6	10.5	12.2	6.1	9.4	1.8	70.4	17.7	8.6	3.3

Note: percentages rounded to the nearest tenth; amounts below 1% omitted.

the table above. Only slightly less surprising are the choices of metres, with an astonishingly small percentage of works in 2/4 and corresponding emphasis on 4/4 or 2/2. It is possible that fuller statistical information or other research on keys and metres would help to explain these curiously individual spectra of preference. For a start one may note the prominence of flat-side keys, with emphasis on Eb and Bb but neglect of A. As for time signatures, the less frequent use of 2/4 may reflect a desire to distinguish the symphony from the high proportion of songs in 2/4. Though these points must await further investigation, one may nonetheless observe that such arcane nonconformities definitely strengthen our sense of a distinctively English approach to the symphony in the eighteenth century.

Thematic index of English symphonies

Charles Cudworth and Jan LaRue

Abbreviations

Sources

Hpd	harpsichord arrangement(s)
MSF	manuscript full score(s)
Org	organ arrangement
PF	printed full score(s)
Pf	pianoforte arrangement(s), manuscript or printed
PP	printed orchestral parts
PV	printed vocal score(s)

Libraries

GB-Cfm	Cambridge, Fitzwilliam Museum
GB-Ckc	Cambridge, Rowe Music Library, King's College
GB-Cpl	Cambridge, Pendlebury Library of Music
GB-Er	Edinburgh, Reid Music Library of the University of Edinburgh
GB-Gu	Glasgow, Euing Music Library
GB-Hb	Hinchingbrook House, Hunts.
GB-Lam	London, Royal Academy of Music
GB-Lbl	London, British Library
GB-Lcm	London, Royal College of Music
GB-Mp	Manchester, Central Public Library, Henry Watson Music Library
GB-Ob	Oxford, Bodleian Library
(T)	(Tenbury MSS, on deposit)
S-Skma	Stockholm, Royal Swedish Academy of Music
US-Ic	Ithaca (N.Y.), Cornell University Music Library
US-PRu	Princeton (N.J.), Princeton University, Harvey S. Firestone Memorial Library
US-Wc	Washington (D.C.), Library of Congress, Music Division

Arne, Michael

1 *Cymon* PV GB-Lbl

Arne, Thomas Augustine

Eight Overtures in 8 parts PP GB-Ckc, Cpl, Lam,
London, Walsh [*c.* 1751] Lbl, Lcm, Mp; US-
  Wc

2 No. 1

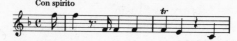

3 No. 2

4 No. 3

= Overture, *Henry and Emma*

5 No. 4

6 No. 5

7 No. 6

8 No. 7

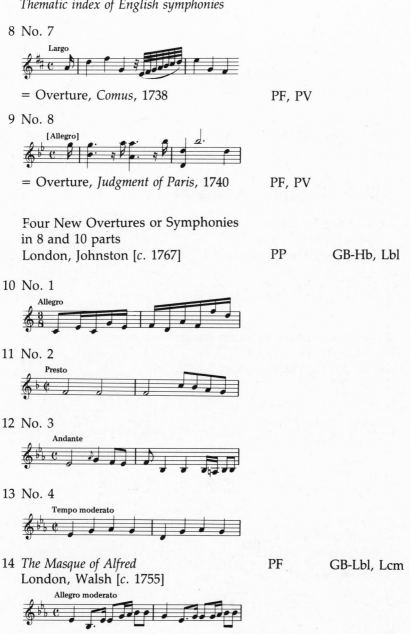

= Overture, *Comus*, 1738   PF, PV

9 No. 8

= Overture, *Judgment of Paris*, 1740   PF, PV

Four New Overtures or Symphonies
in 8 and 10 parts
London, Johnston [*c.* 1767]   PP   GB-Hb, Lbl

10 No. 1

11 No. 2

12 No. 3

13 No. 4

14 *The Masque of Alfred*   PF   GB-Lbl, Lcm
London, Walsh [*c.* 1755]

15 *Eliza*   PF   GB-Lbl, etc.
London, Walsh [1758]

II. Allegro con spirito

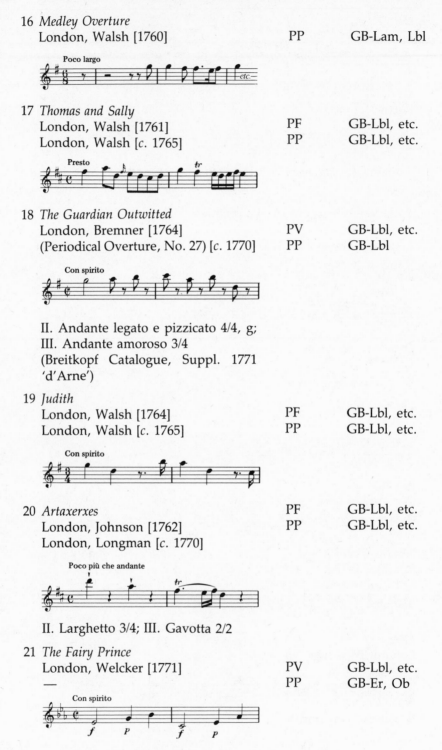

16 *Medley Overture*
   London, Walsh [1760]   PP   GB-Lam, Lbl

17 *Thomas and Sally*
   London, Walsh [1761]   PF   GB-Lbl, etc.
   London, Walsh [c. 1765]   PP   GB-Lbl, etc.

18 *The Guardian Outwitted*
   London, Bremner [1764]   PV   GB-Lbl, etc.
   (Periodical Overture, No. 27) [c. 1770]   PP   GB-Lbl

   II. Andante legato e pizzicato 4/4, g;
   III. Andante amoroso 3/4
   (Breitkopf Catalogue, Suppl. 1771
   'd'Arne')

19 *Judith*
   London, Walsh [1764]   PF   GB-Lbl, etc.
   London, Walsh [c. 1765]   PP   GB-Lbl, etc.

20 *Artaxerxes*   PF   GB-Lbl, etc.
   London, Johnson [1762]   PP   GB-Lbl, etc.
   London, Longman [c. 1770]

   II. Larghetto 3/4; III. Gavotta 2/2

21 *The Fairy Prince*
   London, Welcker [1771]   PV   GB-Lbl, etc.
   —   PP   GB-Er, Ob

22 *The Cooper*
London, Napier [1772]   PV   GB-Lbl, etc.
—   PP   GB-Lam, Lcm, Ob

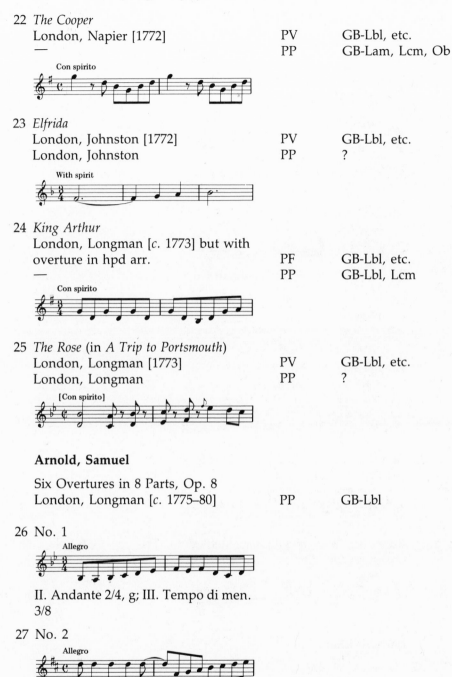

Con spirito

23 *Elfrida*
London, Johnston [1772]   PV   GB-Lbl, etc.
London, Johnston   PP   ?

With spirit

24 *King Arthur*
London, Longman [*c.* 1773] but with
overture in hpd arr.   PF   GB-Lbl, etc.
—   PP   GB-Lbl, Lcm

Con spirito

25 *The Rose* (in *A Trip to Portsmouth*)
London, Longman [1773]   PV   GB-Lbl, etc.
London, Longman   PP   ?

[Con spirito]

Arnold, Samuel

Six Overtures in 8 Parts, Op. 8
London, Longman [*c.* 1775–80]   PP   GB-Lbl

26 No. 1

Allegro

II. Andante 2/4, g; III. Tempo di men.
3/8

27 No. 2

Allegro

II. Largo andante 3/4; III. Rondo:
Vivace 2/2

28 No. 3

II. Andante 2/4, Bb; III. Vivace 3/8

29 No. 4

II. Un poco andante 3/4, G; III. Allegro 3/8

30 No. 5

II. Andantino 2/4, D; III. Allegro 6/8

31 No. 6

32 *The Agreeable Surprise*, Op. 16 London, Bland [*c.* 1781]	PV	GB-Lbl

33 *False and True*, Medley Overture, Op. 46 London, Author [1798]	Pf	GB-Lbl

34 *Review* or *Ways of Windsor*, Medley Overture, Op. 52	Pf	GB-Lbl

Bates, William

35 *Pharnaces* London, Welcker [1765]	PV	GB-Cpl, Lbl

Boyce, William

| Eight Symphonys in 8 parts, Op. 2 London, Walsh [*c.* 1760] | PP | GB-Cfm, Lam, Lbl, Lcm |

36 No. 1

= New Year's Ode, 1756   MSF   GB-Ob

37 No. 2

= Birthday Ode, 1756   MSF   GB-Ob

38 No. 3

= *The Chaplet*, 1749   PF, PV   GB-Lbl, etc.

39 No. 4

= *Shepherd's Lottery*, 1751   PF, PV   GB-Lbl, etc.

40 No. 5

= Ode on St Cecilia's Day 'See, fam'd Apollo'   MSF   GB-Ob

41 No. 6

= *Solomon*, 1743   PF, PV   GB-Lbl, etc.

42 No. 7

= Pindaric Ode   MSF   GB-Ob

43 No. 8

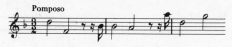

= Worcester Festival Overture   MSF   GB-Ob

Twelve Overtures
privately printed, 1770   PP   GB-Lbl, Mp (both
imperfect)

44 No. 1

= Birthday Ode, 1762   MSF   GB-Ob

45 No. 2

= Birthday Ode, 1765   MSF   GB-Ob

46 No. 3

= New Year's Ode, 1763   MSF   GB-Ob

47 No. 4

= 'Peace' Ode, 1763   MSF   GB-Ob

48 No. 5

= New Year's Ode, 1762   MSF   GB-Ob

49 No. 6

= The Secular Masque [?1750]   MSF   GB-Lbl

50 No. 7

= New Year's Ode, 1765   MSF   GB-Ob

51 No. 8

= Birthday Ode, 1761   MSF   GB-Ob

52 No. 9

= New Year's Ode, 1768   MSF   GB-Ob

53 No. 10

= Birthday Ode, 1764   MSF   GB-Ob

54 No. 11

= Birthday Ode, 1766   MSF   GB-Ob

55 No. 12

= New Year's Ode, 1767   MSF   GB-Ob

56 The Cambridge Ode
[London, 1749]   PF   GB-Lbl, etc.

Charke, Richard

57 Medley Overture   PP   GB-Lbl, etc.

No. 3 of 6 Medley Overtures

Collett, John

Six Simphonies or Overtures in 8 and
10 parts, Op. 2
London, Johnston, etc.   PP   GB-Lam; US-Pru,
                                                    Wc

— [c. 1753–5]   PP   GB-Mp

58 No. 1

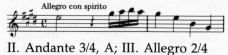

II. Andante 3/4, A; III. Allegro 2/4

59 No. 2

II. Andante sempre legato 2/4, A♭;
III. Allegretto 3/4

60 No. 3

II. Andante 3/4, C; III. Presto 3/8
= Overture, *Midas*, 1765

61 No. 4

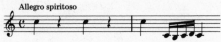

II. Andante 2/4, F; III. Allegro 3/4

62 No. 5

II. Andante 2/4, B♭; III. Tempo di
men. 3/4 [no trio]; IV. Presto 3/8

63 No. 6

II. Andante 2/4, C; III. Presto 3/8

64 Overture in *The Hermit*, or *Harlequin at Rhodes*   MSF   GB-Lbl
   — [*c.* 1770]   PP   GB-Ob

65 **Crotch, William**

  Overture in A major, 1795   MSF   GB-Lbl

66 Symphony No. 2   Org?   US-Wc

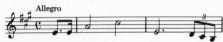

  Dibdin, Charles

67 *The Padlock*
  London, Johnston [1768]   PV   GB-Lbl, etc.
  —   PP   GB-Lbl, Mp, Ob

  II. Andantino 3/4, E♭; III. Presto 3/8

68 *The Blackamoor*
  London, Johnston [1770]   PV   GB-Lbl, etc.
  —   PP   ? lost

  II. Allegretto 3/8; III. Allegro assai 4/4 ('A favorite concert for the German flute or oboe . . .')

69 *The Institution of the Garter*
  London, Longman [1771]   PV   GB-Lbl, etc.
  — PP   GB-Mp

Fisher, John Abraham

Six Symphonies in 8 parts   PP   GB-Lcm
London, Longman [*c.* 1770]

70 No. 1

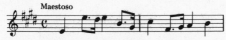

II. Andantino 2/4, A; III. Prestissimo 3/8

71 No. 2

II. Largo e pomposo 3/4; III. Presto assai 3/8

72 No. 3

II. Andantino 2/4, c; III. Presto 3/8

73 No. 4

II. Adagio molto affettuoso 3/4, E♭; III. Tempo di men. 3/4 [no trio]

74 No. 5

II. Andantino 2/4, G; III. Allegro di molto 2/4

75 No. 6

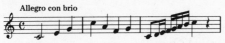

II. Adagio 2/4, G; III. Tempo di men. 3/4 [no trio]

76 Overture in *The Golden Pippin*, 1773   PV   GB-Lbl

77 Overture in *The Syrens*
London, Portal [1777]   PP   GB-Lbl

II. Grave 3/2; Allegretto 2/4

Greene, Maurice

Six Overtures in 7 parts
London, Walsh [*c.* 1745] (privilege   PP   GB-Lbl, Mp
date 1741/2)   Hpd   GB-Lbl, Ob(T)

78 No. 1

79 No. 2

80 No. 3

81 No. 4

82 No. 5

83 No. 6

84 *Florimel* or *Love's Revenge*, 1734   MSF   GB-Lbl, Lcm

85 New Year's Ode, 1740   MSF   GB-Ob

86 New Year's Ode, 1746   MSF   GB-Ob

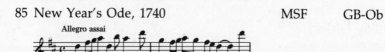

Haigh, Thomas

87 A Favorite Symphony in 9 parts
London, Cahusac [c. 1790]   PP   GB-Lbl

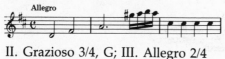

II. Grazioso 3/4, G; III. Allegro 2/4

Hook, James

88 *The Lady of the Manor*, Op. 20
London, Thompson [1778]   PV   GB-Lbl, etc.
—   PP   GB-Mp

II. Largo 3/4; III. Allegretto 6/8

Howard, Samuel

89 *The Amorous Goddess*
London, Walsh [1744]   PV   GB-Lbl, etc.

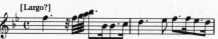

Jackson, William, *of Exeter*

90 *Ode to Fancy*, Op. 8
London [c. 1769]   PF   GB-Lbl, etc.

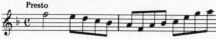

91 *The Metamorphosis*, Op. 14
London, Longman [1783] Pf GB-Lbl

II. Andante 3/4; III. Allegro 2/4

Kelly, Thomas Alexander Erskine, *6th Earl of*

Six Overtures in 8 parts, Op. 1
London, Bremner [*c.* 1761–2]

PP GB-Cpl, Gu, Lbl,
92 No. 1 Lcm, Mp, Ob

93 No. 2

94 No. 3

95 No. 4

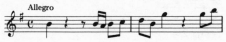

96 No. 5

97 No. 6

Six Simphonies in 4 parts by
Stamitz, his Pupil the Earl of Kelly
and others . . .[1]
London, Bremner [*c.* 1765] PP GM-Lcm

1. These works are probably not by Kelly, according to my 'A Union Thematic Catalogue of 18th-Century Symphonies', *Fontes Artis Musicae*, VI (1959). See also my forthcoming article '18th-century Symphonies of Disputed Paternity'. [LaRue]

98 No. 1

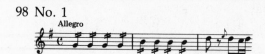

99 No. 2

100 No. 3

101 No. 5

Periodical Overtures
London, Bremner [c. 1766–70]   PP   GB-Lbl,

102 No. 13   Mp

II. Adagio ma non troppo 4/4, Ab;
III. Allegro 3/8, G

103 No. 17

II. Andantino 3/4, c; III. Presto 2/4

104 No. 25

II. Andante 2/4, A; III. Presto 6/8

105 No. 28

II. Adagio ma non troppo 4/4, F; III.
Minuetto 3/4
= Overture, *The Maid of the Mill*,
1765

Linley, Thomas, *the elder*

106 *The Royal Merchant*
London, Welcker [1768]   PV   GB-Lbl, etc.

Con spirito

107 Symphony   PF   GB-Lbl

Allegro

II. Andante 4/4, d; Allegro 2/2

Linley, Thomas, *the younger*

108 *The Duenna*
London, Thompson [1775]   PV   GB-Lbl, etc.
                                 PP   ?
—

Allegro   *tr*   *tr*

Marsh, John[2]

A Favorite Symphony, Nos. 1–6
London, Culliford [*c.* 1795]

109 No. 1   PP   ? lost

Allegro

110 No. 2   PP   ? lost

Allegro

111 No. 3   PP   ? lost

Allegro   *tr*

112 No. 4   PP   GB-Lbl
                               (RM 17.c.1)

Allegro

2. See the Addendum on p. 244.

113 No. 5   PP   ? lost

114 No. 6   PP   GB-Lbl (flauto
                                                          only)

II. Andante 2/4, G; III. Min. Allegro,
Trio; IV. Allegro scherzando

Three Overtures, Op. 37 (arr. as
quintets)
London, Goulding, Phipps and
D'Almaine [after 1800]   PP   GB-Mp

115 No. 1

116 No. 2

117 No. 3

118 *A Conversation Sinfonie* (published
under the name of J. Sharm)
London, Preston [*c.* 1786]   PP   GB-Mp

(for two orchestras)

119 Celebrated Overture, *La Chasse*
London, Preston [*c.* 1795]   PP   GB-Mp

Mazzinghi, Joseph

120 *Paul and Virginia*, Op. 17
     London, G. Goulding [1795]   Pf   GB-Lbl

121 *Ramah Droog* (Country Concerts,
     No. 1)
     London, Goulding, Phipps and
     D'Almaine [after 1800]   PP   GB-Mp

122 *The Exile*   Pf   GB-Lbl

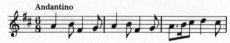

123 *The Wife of Two Husbands*, Op. 50   Pf   GB-Lbl

Moze, Henry

124 Overture to the entertainment of
     The Witches; or *Harlequin's Trip to
     Naples*
     London, Thompson [*c.* 1770]   PP   GB-Lbl, Mp
     —   Hpd   GB-Lbl

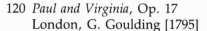

Norris, Thomas

Six Simphonies, in 8 parts, Op. 1
London, the Author [*c.* 1765]   PP   GB-Lbl, Lcm, Mp

125 No. 1

II. Andante moderato 2/4, A; III.
Vivace 3/8

126 No. 2

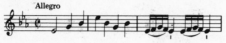

II. Andante moderato 2/4, Bb; III.
Men. 3/4 [no trio]

127 No. 3

II. Andante, 'Slow' 3/4, Eb; III.
Presto 3/8

128 No. 4

II. Largo andante 4/4, C; III. Men. &
Trio 3/4

129 No. 5

II. Andante moderato 2/4, G; III.
Allegro 6/8

130 No. 6

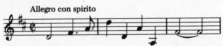

II. Andante moderato 3/4, A; III.
Allegro – Rondo 2/2

Oswald, James

131 *Queen Mab*, Overture
London, Henry Thorowgood [*c.* 1770]   PP   GB-Lbl

II. Affettuoso 3/4, c; III. Allegro
moderato 12/8

Reeve, William

132 *Harlequin and Oberon*
London, Wheatstone, 1796   PP   GB-Mp
—   Pf, PV   GB-Lbl, etc.

133 *The Turnpike Gate* (Country
Concerts, No. 5)
London, Goulding, Phipps and
D'Almaine, 1799   PP   GB-Mp
—   Pf, PV   GB-Lbl, etc.

Rush, George

134 *The Capricious Lovers*
London, Welcker [1764]   PV   GB-Lbl; S-Skma; etc.
—   PP   ? lost

135 *The Royal Shepherd*
London, Welcker [1764]   PV   GB-Lbl; S-Skma; etc.
—   PP   GB-Er, Lam, Lcm,
     Ob

Shaw, Thomas

136 *Cymon*
London, Thompson [c. 1780]   PV   GB-Lcm; US-Ic
—   PP   ? lost

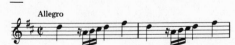

137 *The Island of St Marguerite*
London, Thompson [c. 1789]   PV   GB-Lbl; Us-Ic
—   PP   ? lost

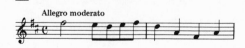

Shield, William

138 *Rosina*, 1783
(many editions)   PV   GB-Lbl, etc.

Smethergell, William

Six Overtures in 8 parts, Op. 2
London, Longman, etc. [*c.* 1775]   PP   GB-Lam, Mp

139 No. 1

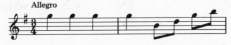

II. Adagio 3/4, c; III. Allegro assai
3/8

140 No. 2

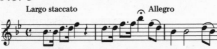

II. Andante 2/4, C; III. Allegro 2/4

141 No. 3

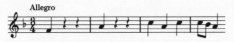

II. Andante 3/4, Eb; III. Presto 3/8

142 No. 4

II. Andante 2/4, Bb; III. Presto 3/8

143 No. 5

II. Andante 2/4, G; III. Presto 6/8

144 No. 6

II. Largo 2/4; III. Tempo di men.
[rondo] 3/4

Six Overtures in 8 parts, Op. 5, A
Second Sett
London, Preston [? 1789–90]   PP   GB-Gu, Lbl, Mp, Ob

145 No. 1

146 No. 2

147 No. 3

148 No. 4

149 No. 5

150 No. 6

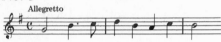

Smith, John Christopher

151 *The Fairies*, Overture
London, Walsh [1755]   PF   GB-Lbl

II. Minuet 3/4, D; III. March 4/4, D

152 *The Tempest*
London, Walsh [1756]   PF   GB-Lbl

II. Minuet andante 3/4

153 *The Enchanter*
London, Walsh [1760]   PF   GB-Lbl

II. Allegro 3/8; III. Gavotte 2/2

Valentine, John

Eight Easy Symphonies, Op. 6
London, Bland [*c.* 1785]   PP   GB-Lbl

154 No. 1

II. Allegro; III. March

155 No. 2

II. Gavot; III. Tempo di men. 3/4

156 No. 3

II. Spiritoso; III. Tempo di men. 3/4

157 No. 4

II. Tempo di men. 3/4; III. March

158 No. 5

II. Minuet & Trio; III. Giga

159 No. 6

II. March; III. Vivace: Rondo

160 No. 7

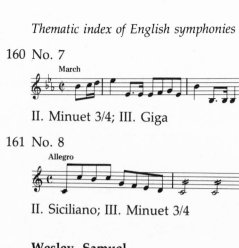

II. Minuet 3/4; III. Giga

161 No. 8

II. Siciliano; III. Minuet 3/4

Wesley, Samuel

Several symphonic works   MSF   GB-Lbl (Add. 35008)

162 Con brio

163 Allegro con brio

164 Allegro maestoso

165 Allegro spiritoso

166 Allegro

167 Allegro

168 Andante

Yates, William

169 *The Choice of Apollo*   MSF   GB-Lcm

[Allegro]

Addendum *by Richard Andrewes*

The Cambridge University Library in 1968 acquired a set of printed parts of works by John Marsh, including items 109–14 and 118–19 above. In this set the imprints for items 109–14 (*A Favorite Symphony* . . . Nos. 1–6) are as follows:

No. 1 London, Preston
No. 2 London, Smart
No. 3 London, Smart
No. 4 London, Longman & Broderip
No. 5 London, Longman & Broderip*
No. 6 London, Longman & Broderip†

* On No. 5 this imprint is crossed out and L. Lavenu's added in longhand.
† On No. 6 this imprint is crossed out and Culliford's added in longhand.
The same set includes printed parts of

> Overture (Country Concerts, No. 3)
> London, Goulding, Phipps and D'Almaine [after 1800]

II. Andante 4/4, C; III. Allegro 2/2

A bibliography of the writings of Charles Cudworth

Compiled by Richard Andrewes

Charles's greatest gift was an ability to communicate his enthusiasm to all sorts of people. This he did with a wit that is evident in his selection of titles, and a clarity that is equally characteristic of his most serious papers. This bibliography attempts to survey both his unpublished and published work and to include most of the latter; it intentionally omits several types of publication, namely shorter record reviews (many of which were written for *Records & Recording* between 1963 and 1975), record and book reviews broadcast by the BBC between 1969 and 1977, book reviews in the *Musical Times, Music & Letters* and elsewhere, sleeve notes for various record companies (in particular for L'Oiseau-Lyre), other programme notes and newspaper articles.

Neither a chronological nor an alphabetical sequence would have indicated the breadth of Charles's range of interests. Hence a subject arrangement, starting with his creative and non-musical writings, then articles on musicology, libraries and general topics, followed by those on music in England and in other countries, and finally those on individual persons, subdivided chronologically into historical periods. (A few articles appear under more than one heading.)

Obituaries for Charles appeared in the *Musical Times*, 119 (1978), p. 263 by Stanley Sadie; in *Fontes*, 25 (1978), p. 107 by Alec Hyatt King; and in *Brio*, 15/1 (Spring 1978),pp. 29–30 by Walter Stock and Brian Redfern. Charles wrote the article on himself in *MGG*, 2 (1952), and *The New Grove* (1980) includes an article on him by Stanley Sadie.

Abbreviations

BBC/MM	British Broadcasting Corporation, Third Programme, Music Magazine
Enc. Brit.	*Encyclopedia Britannica* (Chicago 1970)
Fontes	*Fontes artis musicae*

Grove 5	*Grove's Dictionary of Music and Musicians*, 5th edn, ed. E. Blom, 9 vols. (London: Macmillan, 1954) and Suppl., 1 vol. (Macmillan, 1961)
GSJ	*Galpin Society Journal*
HF	*High Fidelity* (Great Barrington, Mass.)
M&L	*Music & Letters*
M&M	*Music & Musicians*
MGG	*Die Musik in Geschichte und Gegenwart*, ed. F. Blume, 16 vols. (Kassel, etc.: Bärenreiter, 1949–79)
MMR	*The Monthly Musical Record*
MT	*The Musical Times*
New Grove	*The New Grove Dictionary of Music and Musicians*, ed. S. Sadie, 20 vols. (London: Macmillan, 1980)
PRMA	*Proceedings of the Royal Musical Association*
R&R	*Records & Recording*

Outline of subject headings

1 Creative works
2 Non-musical subjects
3 Libraries, sources and settings
4 Music and other subjects (miscellany)
5 Christmas music
6 Historical periods: Gothic–Renaissance
7 Historical periods: Baroque–Classical
8 Music in England
9 Music of other countries
10 Musicians of the early Baroque (born before 1670)
11 Musicians of the later Baroque (born 1670–1720)
12 Musicians of the classical age (born 1720–1770)
13 Musicians of the nineteenth century (born 1770–1870)
14 Musicians of the twentieth century (born after 1870)
15 Editions of music

Order within sections: 1–2, chronological; 3–9, alphabetical (titles, but with some words transferred to headwords, e.g. all articles on Cambridge in section 8); 10–14 alphabetical (surnames).

1. Creative works

Most of the following plays were written during fire-watching duty in the war and were performed locally by amateurs for amusement. Some of the longer plays were read through at meetings of the Mackenzie Society and the Workers' Educational Association in Cambridge.

    1937   The Chastening
    1938   The Beloved Saxon [i.e. Handel]

1940   The Sleeping Princess
1941   No Polo Today
1941   Quit Your Dream
1942   Mr Bach of London
1943   Troubled Harvest
1944   The Singing Tower
1945   Seneca Died Slowly
194–?   Dutch Interlude
194–?   Enter Alexis

A number of poems from the war years and short stories about life in the Fens after the manner of W. W. Jacobs also survive in manuscript. A full-length novel called *The Silken Chord*, about a seventeenth-century musician, was also written at this time.

Patrick Hadley was a close and valued friend for whom Charles wrote the following librettos (Hadley's autographs are in the Fitzwilliam Museum Library):

Cantata for Lent

Connemara

Fen and Flood (vocal score O.U.P. 1956)

The Gate Hangs High

The Suffolk Lady: A Ballad of the Waveney (vocal score A. & C. Black 1948)

2. Non-musical subjects

'The Dutch influence in East Anglia', *Cambridge Antiquarian Society Proceedings*, 37 (1935–6), 24–42

'Dutch gables in East Anglia', *Architectural Review*, 85 (1939), 113–18

'Cambridge in the eighteen-thirties: some notes extracted from an old guide-book', *Cambridge Public Library Record*, 12 (1940), 49–66

'East Anglia and the Netherlands', *Britain and Holland*, 6 (1954), 84–90

'The way to Wind'm', *East Anglian Magazine*, 17 (1958), 492–6; revised version in *1969 East Anglian and Essex Countryside Annual* (Ipswich 1969)

3. Libraries, sources and editing

'Americans in European music libraries (and elsewhere): an after dinner fantasia', *Notes*, 19 (1961), 31–8

'Bless thee! thou art translated', *HF*, 10 (November 1960), 53–5 ['An uncharitable disquisition on the horrors perpetrated by translators of opera librettos']

'From document to disc', *R&R*, 11 (May 1968), 18–19 [on sources and editing]

'The historical quest II', *R&R*, 18 (November 1974), 17

'Libraries' in *Grove 5* (1954)

'The music at Burghley House', *MT*, 104 (1963), 412

'Music libraries and the research worker', *Fontes*, 2 (1955), 118–22
'Music on microfilm', *Music*, 1/9 (August 1952), 22–5
'Un "Répertoire de documents musicaux": secondary report',*Fontes*, 12 (1965), 145
'The scare du printemps; or, The frite of spring', *HF*, 8 (April 1958), 46–8, 131–2
'Watch your jacket: the art of record annotation', *HF*, 12 (March 1962), 58–60, 113
'Ye olde spuriosity shoppe; or, Put it in the Anhang', *Notes*, 12 (1954–5), 25–40, 533–53

4. Music and other subjects (miscellany)

'Art and music', *R&R*, 14 (January 1971), 42–4 [review of *Music, Mirror of the Arts* by Alan Rich (London: Pitman, 1970)]
'Humour and music', *Music*, 1/10 (September 1952), 11–13

5. Christmas music

'Christmas music', *Music*, 2/1 (December 1952), 11–13
'For Christmas night', *BBC/MM*, 24 December 1961
'Per la notte di natale', *MT*, 112 (1971), 1165–6
'Sound of Christmas', *HF*, 12 (December 1962), 38–41
'The true *Stille Nacht*', *MT*, 105 (1964), 892–4

6. Historical periods: Gothic–Renaissance

'From Gothic to Rennaissance, *R&R*, 12 (September 1969), 22–4 [review of two records of early music]

7. Historical periods: Baroque–Classical

'Baroque, Rococo, Galant, Classic', *MMR*, 83 (1953), 172–5
'Cadence galante: the story of a cliché', *MMR*, 79 (1949), 176–8
'Cantata' in *Enc. Brit.* (1970)
From Baroque to Classical: the periods in perspective, Open University course A304, *The development of instruments and their music*, unit 06 (Milton Keynes 1973): sound recording (18' 28")
'G minor: "The key of Fate"', *Music*, 1/6 (May 1952), 13–15 [on symphonies in G minor]
Galant music, Open University course A304, *The development of instruments and their music*, unit 07 (Milton Keynes 1973): sound recording (18' 26")

8. Music in England

'Ballad opera' in *Enc. Brit.* (1970)
'Cambridge' in *MGG*, 2 (1952)

— 'Cambridge' in *New Grove* (1980)
— 'Five centuries of music degrees', *BBC/MM*, 16 February 1964
— '500 years of music degrees', *MT*, 105 (1964), 98–9
— 'A musical profile of King's College Chapel Choir', *BBC/MM*, 1 January 1967
'Coronation music', *Music*, 2/6 (May 1953), 7–9, 21–3
'England', E: '18. und frühes 19. Jahrhunderts' in *MGG*, 3 (1954)
'England's Golden Age', *R&R*, 6/9 (June 1963), 14–15, 77 [review of recordings of music of Shakespeare's time]
'The English organ concerto', *Score*, 8 (September 1953), 51–60
'The English symphonists of the eighteenth century', *PRMA*, 78 (1951–2), 31–51
— Appendix to the preceding: *Thematic Index of English Eighteenth-Century Overtures and Symphonies* (London: Royal Musical Association, 1953; repr. Liechtenstein: Kraus, 1969): see pp. 219–44 in the present volume
'The Fitzwilliam Museum in Cambridge', *BBC/MM*, 6 February 1966
— 'A Cambridge anniversary: the Fitzwilliam Museum and its music-loving founder', *MT*, 107 (1966), 113–17, 209–10
— 'Fitzwilliam and French music of the Baroque' in *French Music and the Fitzwilliam* (Cambridge: Fitzwilliam Museum, 1975), 7–11
— 'Fitzwilliam and Handel' in *Handel and the Fitzwilliam* (Cambridge: Fitzwilliam Museum, 1974), 7–9
— 'Fitzwilliam and the Italian style' in *Italian Music and the Fitzwilliam* (Cambridge: Fitzwilliam Museum, 1976), 7–9
— 'Richard, Viscount Fitzwilliam and the French Baroque music in the Fitzwilliam Museum', *Fontes*, 13 (1966), 27–31
'Great Britain' in *Algemene muziekencyclopedie*, ed. A. Corbet and W. Paap (6 vols., Antwerp 1957–63) [in Dutch]
Housman, A. E. 'The "Shropshire Lad" and English music', *Music*, 1/12 (November 1952), 11–14
King's Lynn. 'Festival at King's Lynn', *Music*, 1/8 (July 1952), 19–20
'London', V: '18. Jahrhundert' in *MGG*, 8 (1960)
'Masters of the Musick', *MT*, 107 (1966), 676–7 [on masters of the Queen's Music]
'The meaning of "vivace" in eighteenth-century England', *Fontes*, 12 (1965), 194–5
'Memoires of musick', *Music*, 2/9 (August–September 1953), 12–14, and 2/10 (October 1953), 8–10, 38
'Norwich' in *MGG*, 9 (1961)
'Pride of Cambridge', *R&R*, 9/12 (September 1966), 21, 68 [review of a recording of a selection from the Fitzwilliam Virginal Book]
Shakespeare, William. 'Hark! What fine change there is in the musicke', *R&R*, 12 (April 1969), 29–31 [review of four recordings of musical settings of Shakespeare]
— 'Shakespeare and English song', *BBC/MM*, 23 April 1961
— 'Shakespeare and the choral singer', *American Choral Review*, 6/3 (1964), 1
— 'Songs and part-song settings of Shakespeare's lyrics, 1660–1960' in *Shakespeare in music*, ed. P. Hartnoll (London: Macmillan, 1964), 51–87
— 'Touches of sweet harmony', *R&R*, 7/7 (April 1964), 16–19, 68

'Symphonie', B: 'Entwicklung . . . im 18. Jahrhundert', v: 'England' in *MGG* 12 (1965).
'The symphony in eighteenth-century Britain', *BBC Third Programme*, 12 December 1957
'The Vauxhall "lists"', *GSJ*, 20 (1967), 24–42
'Wanted . . . An English Music Society', *Music*, 2/2 (January 1953), 11–13

9. Music of other countries

France. 'Age of splendour', *M&M*, 13 (July 1965), 30–1, 50 [an introduction to the main figures of the French Baroque featured in the English Bach Festival, 1965]
— '"Baptist's vein": French orchestral music and its influence from 1650 to 1750', *PRMA*, 83 (1956–7), 29–47
— 'Fitzwilliam and French music of the Baroque' in *French Music and the Fitzwilliam* (Cambridge: Fitzwilliam Museum, 1975), 7–11
— 'Introduction' to F. Raguenet, *A Comparison between French and Italian Musick and Operas* (Farnborough: Gregg, 1968), facsimile reprint of the 1709 edn
— 'Richard, Viscount Fitzwilliam and the French Baroque music in the Fitzwilliam Museum', *Fontes*, 13 (1966), 27–31
Italy. 'Fitzwilliam and the Italian style' in *Italian Music and the Fitzwilliam* (Cambridge: Fitzwilliam Museum, 1976), 7–9
— 'Italian trio sonatas', *BBC/MM*, 20 March 1966
Portugal. 'Portugal's Golden Age', *R&R*, 10/7 (April 1967), 32–3 [review of four recordings of eighteenth-century music]
United States of America. 'The Californian missions, 1769–1969', *MT*, 110 (1969), 194–6
— 'Land of the free', *R&R*, 18 (March 1975), 14 [review of three recordings of American music]

10. Musicians of the early Baroque (born before 1670)

'Akeroyde, Samuel' in *MGG*, 15 (1973)
Ariosti. 'Attilio Ariosti', *BBC/MM*, 6 November 1966
Campra, André. 'Campra', *BBC/MM*, 4 December 1960
Cavalieri, Emilio de'. 'Body and soul', *R&R*, 14 (April 1971), 50–1 [review of a recording of *La rappresentatione di anima e di corpo*]
Cavalli, (Pietro) Francesco. 'Baroque on stage', *M&M*, 15 (June 1967), 24–5 [on the staging of *Ormindo* and of Rameau's *Zéphire*]
Colonna. 'Giovanni Paolo Colonna', *BBC/MM*, 7 November 1971
Corelli. 'The concerti grossi of Arcangelo Corelli', *Music*, 2/8 (July 1953), 33, 35 [record review]
Couperin, François. 'Couperin and his times', *BBC/MM*, 10 November 1968
Delalande. 'Michel Richard Delalande', *BBC/MM*, 22 December 1957
'Fux, Johann Joseph' in *Enc. Brit.* (1970)

'Gallo, Domenico' in *New Grove* (1980)

'Hart, James' in *MGG*, 5 (1956)

'Holder, William' in *MGG*, 6 (1957)

Lawes. 'Henry Lawes', *BBC/MM*, 10 January 1971

'Marais, Marin' in *Enc. Brit.* (1970)

'Muffat, Georg . . .' in *Enc. Brit.* (1970)

'Pepusch, Johann Christoph' in *MGG*, 10 (1962)

— 'Pepusch, John Christopher' in *Enc. Brit.* (1970)

Purcell, Henry. *'Dido and Aeneas'*, *R&R*, 10/1 (October 1966), 26–7 [review of the de los Angeles/Barbirolli recording]

— 'Purcell's *Fairy Queen'*, *R&R*, 15/4 (January 1972), 33–6 [review of Britten's recording]

— 'Purcell's music for royal occasions', *BBC/MM*, 31 December 1972

— 'The unfamiliar Purcell', *R&R*, 6/10 (July 1963), 15–17

'Richardson, Vaughan' in *MGG*, 11 (1963)

— 'Richardson, Vaughan' in *New Grove* (1980)

'Torelli, Giuseppe' in *Enc. Brit.* (1970)

'Tucker, Edmund/Edward' in *MGG*, 13 (1966) [including William Tucker]

Tunder. 'Franz Tunder', *BBC/MM*, 5 November 1967

11. Musicians of the later Baroque (born 1670–1720)

'Alberti, Domenico' in *Enc. Brit.* (1970)

'Albinoni, Tommaso' in *Enc. Brit.* (1970)

'Arne, Thomas Augustine. 'Arne', *BBC/MM*, 6 March 1960

— 'Boyce and Arne: the "generation of 1710"', *M&L*, 41 (1960), 136–45

— 'Two Georgian classics: Arne and Stevens', *M&L*, 45 (1964), 146–53

'Avison, Charles' in *Enc. Brit.* (1970)

— 'Avison, Charles' in *MGG*, 15 (1973)

— 'Avison of Newcastle, 1709–1770', *MT*, 111 (1970), 480–3

— 'Charles Avison', *BBC/MM*, 10 May 1970

Bach, Carl Philipp Emanuel. 'Two sons of music', *M&M*, 13 (November 1964), 14–15, 45 [on Rameau and C. P. E. Bach]

'Benda, family' in *Enc. Brit.* (1970) [including František (Franz)]

Bickham, George, jnr. 'Preface' to a reprint of *The Musical Entertainer* (London: Sudbrook, [196?])

'Boyce, William' in *Enc. Brit.* (1970)

— 'Boyce, William' in *MGG*, 15 (1973)

— 'Boyce', *BBC/MM*, 7 February 1960

— 'Boyce and Arne: the "generation of 1710"', *M&L*, 41 (1960), 136–45

— 'The symphonies of Dr William Boyce', *Music*, 2/3 (February 1953), 27–9

'Clari, Giovanni Carlo Maria' in *Enc. Brit.* (1970)

'Clarke, Jeremiah' in *MGG*, 2 (1952)

— 'Jeremiah Clarke and the "Trumpet Voluntary"', *Music*, 1/5 (April 1952), 16, 36

— 'Some new facts about the Trumpet Voluntary', *MT*, 94 (1953), 401–3
— 'The Trumpet Voluntary', *M&L*, 41 (1960), 342–8, written in collaboration with F. B. Zimmerman; reprinted in *Music* (USA), 3 (September 1969), 29–30
'Daquin, Louis Claude' in *Enc. Brit.* (1970)
'Durante, Francesco' in *Enc. Brit.* (1970)
'Felton, William' in *MGG*, 4 (1955)
— 'Felton, William' in *Enc. Brit.* (1970)
'Festing, Michael Christian' in *MGG*, 4 (1955)
'Galuppi, Baldassare' in *Enc. Brit.* (1970)
'Giardini, Felice (de)' in *MGG*, 5 (1956)
— 'Giardini, Felice de'' in *Enc. Brit.* (1970)
'Gibbs, Joseph' in *MGG*, 5 (1956)
— 'Gibbs, Joseph' in *New Grove* (1980)
'Giordani, Carmine' in *MGG*, 5 (1956)
'Graun, Karl Heinrich' in *Enc. Brit.* (1970)
'Handel, George Frederick' in *Enc. Brit.* (1970)
— 'Fitzwilliam and Handel' in *Handel and the Fitzwilliam* (Cambridge: Fitzwilliam Museum, 1974), 7–9
— *Handel: A Biography with a Survey of Books, Editions and Recordings*, Concert-Goers Companions (London: Bingley, 1972)
— *Handel*, Great Musicians series 67–9 (London 1970): with gramophone records
— 'Handel and the French style', *M&L*, 40 (1959), 122–31
— 'Handel in Egypt', *R&R*, 7/12 (September 1964), 15, 44 [review of Sutherland's recording of *Giulio Cesare*]
— 'Handel's *Belshazzar*', *The Listener*, 76 (22 September 1966), 434
— *Handel's Messiah*, Open University course A100, *Foundation course in the humanities: history and authenticity*, unit 27 (Milton Keynes, 1970): sound recording (23' 47")
— 'The imperishable wag', *HF*, 9 (April 1959), 53–5, 135–6, 138–9 [on Handel's popularity in England]
— 'Laying Handel's ghost', *The Listener*, 59 (1958), 297
— 'Mythistorica Handeliana' in *Festskrift Jens Peter Larsen* (Copenhagen 1972), pp. 161–6
— 'St Cecilia, Dryden and Handel', *BBC/MM*, 21 April 1963
— 'Two Handelian anecdotes' in *Festschrift Otto Erich Deutsch zum 80. Geburstag*, ed. W. Gerstenberg (Kassel, etc.: Bärenreiter, 1963), pp. 49–50
— 'Two unusual plays: (1) Telemann in Tavistock Place, and (2) Handel at Audley End', *Music*, 2/7 (June 1953), 15–16 [review of a performance of *Acis and Galatea*]
— 'The unfamiliar Handel', *R&R*, 6/6 (March 1963), 15–17, 58
'Hart, Philip' in *MGG*, 5 (1956)
'Hasse, Johann Adolph' in *Enc. Brit.* (1970)
'Hawdon, Mattias' in *MGG*, 5 (1956)
'Heighington, Musgrave' in *MGG*, 6 (1957)
— 'Heighington, Musgrave' in *New Grove* (1980)

'Hine, William' in *MGG*, 6 (1957)
'Howard, Samuel' in *MGG*, 6 (1957)
'Immyns, John' in *MGG*, 6 (1957)
'Jomelli, Niccolo' in *Enc. Brit.* (1970)
'Keeble, John' in *MGG*, 7 (1958)
'Kelway, Joseph' in *MGG*, 7 (1958)
'Kent, James' in *MGG*, 7 (1958)
'King, Charles' in *MGG*, 7 (1958)
'Lampe, Johann Friedrich' in *MGG*, 8 (1960)
'Leo, Leonardo' in *Enc. Brit.* (1970)
'Leveridge, Richard' in *MGG*, 8 (1960)
Marcello. 'Alessandro Marcello: a tercentenary note', *MT*, 109 (1968), 1231–2
'Marcello, Benedetto' in *Enc. Brit.* (1970)
'Martini, Giovanni Battista' in *Enc. Brit.* (1970)
'Marpurg, Friedrich Willhelm' in *Enc. Brit.* (1970)
'Mason, William', *MGG*, 8 (1960)
'Muffat, . . . Gottlieb' in *Enc. Brit.* (1970)
'Mudge, Richard' in *MGG*, 9 (1961)
'Nares, James' in *MGG*, 9 (1961)
'Paradies, (Pietro) Domenico' in *MGG*, 10 (1962)
— 'Paradisi, Pietro Domenico' in *Enc. Brit.* (1970)
'Pasquali, Niccolo' in *MGG*, 10 (1962)
'Pellegrini, Ferdinando' in *MGG*, 10 (1962)
'Pergolesi, Giovanni Battista' in *Enc. Brit.* (1970)
— *Pergolesi*, Great Musicians series 51–2 (London 1970): with gramophone records
— 'Pergolesi, Ricciotti and the Count of Bentinck' in *Société Internationale de Musicologie, 5ème Congrès, Utrecht 1952: compte rendu* (Amsterdam 1953), pp. 127–31
— 'Notes on the instrumental works attributed to Pergolesi', *M&L*, 30 (1949), 321–8
'Porpora, Nicola' in *Enc. Brit.* (1970)
'Prelleur, Peter' in *MGG*, 10 (1962)
'Quantz, Johann Joachim' in *Enc. Brit.* (1970)
Rameau, Jean-Philippe. 'Rameau after 200 years', *R&R*, 7/8 (May 1964), 14–15, 72
— 'Rameau's Baroque Arcadia', *R&R*, 9/6 (March 1966), 26–7 [review of a recording of *Hippolyte et Aricie*]
— 'Rameau's chamber music', *BBC/MM*, 3 May 1964
— 'Two sons of music', *M&M*, 13 (November 1964), 14–15, 45 [on Rameau and C. P. E. Bach]
— 'Baroque on stage', *M&M*, 15 (June 1967), 24–5 [on the staging of *Zéphire* and of Cavalli's *Ormindo*]
'Randall, John' in *MGG*, 10 (1962)
Ricciotti, Carlo. 'Pergolesi, Ricciotti and the Count of Bentinck' in *Société Inter-*

nationale de musicologie, 5ème Congrès, Utrecht 1952: compte rendu (Amsterdam, 1953), pp. 127–31

'Robinson, John' in *MGG*, 11 (1963)

'Sammartini' [i.e. Giuseppe and Giovanni Battista] in *Enc. Brit.* (1970)

'Stamitz, family' [Johann Wenzel Anton] in *Enc. Brit.* (1970)

'Stanesby, Thomas I' in *MGG*, 12 (1965) [including Thomas Stanesby II]

'Tartini, Giuseppe' in *Enc. Brit.* (1970)

— 'Giuseppe Tartini', *BBC/MM*, 22 February 1970

Telemann, Georg Philipp. 'Music for seven courses', *R&R*, 8/8 (May 1965), 19, 21 [review of a recording of Telemann's *Tafelmusik*]

— 'Tribute to Telemann', *R&R*, 10/9 (June 1967), 14–15 [review of four records of recorder music]

— 'Two unusual plays: (1) Telemann in Tavistock Place, and (2) Handel at Audley End', *Music*, 2/7 (June 1953), 15–16 [review of performances of *Ino* and *Pimpinone*]

Tischer, Johann Nikolaus. 'Renowned Tischer: a fantasy on a forgotten theme', *Music*, 3/2 (February 1954), 7–9

'Travers, John' in *MGG*, 13 (1966)

— 'Travers, John' in *New Grove* (1980)

'Vincent, Richard (I)' in *MGG*, 13 (1966) [including Isabella Vincent, Richard Vincent (II), Thomas Vincent (I) and (II), *et al.*]

'Vinci, Leonardo' in *Enc. Brit.* (1970)

'Visconti, Gasparo' in *MGG*, 13 (1966)

'Vivaldi, Antonio' in *Enc. Brit.* (1970)

'Walther, Johann Gottfried' in *Enc. Brit.* (1970)

'Webb, Daniel' in *MGG*, 14 (1968)

'Woodcock, Robert' in *MGG*, 14 (1968)

'Worgan, Familie' in *MGG*, 14 (1968)

— 'Worgan family' in *New Grove* (1980)

'Yates, William' in *MGG*, 14 (1968)

12. Musicians of the classical age (born 1720–1770)

'Abel, Karl Friedrich' in *Enc. Brit.* (1970)

'Adams, James B.' in *MGG*, 15 (1973)

'Addison, John' in *MGG*, 15 (1973)

'Albrechtsberger, Johann Georg' in *Enc. Brit.* (1970)

'Anspach, Elizabeth' in *New Grove* (1980), co-author

'Arnold, Samuel' in *Enc. Brit.* (1970)

— 'Arnold, Samuel' in *MGG*, 15 (1973)

'Ashley, Familie' in *MGG*, 15 (1973)

'Ayleward, Theodore' in *MGG*, 15 (1973)

Bach, Johann Christian. 'Bach's songs', *BBC Third Programme*, 195– (?)

— 'Mr Bach of London', *HF*, 12 (June 1962), 35–7

'Battishill, Jonathan' in *Enc. Brit.* (1970)

'Benda, family' in *Enc. Brit.* (1970) [incl. Jiří Antonín (Georg)]

Burney, Charles. 'Dr Burney's musical tours in Europe', *BBC/MM*, 1 November 1959

Casanova, Giovanni Jacopo. 'Casanova and the food of love', *M&M*, 20 (March 1972), 30–2

'Cimarosa, Domenico' in *Enc. Brit.* (1970)

— 'Cimarosa al cembalo', *R&R*, 15 (April 1972), 40–1

— 'Cimarosa's keyboard sonatas', *BBC/MM*, 1 December 1963

— 'Marriage Cimarosa-style', *M&M*, 13 (May 1965), 28–9

'Clementi, Muzio' in *Enc. Brit.* (1970)

'Dittersdorf, Karl Ditters von' in *Enc. Brit.* (1970)

'Dussek, Jan Ladislav' in *Enc. Brit.* (1970)

'Fischer, Johann Christian' in *MGG*, 4 (1955)

'Fisher, John Abraham' in *MGG*, 4 (1955)

'Fitzwilliam, Richard, 7th Viscount Fitzwilliam of Meryon' in *MGG*, 16 (1979)

— See also under Fitzwilliam Museum on p. 249 above

'Forkel, Johann Nikolaus' in *Enc. Brit.* (1970)

Gainsborough, Thomas. 'Gainsborough and his musical friends', *East Anglian Magazine*, 36 (1977) 366–7

— 'Gainsborough and music' in *Gainsborough, English Music and the Fitzwilliam* (Cambridge: Fitzwilliam Museum, 1977), pp. 11–16

'Garth, John' in *MGG*, 4 (1955)

'Giordani, Giuseppe' in *MGG*, 5 (1956)

'Giordani, Tommaso' in *MGG*, 5 (1956)

— 'Giordani, Tommaso' in *New Grove* (1980), co-author

'Gladwin, Thomas' in *MGG*, 5 (1956)

'Gow, Neil' in *Enc. Brit.* (1970)

Gray, 'Thomas Gray and music', *BBC/MM*, 4 July 1971

— 'Thomas Gray and music', *MT*, 112 (1971), 646–8

'Greatorex, Thomas' in *MGG*, 5 (1956)

'Green, Samuel' in *MGG*, 5 (1956)

'Guerini, Francesco' in *MGG*, 5 (1956)

'Hague, Charles' in *MGG*, 5 (1956)

'Haigh, Thomas' in *MGG*, 5 (1956)

'Hamilton, Catherine' in *MGG*, 5 (1956)

'Harington (Harrington), Henry' in *MGG*, 5 (1956)

Hawkins, John. 'Introduction' to a reprint of *A General History of the Science and Practice of Music* (New York: Dover, 1963)

Haydn, Joseph. 'Haydn and the quartet', *R&R*, 8/10 (July 1965), 18–19

— 'The unfamiliar Haydn', *R&R*, 7/4 (January 1964), 61–3, 72

'Hellendaal, Pieter' in *MGG*, 6 (1957)

'Herschel, (Sir) William' in *MGG*, 6 (1957)

— 'Herschel, William' in *New Grove* (1980), co-author

'Hiller, Johann Adam' in *Enc. Brit.* (1970)

'Hook, James' in *Grove 5* (1954)

— 'Hook, James' in *MGG*, 6 (1957)

— 'Hook, James' in *Enciclopedia dello spettacolo*, 6 (1959)
— 'Hook, James' in *Enc. Brit.* (1970)
— 'Hook, James' in *New Grove* (1980)
— 'James Hook of Norwich: crippled boy who became famous musician', *The Journal* (24 August 1946), issued as part of *Norwich Mercury* and other East Anglian newspapers
'Hopkins, Familie' in *MGG*, 6 (1957)
'Ireland, Francis' in *MGG*, 6 (1957)
'Jackson (of Exeter), William' in *MGG*, 6 (1957)
— 'Jackson, William' in *Enc. Brit.* (1970)
'Jones (of Nayland), William' in *MGG*, 7 (1958)
'Jozzi, Giuseppe' in *MGG*, 7 (1958)
'Kammel, Antonín' in *MGG*, 7 (1958)
'Knyvett, Familie' in *MGG*, 7 (1958)
'Koczwara, Franz' in *MGG*, 7 (1958)
'Kozeluch, Leopold' in *Enc. Brit.* (1970)
'Langdon, Richard' in *MGG*, 8 (1960)
'Latour, T.' in *MGG*, 8 (1960)
'Latrobe, Christian Ignatius' in *MGG*, 8 (1960)
'Linley, Thomas [I]' in *MGG*, 8 (1960) [including Thomas Linley [II] *et al.*]
'Mahon, Familie' in *MGG*, 8 (1960)
Marsh, John' in *MGG*, 8 (1960)
— 'Marsh, John' in *Enc. Brit.* (1970)
— 'An essay by John Marsh', *M&L*, 36 (1955), 155–64
— 'Hints to young composers of instrumental music, by J. Marsh (written about 1806)', *GSJ*, 18 (1965), 57–9
— 'John Marsh on the subscription concert', *GSJ*, 19 (1966), 132–4
Méhul, Etienne (Nicolas). 'Méhul', *BBC/MM*, 9 June 1963
'Miller, Edward' in *MGG*, 9 (1961)
'Moore, Thomas' in *MGG*, 9 (1961)
'Moorehead, John' in *MGG*, 9 (1961)
'Noferi, Giovanni Battista' in *MGG*, 9 (1961)
'Norris, Thomas' in *MGG*, 9 (1961)
'Overend, Marmaduke' in *MGG*, 10 (1962)
'Page, John' in *MGG*, 10 (1962)
'Parke, Familie' in *MGG*, 10 (1962)
'Percy, John' in *MGG*, 10 (1962)
'Piozzi, Gabriele Mario' in *MGG*, 10 (1962)
'Potter, John' in *MGG*, 10 (1962)
'Power, James' in *MGG*, 10 (1962)
'Rawlings, Familie' in *MGG* 11 (1963)
'Reeve, William' in *MGG*, 11 (1963)
'Ricci, Francesco Pasquale' in *MGG*, 11 (1963)
'Rush, George' in *MGG*, 11 (1963)

'Sale, Familie' in *MGG*, 11 (1963)
'Salieri, Antonio' in *Enc. Brit.* (1970)
'Sarti, Giuseppe' in *Enc. Brit.* (1970)
'Savage, Jane' in *New Grove* (1980)
'Savage, William' in *MGG*, 11 (1963)
— 'Savage, William' in *New Grove* (1980), co-author
'Schröter, Familie' in *MGG*, 12 (1965), co-author
'Smart, Familie' in *MGG*, 12 (1965), co-author
'Stamitz, family' [Carl Philipp] in *Enc. Brit.* (1970)
'Stevens, Richard John Samuel' in *MGG*, 12 (1965)
— 'R. J. S. Stevens', *BBC/MM*, 23 September 1962
— 'R. J. S. Stevens, 1757–1837: the memories and music of an English pre-romantic', *MT*, 103 (1962), 754–6
— 'An 18th century musical apprenticeship', *MT*, 108 (1967), 602–4
— 'Two Georgian classics: Arne and Stevens', *M&L*, 45 (1964), 146–53
'Taylor, Raynor' in *MGG*, 13 (1966)
'Taylor, Richard' in *MGG*, 13 (1966) [including Thomas Taylor]
'Vernon, Joseph' in *MGG*, 13 (1966)
'Warren (später Warren Horne), Edmund Thomas' in *MGG*, 14 (1968)
'Weichsell, Familie' in *MGG*, 14 (1968)
'Wright, Thomas' in *MGG*, 14 (1968)

13. Musicians of the nineteenth century (born 1770–1870)

Berlioz, Hector. 'Berlioz and Wiertz: a comparison and contrast', *Revue belge de musicologie*, 6 (1952), 275–82
'Dickens and music', *MT*, 111 (1970), 588–90
— 'Charles Dickens and music', *BBC/MM*, 7 June 1970
Foster, Stephen (Collins). 'Songs of a Yankee minstrel', *R&R*, 16/7 (April 1973), 34, 91
'Griesbach, John Henry' in *MGG*, 5 (1956)
'Hart, Joseph Binns' in *MGG*, 5 (1956)
'Holmes, Edward' in *MGG*, 6 (1957)
— 'Introduction' to a reprint of *A ramble among the Musicians of Germany* (New York: Da Capo, 1969)
'Kemp, Joseph' in *MGG*, 7 (1958)
'King, Matthew Peter' in *MGG*, 7 (1958)
— 'King, Matthew Peter' in *New Grove* (1980)
'Kitchiner, William' in *MGG*, 7 (1958)
'Lacy, John' in *MGG*, 8 (1960)
'Lanza, Francesco Giuseppe' in *MGG*, 8 (1960) [including Gesualdo Lanza]
'Linley, Francis' in *MGG*, 8 (1960) [including George Linley]
'Moore, Thomas' in *MGG*, 9 (1961)
'Powell, Thomas' in *MGG*, 10 (1962)

'Russell, William' in *MGG*, 11 (1963)
'Warren, Joseph' in *MGG*, 14 (1968)

14. Musicians of the twentieth century (born after 1870)

'Hadley, Patrick Arthur Sheldon' in *MGG*, 5 (1956)
Hanson Dyer, Louise, 'A great patroness', *R&R*, 6/4 (January 1963), 25, 59 [obituary]
'Morris, Reginald Owen' in *MGG*, 9 (1961)
'Naylor, John' in *MGG*, 9 (1961) [including Edward Woodall Naylor and Bernard Naylor]
'Picken, Laurence Ernest Rowland' in *MGG*, 10 (1962)
'Rootham, Daniel Wilberforce' in *MGG*, 11 (1963) [including Cyril Bradley Rootham]
'Schnapper, Edith' in *MGG*, 11 (1963)
Shaw, George Bernard. 'An introduction to Corno di Bassetto', *Music*, 1/7 (June 1952), 15–16
Vaughan Williams. 'Ralph Vaughan Williams', *Music*, 1/11 (October 1952), 9–12
'Williams, Charles Francis Abdy' in *MGG*, 14 (1968)

15. Editions of music

Handel, G. F. *The Music for the Royal Fireworks*, Eulenburg edn no. 1307 (London 1958)
Mozart, W. A. *Symphony, A major, K. 201*, Eulenburg edn no. 546 (London 1958)
Although these were the only two musical editions actually published, the Oxford University Press proofs exist of a third: Pergolesi's Concerto No. 3 in A major, now known to be by Count Unico Wilhelm van Wassenaer, edited by Charles in association with Reginald Jacques in 1964–5.

From the 1940s onward Charles copied much music which is now in the Pendlebury Library of Music and in Wolfson College Library in Cambridge, unsorted and uncatalogued. Throughout the 1950s and '60s he was constantly preparing eighteenth-century music for both live and recorded performances. Much of this material cannot easily be ascribed to his editorship since it was often prepared by anyone whom Charles could persuade to copy for him, and he rarely named himself as editor on any manuscript score. He gives a list of his editions in his *MGG* article of 1952, but these do not seem to have survived.

Index

by Frederick Smyth

Bold figures indicate the more important references; *italic* figures denote illustrations or their captions; 'q.' stands for 'quoted'. Music publishers and owners of manuscripts are indexed selectively (e.g. omitting most references on pp. 176–87); pp. 219–58 are not indexed.